MUSSOLINI
IN THE MAKING

(*Topical Press Agency*)

MUSSOLINI AT THE AGE OF 22 YEARS.

MUSSOLINI
IN THE MAKING

BY

GAUDENS MEGARO

NEW YORK

Howard Fertig

1967

First published in 1938

HOWARD FERTIG, INC. EDITION 1967
Published by arrangement with Houghton Mifflin Company

Library of Congress Catalog Card Number: 67-13634

PRINTED IN THE UNITED STATES OF AMERICA
BY NOBLE OFFSET PRINTERS, INC.

TO

THE MEMORY OF

EDWARD RAYMOND TURNER

WHO INSPIRED THE AUTHOR

TO STUDY THE HISTORY

OF ITALY

Ex ore tuo, te iudico.

MUSSOLINI, July 8, 1912.

A PERSONAL NOTE

WHATEVER one may think of the character and work of Benito Mussolini, there can be little doubt that he has already achieved a prominent place among the commanding political figures of modern times. His career has inspired unbounded admiration and unbounded repugnance and has given rise to passionate controversy which bids fair to continue unabated for a long time to come. The history of his life and an understanding of his personality have been obscured by a rapidly growing mythology which has steadily been fed either by exaggerated eulogy or by exaggerated defamation. Is it necessary to wait decades for the so-called "facts" about Mussolini when it is possible to ascertain them now through careful and exhaustive research?

The key to an understanding of Mussolini, the Duce of Italian socialism as well as the Duce of Italian fascism, lies in a full explanation of his early life and career. It is the prime object of this book to reconstruct his origins and his development into a mature political personality on the basis of primary and untapped sources of information which the author has succeeded in consulting. To know Mussolini the fascist, one must know Mussolini the socialist.

The author's task has been rendered extremely difficult by the fact that Mussolini and the fascist government have done everything in their power to destroy or conceal the sources of information on his early life. The meagre data which have appeared in book form have generally been presented in such a warped, tendentious or factious manner as to confuse those who desire a sure knowledge of the facts. Simple chronological events have been turned topsy-turvy and distorted; passages have been torn out of their context, falsified or invented; a multitude of legends and apocryphal details has been circulated; irresponsible opinions without any sound basis have been offered to the public in the guise of ascertainable truths; fiction has been hidden under the mask of "impartial history"; so-called psychographic portraits have failed to conceal the abysmal ignorance of their authors; plagiarism has been surprisingly common; textbooks have perpetuated innumerable errors; and the muse of history has been degraded by self-styled historians and social scientists. In 1928 Mussolini made a signal contribution to the hagiographic literature about himself when he permitted the publication of his "Autobiography" in English, but not in Italian. Although the public received this book as the work of Mussolini, it was really written not by him, but by Richard Washburn Child, who was American Ambassador to Italy during the Harding Administration. Three years ago there began to appear what now constitutes the "definitive" edition of Mussolini's works in nine volumes, but, as the present writer has shown in the *Political Science Quarterly* and the *Journal of Modern History*, this edition is in no sense definitive, for it is characterized by extensive omissions and by unconscionable tampering with the texts. Not a single word uttered by Mussolini before November 1914 is contained in this edition which, unfortunately, is being translated into French, German, and Spanish.

If the following pages contain a vast amount of authentic material which has hitherto been unknown to the public, the reason is that the author has spared no pains, no risk, and no expense to find and study at first hand the most inaccessible data on Mussolini's life. In the year 1925–1926 he went to Italy with the object of making an intensive study of that country's history from the eighteenth century to the present time. Mussolini had already survived the most crucial crisis of his career, the murder by fascists of the reformist socialist deputy Giacomo Matteotti, and he was already laying the foundations of the fascist totalitarian state, with its attendant suppression of every vestige of personal liberty and with its extensive system of espionage. As the author proceeded in his research and began to study the revolutionary milieu of pre-war Italy in which Mussolini was born, reared, and steeped, he frequently encountered Mussolini's name at a time when it was quite obscure; and he then decided to concentrate his attention on the most striking

Italian political figure since Cavour. After establishing in 1925–1926 the foundations for his research on Mussolini, he returned to Italy and other parts of Europe and pursued his historical investigations during the summers of 1927 and 1928 and again during the year 1932–1933. In the course of these trips he was able to conclude his study of Mussolini and of other aspects of Italian history. The writing of the present volume was completed in the winter of 1935–36, and no changes have since been made except to mention such recent events as the war in Ethiopia and the Spanish civil war.

It is needless to say that the research on Mussolini was carried on under the most trying conditions. On four occasions the author was searched by the Italian police and on at least ten other occasions he was questioned by them. In one instance a persistent chief of police of an Italian town began to examine the author's baggage, but somehow he became so interested in the author's improvised "oration" on the historical glories of the peninsula that he discontinued his investigation, thus failing to discover a large set of notes on Mussolini at the bottom of a valise. Thereafter, at different places, the author resorted to various expedients in taking notes and in mailing them to relatives and friends in the United States. This book is testimony to the fact that it was possible to gain access to the "suppressed" body of material on Mussolini despite the vigilance of the fascist government and police.

The author made every effort to see those persons who had been associated with the Duce, especially before the Great War. This was done at great risk, for in fascist Italy those who have not bowed to Mussolini's will are ostracized from Italian society, and particularly in small provincial towns the visits of a foreigner to them are carefully watched by the police. On the whole the author learned little from his conversations with these persons. He has not blindly accepted any oral or written statement about Mussolini without carefully checking it. In three or four cases where he was aided by the recollections of former acquaintances of

Mussolini, who are still living in Italy, he has intentionally avoided the mention of their names in the present volume lest it expose them to reprisals on the part of the fascist government. He has also refrained from mentioning the location of the rare documentary sources of his information in order not to make it easier for the fascist government to seize them.

The author's research on Mussolini and on the recent history of Italy has been supplemented by interviews and conversations with Mussolini, King Victor Emmanuel, ex-Prime Ministers Giolitti and Salandra, several ex-ministers of state, and leaders of the anti-fascist movement abroad and in Italy. He takes this occasion to thank those who have helped him, even unwittingly, in his investigations, particularly in Italy, Austria, and Switzerland.

What most impressed the author during his research was the wealth of valuable data on Mussolini and on his background, which had generally been regarded as non-existent, destroyed, or inaccessible. While he does not presume to have seen every scrap of material on the period covered in this volume, he thinks that, aside from mutilated collections of newspapers and aside from records removed from their proper places by Mussolini, few documents have escaped his notice. What can be called the "suppressed" body of Mussolini's writings and speeches alone, which he has consulted, is so voluminous that, even excluding Mussolini's writings and speeches since his accession to power as Prime Minister in 1922, it would take perhaps about fifty volumes to publish it in its bare form, without any attempt at a critical text or a critical evaluation.

In preparing this volume the author necessarily had to make the sort of selection best suited to convey a true picture of the Duce in the making. Every chapter is mainly or almost entirely based on new evidence which has enabled the author to remove the veil of mystery enveloping a multitude of incidents in the Duce's early life. The character of his father, the reasons for his expulsion from two Swiss cantons and from Austria-Hungary, the details of his prison record, the beginnings of his journalistic career, the foundations of his culture in the light of contemporary political and intellectual currents in Italy and Europe, and the background of his meteoric rise to political leadership are amply described. To Americans the Duce's deprecatory opinions of the United States should be of special interest. A matter of curiosity in this connection is that as early as 1903, when he was nineteen years old, Mussolini contributed several articles to an Italian socialist paper published in New York.

Either categorically by direct statement or indirectly by implication, the author has disposed of many legends which abound in books written by Mussolini's apologists and detractors. Since his purpose is to write history, he has not disdained to make use of material that might be damaging to Mussolini, as his apologists have done, or to make use of material that might be complimentary to Mussolini, as his detractors have done. In declaring his own opinion at various points throughout this volume, especially in the last chapter, he has sought to distinguish between what is ascertainable fact and what is matter of personal judgment and to offer an interpretation of the man who was the Duce of Italian socialism and who became the Duce of Italian fascism.

Finally, the author wishes to express his gratitude to his brother, Joseph C. Megaro, for his abiding and critical interest in this work since its inception.

GAUDENS MEGARO

HARVARD UNIVERSITY

CONTENTS

ILLUSTRATIONS

MUSSOLINI IN THE MAKING

CHAPTER I

HIS FATHER'S SON

BENITO MUSSOLINI is a son of the Romagna, that region in central Italy so long famed for the violence of its political passions that it has appropriately been called the Sicily of continental Italy. Nowhere in Italy is the sectarian political spirit more intense than in the Romagna, and many writers from Dante to Byron have spoken of the combative nature of its people. Among the Romagnuoles, the feeling of solidarity binding the members of a political party is almost as strong as the family tie and, if need be, they do not hesitate to resort to the knife in defence of a political faith. And yet with all their pugnacity, they are a hospitable and generous people.

A classic land of political violence, the Romagna has been since the French Revolution a battleground of extreme radical doctrines and a stronghold of Jacobinism, Carbonarism, Mazzinian republicanism and insurrectionism, anarchism, and revolutionary socialism. During the Italian Risorgimento, the Romagna yielded the most fervent republicans and followers of Mazzini, but after the annexation of Rome in 1870 under the auspices of the House of Savoy, the question of the form of government receded in importance, and as social and economic issues became more pressing, a goodly number of enthusiastic Romagnuoles turned from Mazzini's gospel to that of the noted anarchist Bakunin, who had begun in the sixties his feverish propagandist agitation in Italy on behalf of the anarchist wing of the First International. An event of cardinal importance in accentuating the marked split between the social revolutionists generally and the Mazzinians was Mazzini's vehement denunciation of the

Paris Commune. The bitter animosity, the factious spirit and the poisonous bile which characterized the feuds between the Guelphs and the Ghibellines in the Middle Ages found three modern variations in the political struggles of the Romagna: the conflicts involving at first the republicans and the monarchists, then the republicans and the social revolutionists of Marxist-socialist or Bakuninist-anarchist persuasion, and later the socialists and the anarchists. In the eighties and nineties, the social revolutionists of this region had two conspicuous martyrs, killed in party feuds with republicans—Francesco Piccinini and Pio Battistini. The memory of the latter was commemorated in one of Benito Mussolini's earliest and most eloquent speeches.

Among the first anarchist-internationalists in the Romagna was the father of the future Duce of Italian socialism and fascism—Alessandro Gaspare Mussolini. At a time when internationalists, anarchists, and socialists were too frequently placed in the category of common criminals, he embraced the cause of social revolution with ardent zeal and faced persecution and prejudice with admirable courage. He was a proud militant among the growing number of social revolutionists who, to adopt his phraseology, were "poor children of the soil, of hunger and of need". Apparently his own father, Luigi Mussolini (1834–1908), had also been interested in politics, and I have it on the authority of Benito Mussolini himself that he had been jailed in a papal prison when the Romagna formed part of the Papal States. Years before he became the Duce of fascist Italy, Benito Mussolini pointed with pride to his own prison record and to that of his father and grandfather. When Alessandro Mussolini died in 1910, his son, Benito, then the fiery twenty-seven-year-old editor of the socialist weekly *La Lotta di Classe* (*The Class Struggle*) of Forlì, wrote the following interesting account of his life:

"I pen these lines—with a trembling hand—not to weave a biography or a panegyric, but simply to pay the last homage of my filial devotion on the grave of my father and to add some documents relating to the history of the International in the Romagna. I feel the duty and perhaps even the right to do so.

"My father was born on November 11, 1854, the son of Luigi Mussolini and Caterina Garduni,[1] on a farm that was then, not now, our property, situated at Villa Montemaggiore in the Commune of Predappio. After his earliest years, he spent some time at Dovadola to learn the blacksmith trade. From Dovadola he moved to Meldola. Now grown older, he went from Meldola to Dovia, at that time a very small village, where he put up a workshop. I do not know in what town or under what influences he embraced the ideas of the International. What is certain is that when at Dovia, he began to support them with great fervour, succeeding in a short time in establishing a branch of the International, very large and feared. This branch, with the very large branch of Predappio, was a part of the Socialist Federation of Predappio. The internationalists at that time were regarded as criminals to be segregated, and my father—guilty of having founded and led a group of the International—was arrested. He spent several months in the old Rocca [prison] of Forlì. Here he became acquainted with many other comrades of his faith. The socialists of the Romagna were then very few and they were harassed on all sides; but they resisted the police tempests and those, no less violent, of their adversaries. They were devoted to one another, protecting and defending each other with a feeling of solidarity that by some super-modern coward might be called morbid. The house of one comrade was the house of all comrades. That was the golden age of Romagnuole socialism.

"One cannot read the documents of that time—be they periodicals, secret bulletins or mere minutes of meetings—without vibrating inwardly with pride and admiration. When my father came out of prison, it was ordered that he be kept under special surveillance. This kind of harsh and exasperating moral imprisonment lasted forty-two months. Here is a document: 'Commune of Predappio, September 21, 1882. Permission is given to the admonished Alessandro Mussolini, of this town, to go to-morrow, the 22nd, to Forlì, under the

[1] Probably a typographical error. The name, I think, was Vasumi, not Garduni.

obligation to return to his own residence on the same day.
For the Mayor—Alderman Monti.' I have found letters
between 1880 and 1885 addressed to my father by all the
best-known internationalists of the time. My Varano home,
which a large number of socialists and republicans of the
region of Forlì certainly remember, afforded asylum and
hospitality to all those who had political accounts to settle
with bourgeois justice. And frequently it was forced to offer
hospitality also to the policemen who came to search for
manifestos and to sequestrate revolutionary emblems, but
always in vain. In the meantime, good seeds bore fruit. The
socialists of the Federation of Predappio did not belie their
reputation as fighters. The tumults that took place at Piazza
del Duomo at Forlì demonstrate this.

"When times became less unpleasant, the socialists participated in municipal life. My father was a town councillor and
mayor of Predappio. In 1893, he founded at Predappio a
co-operative association that comprised all the workers of the
town. Article 2 of the Constitution defined the character of the
society that '*had a purely economic purpose and eschewed any
activity that was not connected with its specific purpose*'. Article 4
fixed the aim of the society: '*The association undertakes to take
on and carry out in a co-operative manner works which are to-day
carried out by contractors, such as masonry work, building of bridges,
railway lines, streets, embankments, excavations, etc., so that every
worker could obtain the fruits of his own labour.*' To gather funds,
appeal was made to the most prominent personages in the
democratic movement. Antonio Fratti [republican leader
and ardent patriot] wrote from Rome on January 12, 1892:
'Dear Mussolini: I received your letter of the 2nd instant,
with the enclosed subscription share that I am very glad to
buy. I wish that your association may live a vigorous and
long life and may emulate the others of our region in honour-
ableness, activity and intelligence. Next month, I shall come
to the Romagna for a while and I shall pay the price of the
share. In the meantime, include me in the list of share-
holders. To me, this will be an honour and a source of
satisfaction.'

THE BIRTH PLACE OF MUSSOLINI.

"The co-operative lived for six active years, I think, and then it dissolved. I have found traces of my father's journalistic activity about this time in socialist as well as republican periodicals, consisting of short articles and correspondence relating to the administrative life of the Commune of Predappio or the political activities of the socialists. If certain works of indisputable public utility, like the improvement of the road of Rocca d'Elmici, the junction of San Zeno road and that of Marsignano, etc., were done, they were due in great part to my father who never tired of insisting upon them to the proper authorities. The political authorities, however, always kept an eye on him. On July 6, 1902, there broke out at Predappio the famous election disturbances in which my father did not in any way participate. This does not matter. He was arrested. I learned this at Chiasso while I was getting ready to cross the frontier and to undertake my foreign peregrinations [in Switzerland]. I thought it was a matter of small importance. Instead, despite the activity of lawyer Bellini who very ably defended my father during the preliminary inquiry and the trial, the authorities did not grant him provisional liberty. The police, the priests and the moderates exaggerated the incidents. A trial was hatched. My father appeared before the Assizes of Forlì on Christmas Eve and was acquitted. But at forty-eight years of age, six months of rigid segregation in a prison are certainly not a wholesome vacation. My father came out of it with his health impaired. Almost two years later, my mother died when still young : at forty-six years of age. This was another very heavy blow. My father retired from the active movement of the party in which, however, he always remained enrolled, at first in the section of Predappio and latterly in that of Ospedaletto.

"My father experienced the joys of party work and also the inevitable bitterness due to the moral pettiness of men. He was a good man and at times excessively altruistic. He did good to comrades and adversaries. In many respects he had a tormented existence. His end was premature. Of worldly goods he has left us nothing; of spiritual goods he has left us a treasure: the Idea. And now, the period of mourning over, Life must go on its way with all its rights!''

The spiritual treasure that Alessandro Mussolini had bequeathed to his children was the Socialist Idea. This poor and obscure blacksmith of the village of Dovia has left traces of his political faith in writings dispersed in local newspapers, now extremely rare and difficult of access. Our discovery of these writings in 1926 enables us to present for the first time a fairly complete picture of this man of character and energy. Only fragmentary and distorted views about him have hitherto been offered to the public by a host of writers. Particularly those views expressed by fascist authors constitute the worst possible monument to the memory of an eminently courageous and upright man who deserved a better fate at the hands of his son's admirers.

The earliest mention of Alessandro Mussolini that I have found is in 1881 as one of the signatories of an eloquent manifesto exhorting fellow socialists to keep together in the struggle for human regeneration and to avoid factional fights within their ranks. He was a constant advocate of unity among social revolutionists, some of whom continued to adhere to the anarchistic tendencies of Bakunin while others, like himself, were drawing away from anarchism and were being attracted to the Marxian type of socialism preached by Andrea Costa. Although it appears that Alessandro Mussolini had decided by the early eighties to champion socialist instead of anarchist principles, he shared in the enthusiasm for Carlo Cafiero and Amilcare Cipriani, two well-known Italian pioneers of the anarchist cause. In 1888, several socialists of Predappio, including Alessandro Mussolini, expressed, on behalf of the revolutionary socialist federation of the town, their joy at the liberation from prison of the "indomitable Carlo Cafiero", whom they hailed as "the rebel hero of the insurrection of Benevento and the future champion of economic struggles". In March 1889, Mussolini reported to a Forlì socialist paper the commemoration by the Predappio revolutionary socialist federation of the anniversary of the Commune, "the glorious Parisian revolution of

1871". The meeting ended with the extolling of the coming social revolution and with a greeting to the "heroic colonel of the Commune, the courageous revolutionist Amilcare Cipriani, glorious survivor of so much greatness". Together with anarchists and socialists, Mussolini cherished the memory of the victims of the "Chicago Massacre"—the social revolutionists August Spies, Albert Parsons, George Engel and Adolph Fischer who had been hanged on November 11, 1887, because of their alleged connection with the famous Haymarket Bomb. He noted in a Forlì socialist weekly that in November 1893, "our socialist federation, on the sixth anniversary of the hanging of our comrades of Chicago, unfurled a flag at half-mast to commemorate the holy victims of the socialist idea, killed by the republicans of overseas". So embittered was he by factional fights and personal rivalries in the revolutionary movement that on one occasion, in 1889, he assailed certain "patriarchs of anarchism", whom he did not name, for indulging in attacks on genuine revolutionists. Nevertheless, as he declared in 1890, he was convinced that despite differences about tactics, all Italian socialists were agreed in accepting revolution as their means and anarchism as their end.

Alessandro Mussolini's passionate enthusiasm for socialism is clearly illustrated in an article he wrote in 1891: "What is socialism? This question is asked by the masses who are ignorant of this noble idea and are frightened by the powerful and mysterious word that echoes resoundingly from one end of the world to the other. Socialism, we answer, is open, violent and moral rebellion against the inhuman order of things as now constituted. It is knowledge and the excelsior that illumine the world. It is reason that supplants faith. It is free thought rebelling against prejudice. It is free love taking the place of a legal contract. It is a free agreement among all men to live a truly decent life. It is true justice that reigns as sovereign over the earth.

"According to us, socialism is a sublime harmony of concepts, of thoughts and of action that precedes the great chariot of human progress in its triumphal march towards the great goal of the beautiful, the just and the true. Socialism —he who denies it is stupid, he who does not understand it is an unfortunate—here, O brother workmen, is described in its major outlines the majestic figure of our ideal, that ideal which resounds so much in your ear and speaks to your heart and which you still do not dare utter. Why? Because the priest and the bourgeois do their utmost to make you believe that we socialists are visionaries, madmen, that we want the property of others, that we are thieves, despicable people fit for prison and the halter. Do not pay any attention to these masters, O brothers of labour. They are our natural enemies; they deceive you; they lie knowing that they are lying. Listen to us who are your real friends because, like you, we find that fortune has been greedy, because, like you, we suffer hunger and all human miseries. Come with us so that you will learn to know and love us, and strong in our faith and in our rights we will attain our complete emancipation. One day the great Brunelleschi [sic] said: 'Give me a fulcrum for a lever and I will move the world.' Well then, we say, let us all unite for the common good. And pressing on the great lever (the Social Revolution) as one man, we will give the last blow to this monstrous and crumbling edifice; and on the remains of the still smouldering ruins, we will build in unison the new kingdom of true civilization, peace and love."

The misery and poverty of the humblest classes of society afflicted Benito Mussolini's father. He seems to have taken advantage of every opportunity to preach the socialist gospel among them. Of the condition of the unemployed and indigent, he wrote:

"It is indeed disheartening!!! Poverty is increasing! For several weeks, throngs of workmen of all ages have been seen passing by here daily on the way to Florence in search of work. Watching these poor pariahs of society who are in a pitiful state, lean, pale, sickly and poorly dressed, one sees stamped on their faces the distress they have been suffering. The pain of having left their families without bread, the anguish caused by the uncertainty of finding any make them so despondent that one would rather not have seen them. Poor humanity!

And to think that at every house they ask for a morsel of bread in order to appease their hunger. To see young and robust workmen in such a state of moral degradation is truly discouraging; but still more discouraging is it to know that they are completely ignorant of all the great social ideas for economic and moral emancipation. A few days ago, when one of these pitiful groups stopped in our neighbourhood to rest a while, I, together with other comrades, went to them, urged on by curiosity to ask them about their enforced pilgrimage. In their moving stories, they frequently blamed God for so much distress and misfortune. We hastened to tell them that God was only a bourgeois expedient, put into circulation by the more cunning to frighten the weak-minded in order then to be able to dominate them and to exploit them as they please in his name. We also told them that for the workman to emancipate himself it is necessary that he associate himself with his working companions and after such a union, abandon every political and religious prejudice and embrace the great liberating ideas of socialism. Socialism has for its foundation the total abolition of every human privilege. Through it the brotherhood and social equality among men can be proclaimed, and through it alone can the kingdom of peace and of love be built, and at last man can live freely among his fellows and attain in such a way his complete material and moral development, thus rising to the height of human perfection."

Alessandro Mussolini also described the pitiful condition of those who were forced to move from their homes: "In these days of moving, or better, of expulsions from their homes, we socialists, men of sympathy, can better understand the sense of profound disgust that is experienced in seeing such hardly edifying reproductions of the movements of modern gypsies. Along the roads there is a constant going and coming of people with carts full of old household goods to be transported to their new huts. A worm-eaten box, a straw mattress, two bed stools and a few other worthless trifles make up the equipment of a poor little family. The father, melancholy and taciturn, precedes his modest convoy. His wife

carries a baby in a little basket. The other children, barefooted and poorly dressed, are clinging to her petticoat.
Meagre and unwholesome nutrition renders them none too
healthy. Poor humanity! But alas! this sad fate is reserved
not only for tenant-farmers but more so for farm-hands. And
to think that these wretched workers in the fields and in the
cities sweat all day to produce the necessary sustenance for
the material maintenance of society, building houses and
carriages, breeding horses, and preparing exquisite foods of
all kinds for the bourgeois class. This class, in exchange for so
many services, denies to these well-deserving human beings
even a hovel to protect themselves from the harsh rigours of
the seasons. And how long will this horrible state of affairs
last? It will last until the people will have learned the new
gospel of socialism, regenerator of human society."

Besides writing for socialist journals, Alessandro Mussolini
occasionally contributed articles to a Forlì republican paper,
Il Pensiero Romagnolo. The seeming incongruity of a Romagnuole socialist writing for a republican paper is explained by
the fact that, especially in periods of reaction like those from
1893 to 1900 under the Prime Ministers Crispi, Di Rudini, and
Pelloux, it was most expedient for the two extreme political
groups in the Romagna, the socialists and the republicans, to
join forces and to establish a "united front" in the struggle for
fundamental political rights. Where the monarchists, the conservatives, and the Catholics were predominant, the socialists,
the republicans, the radicals, and the democrats often formed
electoral coalitions in order to gain political representation
for their relatively advanced views. Many of them had been
victimized by reactionary governments, and in small com-
munities, like Predappio and Forlì, it was not uncommon
for a socialist and a republican to be on terms of close friendship. It is certain that Giuseppe Gaudenzi, the editor of *Il
Pensiero*, and Alessandro Mussolini were personal friends. In
1898 the latter wrote an article for *Il Pensiero* in which he
noted the increasing emigration of indigent workmen to the
Americas:

"Everybody to America!—These are the words that pass

from mouth to mouth in these days among the general mass of our workers. This morning, here at the village of Dovia, nine families, all together about fifty persons, left for S[ão] Paulo in Brazil. They were grieved by the pain caused by their departure, and they moved every noble heart as they greeted their relatives and friends. They leave, venturing their fortunes on the other side of the ocean, in lands that are almost unknown, to see if they can find there, by means of the honest labour of their own hands, that morsel of bread that the third Italy, the bourgeois Italy, denies to the poor workers. For the same destination, other local families had already left and still others are preparing to start off within a few days. Oh! power of harsh necessity, how unhappy is the present hour! These poor pariahs of a frivolous and decrepit society seek flight in distant lands, perhaps running into yellow fever and exploitation by some speculator, without our being able to dissuade them. And how could we? How can one have the courage to counsel poor unemployed workers, without bread and shelter, to remain here, where all the necessities of life are lacking? And to think that if bourgeois Italy should plough and put into cultivation the immense area of uncultivated and marshy land that we have in Italy, bread would certainly not be lacking to any of its workers and Italy could still rightly boast of its being called by the beautiful name of the garden of Europe! But what can one hope from a government . . . that for several years has initiated on behalf of the working class its glorious records at Conselice, Caltavuturo, Melzi, Troina and Modica,[1] where many still smoking corpses, of different ages and sex, demonstrate to the civilized world and to the common people of Italy the horrible spectacle of having been answered with lead when they were asking for bread?

"Ah! certainly it was not worth while that so many heroes should have left their lives on the gallows, in prisons and on the fields of war, in order to create a fatherland like this! This is certainly not the Italy envisioned by those great men

[1] Towns where persons, generally workmen, were killed in conflicts between the police and workers seeking better economic conditions.

like Pisacane, Mazzini and Garibaldi. But all is not lost; we still have a life to offer . . . [to the cause of the social revolution].[1] We trust to better days!

"Coming back to our emigrants, all of them are leaving animated by the comforting hope of making their fortune. We wish it for them most heartily. But alas! who knows what and how many disillusionments await them in those distant lands! To these unfortunate folk, our greetings, accompanied by the most sincere good wishes that they may happily see again their native land when it will no longer be contaminated by grafters and swindlers in the manner of to-day and when it will instead be the land of the people, for the people."

Alessandro Mussolini was vehement in his denunciation of the bourgeoisie and the Catholics. Like most socialists in the Romagna, he was at once an anti-Catholic and an atheist. He was one of the few in his town who stayed away from Christmas Mass. The local politics of Predappio centred around a struggle between Catholics and socialists; monarchists of a democratic turn of mind were scarce and there were virtually no republicans. The burden of combating the influence of the clergy and the Catholic laity in the town rested on the socialists, among whom Alessandro was a conspicuous leader. He sarcastically referred to Pope Leo XIII as "the poor prisoner Gioacchino Pecci", and he expressed his contempt and hatred for the "Black Sect" more fully in connection with a sermon by "a certain Father Agostino *** who, during the recent Lent period, proclaimed from the pulpit the divine word, boasting in calling it the gospel of truth. The enthusiasm of our Catholic imbeciles, aroused to a point of delirium, showed itself in public praise on printed leaflets in which an apotheosis was made of the eloquence and learning of the black orator who, moved to compassion, invoked from heaven a deluge of benedictions on behalf of his sheep-like congregation and especially of the town officials. Strange and ridiculous is this *réclame* made for a priest who

---

[1] The dots in this and other quotations throughout this volume are parts of the original documents. I use three asterisks to indicate my omissions from the documents.

is and forever will be nothing but a nullity. One example will suffice: in the last sermon, the theme of which was *faith and reason*, this apostolic Cicero declared that the real and sole cause that torments the human family must be sought exclusively in the diabolical doctrine that is prevalent at present, that is to say, *reason substituted for faith*. If the opposite were true, he said, evils would disappear and social welfare would be fully realized. This example is more than sufficient to show how far the ignorance or the craftiness of this black *uncastrated cantor* goes. You should have heard with what passion he supplicated the celestial ire and implored its fulminations against progress, liberty and certain reprehensible as well as cursed organizations. And the cursed organizations to which he referred are we socialists who care not for his inflammatory and viperous words or for the anathemas hurled with the ferocity of a Torquemada.***

"Our aim is clear: economic, political, intellectual and moral emancipation; therefore, abolition of everything that is contrary to reason and to the harmony and laws of nature—this is our ideal. O priests, the day is not distant when you will cease to be useless and false apostles of a deceitful religion and when, leaving behind obscurantism and falsehood, you will embrace truth and reason, and you will throw your tunics in the purifying flame of progress to put on the honoured doublet of the workman, very happy to understand and to pursue with us the high mission of life."

As a militant leader of the Predappio socialists, Alessandro Mussolini was very active in town politics and fought for progressive causes. He was a town councillor, and although his son, Benito, stated that he was also mayor, I think he was only vice-mayor for a short time. Among other things, he favoured an immediate amnesty for all political offenders including, of course, the numerous victims of the Italian government's reactionary measures in connection with the tumults of 1898.

When the Predappio town council was planning certain minor public works, he castigated in a Forlì socialist paper a rich business man, Livio Zoli, for his callousness and maliciousness in underbidding a poor artisan by a slight margin. Occasionally, he reported the outcome of communal and provincial elections, especially when notable victories for the working and democratic elements were achieved. In 1889, commenting on one of these victories, he declared: "The well-fed bourgeoisie that had up to now always ruled despotically at Predappio, realizing that it has been completely beaten, bestirs itself, shrieks, and vomits its poisonous rage. But what good is it? Keep on fighting, O mendacious dogs, your star is on the decline. These are the first skirmishes of the final battle and the first funeral-knells of your agony." On a similar occasion in the following year, when some prominent lawyers and wealthy men were defeated by humble workmen, he wrote: "The time is past, and the electors have understood it, of following those who have titles and money. A new era has risen, which aspires to new life, to ideals that are higher and far different from those of the wheedlers of the masses. There is a desire for progress in spite of those who do not want it. There is a desire to march on, and the conservative masters who do not have good legs will be left behind."

The bitter electoral feuds between the Catholics and the socialists at Predappio culminated in the breaking of the ballot boxes on the town election day, July 6, 1902. Several socialists, among them Alessandro Mussolini, were arrested for having instigated and committed this act of violence. Since the authorities refused to grant provisional liberty to Mussolini, he was kept in prison for almost five months, until December 1902, when a jury at the Assizes of Forlì acquitted him and his comrades. This rather long and unwarranted stay in prison had a bad effect on his health. About three and a half years after the death of his wife in 1905, he moved to the nearby city of Forlì where he began to earn his living as a tavern-keeper.

The most interesting press comments dealing with the electoral disturbances at Predappio were published in a Forlì clerical weekly, *Il Lavoro d'Oggi* (*The Work of To-day*). A biting editorial entitled "Electoral Musolinism" suggested a

similarity between Mussolini and Musolino, a notorious Italian
brigand who attained a popular reputation in Italy not unlike
that of Al Capone in the United States, and attacked the
liberal government for not maintaining order at the polls
and for not checking the excesses of the socialists. Among
those arrested at Predappio, it said, was "a ringleader who,
in addition to his deeds, also bears by fate the name of
Musolino". Farther on, the editorial made this appeal to the
local Catholics: "Catholics, it is time to awaken ourselves
from the long sleep we have had up to now. Liberalism,
with all its coffers, has not the means to make amends for the
ruins it has piled up. It is up to us to go united to the polls in
order to sweep away from the municipal and provincial
halls all that rubbish of Musolinism that has invaded them."

The same paper published an article written in extremely
poor Italian by a correspondent from Predappio, who, while
giving a very prejudiced account of the disturbances, further
acquaints us with the general repute of Mussolini among the
reactionaries and clericals of his town. He asserted that in
the formation of the election vote committee, "as though
two men were not sufficient to check on the work of the president, a third person, very notorious for his brutishness
especially when he is drunk, wanted to take part in it; on
account of his silly comments he was put out of the hall by
the president. To speak of how they [the socialists] sought
to corrupt our supporters is not an easy matter. When the
voting started, one of the *known* chiefs . . ., probably having
a presentiment of defeat, said in the presence of the president
of the election committee and of many voters: 'We are ready
in the last resort to *smash* the ballot boxes.' Since one of our
men held Mussolini responsible for anything that might occur,
he begged the president to take note of the statement of Mussolini and to take the steps he thought best. But their order
was to break the ballot boxes."

The correspondent continued to say that about thirty
socialists, in a demonstration, shouted: "Down with the
Pope! Down with the King! Down with the House of Savoy!
Long live the revolution!" After some forty ballots had

been counted, an assault on the boxes was attempted, but this was checked. "The usual leader appeared on the large staircase of the city hall and shouted out loudly: 'Comrades, be calm because we do not yet know who will be victorious. If victory is not ours, we will *smash* the ballot boxes.' These words were received with noisy and frantic applause." Shortly afterwards, socialists forced themselves into the election hall and destroyed the ballot boxes.

The "usual leader" was Alessandro Mussolini. That the correspondent also meant him in speaking of the drunkard is difficult to ascertain. In its report of the trial, which it called a "comedy", *Il Lavoro* observed, without mentioning any names, that "the jurors admitted only the drunkenness of one of the defendants".

After the incidents of 1902, Mussolini was not as active in the socialist movement as he had previously been. There was, however, no abatement in his devotion to the socialist cause. One of his articles, written in 1905, deals with "fraudulent voters" or "cow-electors", as they were called in his locality to describe the practice of certain parties which registered "cows" instead of genuine electors in the voting lists. Voters of Meldola, a town near Predappio, had protested to the authorities against the illegal registration of residents of Predappio in their elections. "This is a trick", wrote Mussolini, "especially devised and put into practice by priests in spite of the penal code and Christian morality." Even at Predappio, as a consequence of the "usual fraudulent subterfuges that are unworthy of a party that respects itself, there are about fifty Meldola *cows* registered in our communal lists. We enthusiastically approve the courageous work of our friends who have accused the high and low tricksters before the public prosecutor, but as to the outcome of the proceedings, we are not optimists like the editors of the *Pensiero Romagnolo*. In view of the dark hour, in the face of the edifying spectacle of the fond embrace of the tiara and the crown, and in the face of the open and impudent marriage of the so-called *liberals* with the *clericals*, for us subversives there is little to hope from the law. We should not want to be prophets, but unfortunately we have reason not to delude ourselves about action on the part of the royal judiciary.

"The trick, organized by those who call themselves the representatives on earth of that man-god who preached to the populace of Galilee that 'my kingdom is not of this world', neither astonishes nor surprises us. History, which is a record of the past, shows us to what means they resorted for well-nigh fifteen centuries in order to seize and maintain power. They used intrigues, betrayals, fraud, iron and fire, and atrocious tortures of all kinds; they used everything that the mind of man had ever, unfortunately, thought of. The means to which they resort to-day, rural banks, organizations of scab-workers, under a *Bonomellian label*,[1] false records of houses and of . . . cows . . . and so on . . . are trifles in comparison with the old methods, but they are designed for the same purpose, that is, of acquiring the rule of this world, since there is time to think of the conquest of the other world . . . in the beyond. Honest people, real people who sweat and work, will strongly prepare themselves not only to combat and to win over these worm-eaten props of the throne, but also to wage the great and decisive final battle with other means that are much more eloquent and persuasive than a piece of paper obtained with more or less legal right from institutions which are not ours and which we suffer by force of circumstances or rather through our own fault."

Alessandro Mussolini returned to the theme of the increasing poverty of the workers and their need for employment: "The meagre vintage of this year—grape is almost the only resource of our little town—and the absolute lack of work for our numerous class of day labourers have contributed to increase poverty." After protesting against the delays of the higher authorities regarding plans for various public works, especially the one concerning the Rocca d'Elmici road which the Provincial Technical Bureau had

---

[1] G. Bonomelli (1831–1914), liberal Catholic priest, was the founder of the Opera Bonomelli, a religious-social organization for Italian emigrants in Europe, and the promoter of other movements for social, political, and religious betterment.

spent many years in studying, he added: "Our bourgeoisie, which is still imbued with all the ignorance of the Middle Ages, will shout against the canaille, against insolence and hooliganism if to-morrow the population should be forced by hunger to occupy the streets and the squares. The bourgeoisie does not wish nor does it know how to help even that part of the ignorant masses who parade the bourgeoisie on their escutcheons and make their appearance only at election time. Thus poverty is always becoming more acute and spasmodic, and discontent will, in the end, burst forth. Hunger is a sad counsellor, and the royal bayonets, to which our bourgeois would gladly resort, will not fill empty stomachs. It is necessary to arrange for and begin those works which have been studied long enough ***. Hope being the last thing to lose, we trust that the Provincial Council, in which there are very upright men who have embraced the cause of the people like Prof. Squadrani, the Hon. Comandini, lawyers Bellini and Ronchi, will give the order so that work on the Rocca d'Elmici road will be finally begun, and thus hundreds of workmen who wait in the terrible imminence of hunger may be employed."

Alessandro Mussolini died in 1910, at fifty-six years of age, remembered by his comrades as one of the "old guard of the International". They had a genuine veneration for him and esteemed him as the "father of Predappio socialism".

Benito Mussolini's mother, Rosa Maltoni Mussolini, was born at San Martino in Strada, a small town about two miles from Forlì, on April 22, 1858, the daughter of Giuseppe Maltoni (1809-1887), a veterinarian, and Marianna Ghetti Maltoni (1819-1896). She was sent to Forlì to complete her studies, and at eighteen, received a diploma qualifying her to teach the first three grades of elementary school. After teaching several months at Modigliana, a town in the province of Ravenna, she became in 1877 a school teacher at Dovia at the modest salary of about fifty lire—ten dollars—a month.

Although it appears that her parents thought she could

have chosen a more well-to-do man, or, at any rate, one who was not such a fervent socialist and atheist, the gentle and dignified school mistress married the village blacksmith in 1882. Unlike her husband, she was a pious Catholic and she was not interested in social and economic questions.

The Mussolinis were miserably poor and their combined efforts barely yielded the necessaries of life. Their continual economic preoccupations were increased by the fact that Alessandro was inclined to be too generous to his needy and persecuted companions for whom his home was a frequent refuge and gathering-place.

When Rosa Mussolini died on February 19, 1905, at forty-six years of age, *Il Pensiero Romagnolo* published the following obituary by a correspondent from Predappio: "Last Sunday, the school teacher Rosa Maltoni, the very beloved wife of our good friend Alessandro Mussolini, one of the most faithful precursors of international socialism amid these hills, died of meningitis at only forty-eight years of age.[1] The entire village deeply shared the mourning of the unfortunate family because the deceased was well liked and esteemed by everyone for her virtues and for the love and intelligence with which she fulfilled her noble function. Never was a more imposing funeral seen at Dovia; about a thousand persons were there. After having followed the coffin of his adored mother, it seemed that young Benito Mussolini wanted to utter a last farewell, but in the painful effort to do so he burst into tears and he was able only to throw some flowers on the sepulchral mound. The sad gathering dispersed amid profound emotion."

Below this correspondence is an editorial note of *Il Pensiero:* "From these columns we extend most heartfelt condolences to Alessandro Mussolini and to his children, to whom a sincere friendship, transcending small partisan differences, binds us."

A week later, the following notice appeared in *Il Pensiero:*

[1] This is an inaccuracy on the part of the correspondent. She was born in 1858 and died in 1905.

"The Mussolini family—moved by the demonstration of affection rendered to the most beloved remains of both wife and mother, Rosa Maltoni, Teacher, thanks from the bottom of its heart all those who by word, letter, or any other manner wished to share in this recent irreparable domestic misfortune."

THE PARENTS OF MUSSOLINI.

CHAPTER II

MUSSOLINI'S EARLIEST YEARS

ALESSANDRO and Rosa Mussolini had three children: Benito, born in 1883; Arnaldo, born in 1885, who died in 1931; and Edvige, born in 1888, who married a draper. The names of the two sons bear witness to Alessandro's revolutionary bent. Arnaldo's name recalled Arnaldo da Brescia, the medieval religious reformer whom many nineteenth-century Italians regarded as an apostle of civil liberty. The full name of the eldest son was Benito Amilcare Andrea Mussolini: Benito after Benito Juarez, the famous Mexican revolutionist who led a revolt against Emperor Maximilian and had this ill-fated Hapsburg executed; Amilcare after Amilcare Cipriani, the Romagnuole anarchist-internationalist; and Andrea after Andrea Costa, another Romagnuole anarchist-internationalist who later became one of the founders of the Italian socialist party. Alessandro Mussolini admired both Cipriani and Costa and it is quite probable that he was personally acquainted with them.

Benito Mussolini was born on Sunday afternoon, July 29, 1883, at Dovia, a village district in the town of Predappio. In a brief autobiographical account which he wrote in prison several years before he became the Duce of fascist Italy, he relates some interesting things about his early boyhood. When he was four or five years old, he began to read. From his sixth to his ninth year, he went first to his mother's school, and then to the school conducted by Silvio Marani, the chief elementary school teacher at Predappio.[1] "I was a restless and pugnacious little rogue. More than once I returned home with my head bleeding from a blow with a stone. But I knew how to avenge myself. I was a very audacious poacher." Once he stole some decoy birds. Pursued by the owner, he ran off and forded a river, but he did not

[1] I am certain that Marani was a socialist.

abandon his booty. He was very fond of birds, the screech-owl in particular. Now and then he blew the bellows in his father's blacksmith shop. Though he used to go to church with his mother and maternal grandmother, both of whom were devout believers, he tells us that he "could never remain long in church especially when great ceremonies were being conducted. The reddish light of the burning candles, the penetrating odour of the incense, the colours of the sacred vestments, the long drawn out singing of the faithful and the sound of the organ disturbed me profoundly."

At the age of nine, Mussolini was sent to a Catholic school for boys, or college as the Italians call it, conducted by Salesian Fathers at Faenza, a town famous for its faience. Although his father was resolutely opposed to having his boy attend a parochial school, he finally consented, apparently to satisfy the deep religious convictions of his wife. Benito informs us that during the weeks before his departure, he was more of a "little rogue" than usual. "I felt within me a vague restlessness. I had a hazy idea that college and prison were almost synonymous. I wanted to enjoy, to enjoy to the utmost, the last days of my freedom in the streets and fields, along ditches, amid vineyards with bunches of ripe grapes. Towards the middle of that October [1892?], everything was ready: clothes, personal effects, money. I do not recall that I was very much grieved over leaving my brother and sister: Edvige was then three years old, Arnaldo was seven. Instead I was profoundly sad at my having to leave behind a goldfinch that I had kept in a cage beneath my window. On the eve of my departure, I quarrelled with a companion and struck at him, but instead of hitting him, I hit a wall and hurt my knuckles. I had to depart with my hand bandaged. At the moment of parting, I wept. My father and I took our places in a small cart drawn by a donkey. We put our luggage under the seat and started out. We had not gone two hundred yards when the donkey stumbled and fell.   'A bad sign!', said my father, but he got the donkey on his feet, and we continued on our way. During the trip, I did not utter a word. I looked at the countryside, which was beginning to lose its greenness, and I followed the flight of the swallows and the course of the river. We passed through Forlì. The city made a great impression on me. I had been there but I did not remember it any more. I knew only that I had got lost and after several hours of anxious search, I had been found sitting quietly on the bench of a shoemaker who had generously given me—a boy scarcely four years old —a half Tuscan cigar to smoke. The deepest impression I got on entering Faenza was evoked by the Ponte di Ferro, the iron bridge thrown across the Lamone which unites the city with the suburbs. It may have been two o'clock in the afternoon when we knocked at the door of the College of the Salesian Fathers. It was opened for us. I was introduced to the rector who looked at me and said: 'He must be a vivacious young fellow.' Then my father embraced and kissed me. He too was deeply moved. When I heard the large entrance door close behind me, I burst into tears.''

Three things stand out in connection with his experiences at the Catholic school: the social discrimination among students, the brevity of his stay, and his expulsion. At the early age of nine, social and economic inequalities were poignantly brought home to him by the fact that for various purposes the students were divided into three classes with the result that he, a child of an extremely poor family, had to lunch and dine at third-class tables. He certainly must have been ready to respond enthusiastically to his father's socialist teachings. The restless, recalcitrant and "tough" boy did not hesitate to stab with a penknife a school companion who had insulted him and he got into so many other difficulties with the authorities that he was finally expelled from the school of the Salesian Fathers about two years after he had entered it.

Mussolini's parents then sent him to the Royal Normal School of Forlimpopoli where he completed his high school training in 1898 and his normal school training in 1901. Here too he was regarded as a lively young fellow. In 1898, during the last year of Mussolini's high school course, Valfredo Carducci, the director of the Normal School and a brother of the famous poet Giosuè Carducci, wrote to Alessandro Mussolini, telling him that the Faculty, in order to uphold the prestige of the school and the respect towards those who attended it, had suspended his son from classes for a period of ten days. The reason was stated: a teacher of Italian had assigned to Mussolini and his classmates the following theme: "Time is money." Mussolini handed in a small piece of paper with the following remarks: "Time is money. Therefore I am going home to study geometry since the examination is near. Doesn't this seem more logical to you?"

There is good authority for saying that Mussolini gathered together his fellow students at Forlimpopoli and delivered an apologia for regicide. I judge that this occurred some time after July 29, 1900, when King Humbert of Italy was assassinated by the anarchist Gaetano Bresci. Incidentally, that day was Mussolini's seventeenth birthday. Later on, in the course of his socialist career, Mussolini expressed his admiration for Bresci and defended at great length the need for violence in political action.

The first published reference to Benito Mussolini that I have found appeared on February 1, 1901, in the *Avanti!* (*Forward!*), the official daily newspaper of the Italian socialist party. The Italian newspapers were full of news and articles on Giuseppe Verdi, the famous Italian composer, who had died on January 27, 1901. The front page of the *Avanti!*, February 1, contained, among many other notices about Verdi, the following brief item, dated Forlimpopoli, January 29, and written by a correspondent who signed himself "b.r.": "Last night [January 28], in the city theatre, the comrade, student Mussolini, commemorated Giuseppe Verdi, delivering a speech that was applauded."

This brief item makes it clear that he was known as a socialist comrade in his teens. It is significant that, in spite of his irregularities at school, his superiors thought well enough of him to choose him from all their students to deliver an oration on Verdi. He was doubtless flattered by the mention of his name in the *Avanti!*, which was a national daily and, to boot, the principal organ of the party he and his father supported. Eleven years later, when he was twenty-nine years old, Benito Mussolini became its editor-in-chief.

Something more should be said about the poverty of the Mussolini family. They lived in a two-room apartment on the second floor of Palazzo Varano, an old building at Dovia. Benito and Arnaldo occupied one of the rooms, where they slept in the same iron bed made by their father—a bed with only a sack of corn leaves for a mattress—and this room served also as the kitchen. In the other room slept Alessandro, his wife and Edvige. The entire apartment was almost bare except for the simplest and most necessary furniture. In order to enter their "home", the Mussolinis had to pass through a third room, which was Rosa Mussolinis school. During the summer holidays, this room was cleared to store the wheat threshed by Alessandro.

The meals of the entire family were very frugal indeed, for on week-days, they had vegetable soup for lunch and plain chicory for dinner and on Sundays, they had a pound of mutton for broth since meat was an extreme rarity. They all ate from a common plate. During the winter months, the apartment was cold and virtually without any heat whatsoever. Such was their poverty that the Mussolinis frequently had to borrow bread, oil and salt. Benito's early diet has doubtless been an important element in making him to this day a very sparing eater.

In 1895, while Mussolini was attending school at Forlimpopoli, his mother wrote a moving letter to the prefect of the province of Forlì who had visited her school and had complimented her on her work: "Ever mindful of that auspicious day for me when Your Excellency deigned to visit my humble school, still recalling that Your Excellency expressed on that occasion words that were too flattering on my behalf, despite my merits, and among the many, that in view of my long service you would propose to the Ministry of Public Instruction a bonus for me, may Your Excellency permit me on this solemn National Holiday[1] to remind you of the kind

---

[1] September 20, the anniversary of the Italian Kingdom's "conquest" of Rome in 1870.

words you expressed, in spite of my merits. Your Excellency may see for yourself that this year the economic crisis in this small town is at its height, owing to the scarcity of crops and the total lack of grape, the sole product of these parts. And it is precisely for the above-mentioned reasons that my poor family again finds itself in such financial straits that we are forced to cut short the studies of our poor little boy of twelve who is now at the Royal Normal School of Forlim-popoli and who, according to his instructors, promises to amount to something. If Your Excellency could propose to the proper authorities a bonus for me, if you could advise me as to what I should do in order to obtain a subsidy for my boy or if you could help me in some way, I should always carry the memory of you engraved and blessed in my heart."

This request was not granted.

Upon his graduation from the Normal School as a licensed elementary school teacher in 1901, Mussolini applied in vain for a teaching post at Predappio and at Castelnuovo Scrivia and for the temporarily vacant post of secretary of the Commune of Predappio. He succeeded, however, in obtaining a post as a substitute teacher in an elementary school situated at Pieve di Saliceto, a village district in the "red" Commune of Gualtieri Emilia. In February 1902 he began teaching thirty-five pupils in the second and third primary grades, receiving a meagre salary, fifty-six lire—about eleven dollars—a month, forty of which went for his board.

In a candid and terse report to the Mayor of Gualtieri on the school year 1901–1902, after noting that out of thirty-five pupils there was a praiseworthy average daily attendance of thirty-three, Mussolini says: "This too is a sign of the times. Education is mounting in the opinion of the masses and is becoming a social necessity." His observations on discipline would not be tolerated in the fascist-controlled schools of to-day: "I have always maintained discipline by very simple means: awakening attention and interest and being watchful. Discipline obtained by coercive methods is not discipline. That sort of discipline represses the child's individuality and generates bad feelings. The teacher must forestall and remove the causes of evil in order not to have to resort to painful repression." As to cleanliness, he writes: "As long as the school and the family are not united in the work of education, real cleanliness will remain a pious and Utopian dream. How can we expect a clean sheet of paper from a boy who, because of dire circumstances, does his home work in a stable? My experience here has had the salutary virtue of making me throw away much, and perhaps cumbersome, idealistic rubbish." He notes an element of bigotry in a reading book used by his students and advises that the book be discarded. By way of concluding his report, he remarks that for reasons independent of his will, the results achieved were not satisfactory, "however much I did not neglect anything to improve the intellectual lot of children slaughtered by many years of scholastic misgovernment". It was a mistake, he continues, to judge a teacher by the number of pupils who pass their examinations. "Why? Because examinations, as they are given to-day, assume the hardly pedagogical characteristics of a judgment of God, and the teachers are not rare who, together with their children, place their trust in the same goddess: luck."

The Commune of Gualtieri had a socialist mayor and town council, which was not unusual, for socialism had made rapid strides in the Emilian region. The temperate and evolutionary character of the Emilian socialist movement made little impression on Mussolini who came from the more violently "red" Romagna and was destined to champion a revolutionary brand of socialism which looked askance at the reformist socialists and their tactics. The only authentic record that I have found of Mussolini's political activity at Gualtieri states that he presided and delivered some "applauded remarks" at a socialist mass-meeting addressed by the socialist mayor of the town.

Realizing that his duties as a substitute teacher at Gualtieri would end in June 1902, Mussolini decided to emigrate to Switzerland, thus following the example of thousands of other poor and unemployed Italians who sought work in the Helvetic Republic. He telegraphed to his mother for money to make the trip and with the forty-five lire that she sent, young Mussolini, who envisaged himself as a "plebeian of the twentieth century", a son of Italy forced by necessity to go abroad, set forth for Switzerland in July 1902 "to try his fortune".

E. P. Dutton & Co.)   (De Fiori " Mussolini, the Man of Destiny "

MUSSOLINI AT THE AGE OF 14 YEARS.

CHAPTER III

SWITZERLAND

1. EARLY EXPERIENCES

THE incidents connected with Mussolini's journey to Switzerland and his first experiences there are described in a letter to a friend dated September 3, 1902:

> "LAUSANNE,
> "3–IX–[1]902

"DEAR FRIEND,
"What I am about to write to you are memories. Sad memories of a hopeless youth which sees everything vanish—even the ideal. You will tell no one of what the llowing pages may contain: only a woman knows my sorrows, and you when you shall have read. I shall curse you if you make it a matter of gossip. My demand for secrecy should not seem to you inexplicable. I begin.

"I started from Gualtieri—saying good-bye only to my lady—on the morning of July 9. It was a Wednesday. From Parma to Milan and from Milan to Chiasso, the unbearable heat nearly made me die of thirst. Chiasso, the first Republican town, harboured me until 10.30 in the evening. While reading the *Secolo*, I experienced surprise in noting the arrest of my father, implicated in electoral disorders. The arrest disturbed me only because if I had known of it at Gualtieri, I would not have set out for

Switzerland, but for the Romagna. Having made the acquaintance of a fellow-traveller, one Tangherone of Pontremoli, I changed my Italian money and got into the train which was to reach Lucerne the next morning— a twelve-hour ride. The coach was full of Italians. Will you believe it? I stood at the window for almost the whole of the journey. The night was splendid. The moon rose behind the very high mountains, white with snow, amidst a silvery smile of stars. Lake Lugano gave out magical reflections like a polished sheet of metal on which beat unknown and enchanting lights. Mount Gothard presented itself to my eyes like a pensive and tranquil giant offering the use of his hidden passage to the serpent of steel which, with dizzying swiftness, was carrying me among new people.

"In the coach all were sleeping. I alone was thinking. What was I thinking on that night which divided two periods of my life? I do not remember. Only in the morning, and it may well have been due to physical fatigue—when we were crossing German Switzerland and a November rain struck us as coldly as the farewell of a doomed man—did I recall, with a heart-pang, the green countrysides of Italy kissed by a sun of fire . . . Was it a first touch of nostalgia? Perhaps. At Lucerne, I changed trains and took a ticket for Yverdon, coaxed by my travelling companion who promised me a post in the service of a relative of his, a draper. I reached Yverdon at 11 on Thursday, the 10th; a 36 hour train ride.[1] Stupified and weary, I made my way into a low-class inn where I had occasion to talk French for the first time. I had something to eat. We went to that Italian merchant. He gave me a lot of idle talk. Nevertheless, he invited me to dine with him. I accepted. More inconclusive idle talk. At last, he gave me a crown. So that he should not imagine he was benefiting me, I left with him as a pledge a very beautiful knife of Arabian design which I had bought at Parma on April 1st in the company of our good and sorrel-headed Romani.

[1] In his autobiographical account referred to above, p. 41, Mussolini says that when he got out at the station of Yverdon, he had two lire and ten centimes in his pocket.

"On Friday, I remained for one hour in front of the statue of Pestalozzi, who was born at Yverdon; and for 23 hours in bed. On Saturday, together with a painter out of employment, I went to Orbe, a neighbouring town, to work as a manual labourer. I found work and on Monday morning, the 14th, I began. Eleven hours' work a day, thirty-two centimes an hour. I made one hundred and twenty-one trips with a hand-barrow full of stones up to the second floor of a *bâtiment* in process of construction. In the evening, the muscles of my arms were swollen. I ate some potatoes baked in ashes and with all my clothes on, I threw myself on my bed: a pile of straw. At five on Tuesday, I awoke and returned to work. I chafed with the terrible rage of the powerless. The boss was making me mad. The third day he said to me: 'You are too well-dressed!' That phrase was meant to be significant. I should have liked to rebel and to crack the skull of that upstart who was accusing me of laziness while the stones were making my bones ache, to shout out in his face: 'Coward, Coward!' And then? Right is always on the side of the man who pays you. Saturday evening came. I told the boss that I intended to leave and that therefore he should pay me. He went into his office; I remained in the lobby. Presently he came out. With ill-disguised rage, he threw into my hands twenty lire and some centimes, saying: 'Here is your pay and it is stolen.' I stood petrified. What should I have done to him? Kill him? What did I do to him? Nothing. Why? Because I was hungry and had no shoes. I had worn a pair of almost new half-boots to pieces on the stones for the building, which had lacerated my hands and the soles of my feet. Almost barefooted, I hurried to an Italian and bought myself a pair of shoes, hobnailed in mountaineer's style. I packed off and on the next morning—Sunday, July 20—I took the train at Chavornay for Lausanne.

"This is not a beautiful city, but it is an attractive one. From the summit of the hill, it extends down to the shore of Lake Geneva with its enchanting suburb of Ouchy. It is full of Italians (6,000) who are not looked upon with much favour, and the Executive Committee of the [Italian] Socialist

Party [in Switzerland] has its headquarters here, and here is issued the weekly journal *Avvenire del Lavoratore* which I edit together with lawyer Barboni.[1]

"But let us proceed in order. In Lausanne, I lived fairly well the first week on the money I had earned at Orbe. Then I was again hard up. One Monday, the only piece of metal I had in my pocket was a nickel medallion of Karl Marx. I had eaten a bit of bread in the morning and I did not know where to sleep that evening. Desperate, I wandered about, and I sat down (the cramps in my stomach prevented me from walking any longer) on the pedestal of the statue of William Tell, which stands in the park of Montbénon. My appearance must have been terrible during these terrible moments, for the people who came to see the monument looked at me with suspicion, almost with alarm. Oh! if De Dominicis had come to preach his morality to me there, with what gusto would I have laid him out![2]

"At five o'clock, I leave Montbénon and direct my steps towards Ouchy. For quite some time, I walk along the Quay (the very beautiful road by the shore of the lake) and meanwhile evening comes on. In the twilight, the last rays of the sun and the last sounds of the old bells take me out of myself. A feeling of infinite sadness assails me, and I ask myself on the shore of the Leman whether it is worth while to live another day . . . I meditate, but a sweet melody, like a mother's lullaby over the cradle of her little boy, diverts the course of my thoughts and I turn back. In front of the imposing *Hôtel Beau Rivage*, an orchestra of forty is playing.[3] I lean against the railings of the garden, peer through the dark green foliage of the firs and listen intently. The music comforts both my brain and my stomach. But the intervals are terrible, the cramps stabbing into my entrails like red-hot

[1] Although Mussolini was a frequent contributor to the *Avvenire*, I found no evidence showing that he edited the paper in any capacity.

[2] I think Mussolini is referring to the educator Saverio De Dominicis, the author of several elementary pedagogical works characterized by an optimistic and moralizing tone.

[3] Mussolini stayed at this hotel in November 1922, when, as Italian Premier, he attended the conference of Lausanne.

pins. Meanwhile, the crowds of pleasure-seekers are moving about on the pathways of the park; the rustle of silks may be heard and the murmur of languages which I do not understand. An elderly couple pass close by me. They look English. I would like to ask them for *l'argent pour me coucher ce soir*. But the words die on my lips. The lady, stocky and smooth-skinned, glitters with gold and precious stones. I have not a soldo; I have no bed; I have no bread. I make off, cursing. Ah! a blessed idea, that of Anarchy of thought and action. Is it not the right of whoever is down to bite him who crushes him?

"From ten until eleven, I stay in the public lavatory of Ouchy, from eleven to twelve, under an old barge. The wind blows from Savoy and is cold. I return to the city and spend the rest of the night under the *Grand Pont* (the connecting link between two hills). In the morning, I look at myself out of curiosity in the windows of a shop. I am unrecognizable. I meet a man from the Romagna. I tell him briefly of my experiences. He laughs about them. I curse him. He puts his hand in his pocket and gives me ten soldi. I thank him. I hasten to the shop of a baker and buy a loaf of bread. I direct my way towards the wood. I feel as though I had a fortune. Having got a long way from the centre of the city, I bite into my bread with the ferocity of a Cerberus. I had not eaten for twenty-six hours.

"I feel a little life flowing through my veins. Courage returns with the flight of my hunger. I decide to fight on. I direct my steps towards the Villa Amina, Avenue de Léman. A professor of Italian, a certain Zini, lives there. Before going into the entrance-way of the charming little house, I clean my shoes and arrange my tie and hat. I enter. Zini has a head of ruffled, grey hair; his nose is phenomenal. I have hardly greeted him in Italian than he receives me with a volley of: 'Daily nuisances, daily nuisances! Holy, holy, holy Christ, etc. What do you want?!! I don't know, I couldn't tell! I shall see, we shall see. Go to Borgatta, rue Solitude. Ah! if I could! But . . . there may be something.'

" 'Go to hell with him who made you! Rascal!' And with this salutation I left him.

"In my next letter, I shall tell you all the rest. It will seem to you a novel, but it was, and is, a reality.

"I have received your postcard. Send me the ode and news of our friends.

"Your friend,

"MUSSOLINI BENITO."

This moving letter of a young emigrant boy of nineteen, forced to work as a manual labourer at thirty-two centimes an hour, chafing with terrible rage at his *padrone*, wandering about aimlessly for shelter and food, bitter and lonely, but none the less responsive to beautiful scenery, is a portrait of the average poor and indigent Italian emigrant in Switzerland, except that Mussolini had the benefit of a formal education and was imbued with a philosophy of life that was calculated to make each trying burden intensify his hatred for the capitalist system. He was fitted, moreover, to communicate his rebellious feelings to his fellow-country-men by his oratory and his writing, and so he was able to spend the larger part of his time as a labour organizer and socialist propagandist. Inasmuch as a normal school education and a gift for talking and writing were uncommon among Italian emigrant workmen, most of whom were illiterate and inarticulate, a youth like Mussolini was likely to eke out a livelihood in this way.

Since Mussolini's "betrayal" of the socialist ideal after his emergence as a fascist leader, his enemies have accused him of having taken unfair advantage of his comrades' hospitality in Switzerland and of having "lived on" them. While it is true that he worked as a manual labourer, a hodman, a butcher's boy, and an errand-boy for a wine merchant, it does not appear that he was engaged in these activities except at very occasional intervals, when he was in great need. He seems never to have held any position for very long or to have had the time or the disposition to learn a trade; he worked as a hodman and as a mason's helper, but he certainly was never a mason, as many writers would wish us to believe.

It is an exaggeration to charge him with "living on" his comrades. This accusation can be levelled against most Italian socialists who carry on propaganda among their compatriots in a foreign country, and we have no reason whatever to attribute to Mussolini the conscious intent of exploiting the socialist ideal in order to "live on" his comrades. One should not forget the feeling of hospitality prevailing in socialist groups, nor should one forget that Mussolini begged for bread on occasion and was arrested for vagrancy at Lausanne in July 1902—incidents which doubtless left an indelible impression on his sensitive mind.

The fascist and apologetic biographies of Mussolini are shamefully silent on his most important activities in Switzerland. In them will be found almost no discussion of the extensive material which we shall presently set forth. Two legends have been studiously circulated about Mussolini's stay in Switzerland, which should immediately be dismissed as sheer invention: one, that he spent most of his time as a manual labourer; the other, that he spent most of his time as a university student. His "manual" or "university" work is variously emphasized according to the fancy of the writer. An appeal to the wealth of documents that have been almost completely ignored will show that Mussolini was for the most part a labour organizer and a socialist propagandist and journalist. Those who were associated with him in Switzerland thought of him not as a manual worker or as a student but as an active revolutionist.

2. THE SOCIALIST AGITATOR. EXPULSION FROM TWO CANTONS

The two years or so that Mussolini spent in the Helvetic Republic were a period of energetic propagandist activity. Wherever he went, he displayed his oratorical and journalistic aptitudes and within a short time, he became well known as an agitator among the Italian inhabitants. On account of his relatively extensive reading and writing, he early gained a reputation as a socialist "intellectual". Less than a month after his departure from Italy in July 1902, he published his first article in a socialist weekly issued by the Italian socialists in Switzerland—*L'Avvenire del Lavoratore* (*The Future of the Worker*).

Mussolini's absorption in the work of organization and propaganda may best be shown by an itinerary of his movements. About August 24, 1902, he delivered his first socialist speech in Switzerland at Montreux; on August 31, he spoke at Vevey and on September 5, at Lausanne. In November, he was secretary of the Italian trade union of masons and masons' helpers at Lausanne and was elected by this union to represent it at a congress of a federation of these workers in the French-speaking part of Switzerland; at this congress, held at Lausanne on November 29, 30, he presented a resolution on a detail of organization. On December 7, at Lausanne, he expatiated on the historical, economic, and moral basis of socialism.

On January 23, 1903, he presented to a socialist meeting at Lausanne a joint resolution with his comrade Barboni criticizing the tactics of the Italian socialist party in an election at Cremona—apparently because socialists had been urged to support the candidacy of a member of the radical party. This doubtless was repugnant to Mussolini's intransigent position that socialists should fight their electoral battles alone and should form no electoral coalitions with "bourgeois" parties.

At Nyon, on February 15, 1903, he spoke before a labour organization on "The Right and Duty to Organize." After

Mussolini had refuted various objections by one of those present, the following resolution was unanimously approved: "The Assembly of Masons and Masons' Helpers of Nyon, after the speech by Mussolini, associates itself with and applauds the anti-militarist campaign undertaken so energetically in Italy and in the entire civilized world by the conscious proletariat, and expresses the wish that the reduction of unproductive expenses will serve to increase the level of education of the Italian workers in order to free them from the shameful sore of illiteracy, now that the most advanced states are about to prohibit the immigration of illiterates into their territories."

From the French part of Switzerland, Mussolini moved on to the German part in the spring of 1903. Bern was the centre of his activity for a few months. On March 8, at a meeting of masons and masons' helpers, he explained the agitation for a boycott movement. We are told that in another speech on that day, he discussed, "with the acumen of a scholar, the sorrows and poverty that afflicted a part of the human race . . ., that part which produces everything. He took a just fling at the ultramontanes, spoke about the causes of so much misfortune, and incited the workers to organize, recalling to them the celebrated phrase that organization would make even the government organic. A great impression and excellent propaganda."

The Italian socialists of Bern were so well impressed with Mussolini that they asked him to stay with them, apparently as their secretary and official propagandist. They expressed the hope that his work would be a source of instruction and of encouragement to the "disinherited" who were fighting for the socialist ideal. This tribute to nineteen-year-old Mussolini is a measure of the confidence that he inspired in his fellow countrymen throughout several socialist centres in Switzerland.

On April 4, 1903, Mussolini addressed Italian socialists at Thun, a town near Bern. A correspondent wrote of this meeting: "The hall of our organization was full of emigrants, among whom were many who had arrived from Italy that morning. Mussolini spoke for an hour and a half on the theme: 'Why we are poor.' His plain and effective speaking was liked and called forth much applause. After the speech, there were several applications for membership, and many paid their back-dues. Mussolini left with the promise to return to speak on socialism and to establish also at Thun a socialist organization. We anxiously await him." It was in the vicinity of Thun that Mussolini's younger brother, Arnaldo, went to work as a hodman and as a gardener and on several occasions the brothers met at Thun, Bern and Fribourg.

On May Day, Mussolini made two speeches at Bern and some days later, he told the workers that the bricklayers at Bern were poorly paid in enterprises conducted by liberals and socialists as well as in those where capitalistic usury was practised. On May 27, at a protest meeting against the pogrom at Kishineff in Russia, he spoke on behalf of the Italian socialists of Bern, concluding his address with the words of the anarchist Kropotkin: The sluggards do not make history, but submit to it. At the Italian socialist organization of Bern, he presented a resolution, on May 30, applauding the combative campaign of the Italian socialist daily, the *Avanti!*, and of its editor, against grafters and exploiters. The editor of the *Avanti!* was Enrico Ferri, the well-known criminologist, whose attempts to expose graft in high government circles eventually involved him in a sensational libel suit with a Cabinet Minister. Some years later, as Ferri drew away from socialist principles, Mussolini freely assailed him and vociferously demanded his expulsion from the socialist party.

The principal event with which Mussolini was connected at Bern was the protracted carpenters' strike. On June 7, at an important meeting held under the auspices of the *Union Latine*, the main speaker, Luigi Bertoni—the noted publisher and editor of *Le Réveil* and *Il Risveglio*, an anarchist weekly issued in Italian and French at Geneva—exhorted the workers to the necessity for solidarity of action. Mussolini advocated a parade of protest by the workers. He was arrested, expelled

from the Canton of Bern and "despatched in a car of vege-
tables" up to the Italian frontier. Protests against these arbitrary acts were of no avail. A correspondent of the *Avanti!*,
reporting the incidents at Bern, said that they had cost the
Italian socialists "a victim, the comrade Mussolini, an
able young man, of ardent zeal ***, a convinced and cultured socialist", not a dangerous anarchist. "The police of
Bern accused him on the pretext that he lacked a proper
residence permit, but the real truth is that Mussolini carried
on undiluted socialist propaganda, and this disturbed the
slumbers of the Swiss authorities who, in order to free themselves of a troublesome guest, did not bother about niceties."
On his expulsion, Mussolini wrote an article entitled "How
Italians are expelled from Switzerland":

"I am arrested on June 18, accused of making threats.
I become number 27. The next day, a member of the Police
Head quarters of Bern comes to see me in my new lodgings
and directs a heap of questions at me, which I answer as
I please. He wants to know who, after the Bertoni speech,
proposed the idea of a protest parade, and then I confess
that it was I. This was sufficient to make me a dangerous
individual. I am called to the anthropometric office, and I
am photographed in two poses; my left arm is studied and
all its peculiarities are observed. I pass another ten days in
my cell. I am informed that the judge no longer has the proofs
of the charge for which I was arrested, and the inquiry
is closed, all costs of the procedure being borne by the
state.

"At the same time, I received notice of the decree for
my expulsion from the Canton of Bern—with a police escort
up to Lucerne. It appears too clearly—and I shall not insist
on it further—that republican justice has faithfully served
the police which, for a long time, awaited a favourable
opportunity to strike me. At Lucerne, a stop of two nights.
I leave and there is another stop of 16 hours at Airolo. *Here
I pay for my food.* They put us, five of us—I say five of us—
in one of those small compartments of trains used for the
rapid transportation of merchandise. We suffocate. In the

tunnels the smoke takes away our breath. Our cries do not move those who have us in custody. We are a lot of poor, putrefied meat. Finally we get off at Chiasso. The Swiss policemen turn us over to their Italian colleagues. After a brief examination—being fortified with a passport—they set me free. I go back to Lugano. As soon as I get off there, I am arrested again. I begin to ask myself whether my face is one for the guillotine. Six hours more under arrest, and they let me go.

"These are the facts. I pass over many details which would render this account more interesting. I leave to the reader the trouble of making comments.

"Moral: Long live the Republic!"

It is well known that although each Swiss canton may expel a foreigner from its borders, such action does not mean expulsion from other parts of Switzerland. Numerous expulsions were ordered by the police without going through the process of a court trial, and in the case of foreign anarchists and socialists of the extreme type, this procedure was very common. Thus Mussolini, after being set free by the Italian police at Chiasso, was able to go to the Canton Ticino, the Italian part of Switzerland, where he continued his socialist propaganda for about three weeks, speaking before Italian stone-workers at Claro and Cresciano, before socialists at Castione, and addressing the socialists of Bellinzona on "Socialists and Religion".

In August 1903, we find Mussolini again at Lausanne. Here he applauded the conduct of Geneva strikers, offered to a Nyon strikers' fund a small sum that he had received for making a speech, and encouraged workers to contribute to the support of the Italian socialist paper in Switzerland. Towards the end of September 1903, it was announced that he would speak at Fribourg, a short distance from Bern, but not in the Canton of Bern from which he had been expelled. Whether or not he made the speech is not recorded, but the announcement is worthy of note because when he went to Flamatt in the Canton of Fribourg ten years later, in 1913, as the editor of the *Avanti!* and one of the most powerful men in the Italian revolutionary movement, he was enthusiastically received by many comrades who had known him as an obscure and youthful agitator in Bern and its vicinity.

At Lausanne, in September 1903, Mussolini took part in a meeting addressed by Taglialatela, an Italian evangelist preacher, and challenged the minister's arguments on religion. He was the principal speaker in a protest meeting against the "massacre" of workers by the Italian police at Torre Annunziata, a town near Naples. Mussolini himself sent a report of this meeting to the *Avanti!* of Rome. Another correspondent wrote: "In this moving speech, in which you perceived feeling and anguish, Mussolini traced the history of atrocities by bourgeois governments. He spoke of the massacres committed by the French reactionaries against the revolutionists of the Commune in 1871; and passed on to the painful episodes against the *Fasci Siciliani* and to the massacre at Milan in 1898, not forgetting the sanguinary repressions at Berra, Candela, Manduria, Giarratana, Putignano, Galatura and finally at Torre Annunziata. Not a few in the audience shivered with horror as they heard him unfold the terrible acts of brutal Italian police officers who had been decorated by the government; and many there were whose eyes became wet with tears at the recital of the textual words of those poor unfortunates who after being wounded, vainly implored mercy."

In this speech Mussolini, like his father, made reference to various incidents in Italian towns involving conflicts between the police and workers where the latter were "massacred". Italian revolutionists had not forgotten Crispi's violent repression of the *Fasci Siciliani*, groups of Sicilian workers striving for economic betterment, or the bloody reaction in Milan under the leadership of General Bava-Beccaris, who was given a special decoration by King Humbert. Symbolical of the popular fury that resulted from the government's policy of persecution was the assassination of King Humbert in 1900. To recall the "massacres" of Italian workers was one of Mussolini's favourite themes throughout his socialist career. Here it is appropriate to suggest that the "massacres" he once condemned were perhaps trifles when compared to the regime of violence which he instituted as the leader of the fascist party and state.

The Swiss sojourn of Mussolini was interrupted in October 1903 by a telegram from his father urging him to return home because of the serious illness of his mother. Upon his departure, the *Avvenire* felt certain that the Italian proletariat in Switzerland had appreciated "his intelligence, faith, and spirit of abnegation".

Back home at Predappio, in the province of Forlì, Mussolini became sufficiently notorious as a revolutionary socialist to influence the Royal Prefecture of Forlì to keep a secret police record of his activities. The first entry in the record contains a summary of his character and his doings up to January 1, 1904, and it is from this entry that we cull the following remarks: "As an individual of rather vivacious and sometimes impulsive and violent character, but because of his meagre education (that is, something the average worker could not boast) has enjoyed a good name. He has shown intelligence and some small culture, having attended the royal normal school of Forlimpopoli, where he took the superior courses. He is a hard worker and is supported by his family. He frequents the company of workmen in order to make proselytes to his party. In family relations behaves well. Until now he has held no office. He is inscribed in the socialist party, in which he has always been active, exercising a slight influence, limited, however, to his native town. He is in relations with the heads of the party in Romagna and with some in Bern, Zurich, and Lausanne ***. He makes an active propaganda among the working class, and earns a little money by it. He is capable of making speeches and has made some, one in Predappio, December 6, 1903, and another in Meldola, the 22nd of the same month. Further, during his residence in Bern, where he made for himself a certain position among our workers who professed advanced opinions, he repeatedly spoke in their public meetings, and especially on the occasion of May first, 1903, so much that he was registered by the Swiss police as a fervid socialist orator.

Towards the authorities he showed himself indifferent. He participates personally in all meetings of the party, and since his return from Switzerland has assumed in Predappio the attitude of party leader."

On January 3, 1904, according to the police record, Mussolini left for Geneva in search of employment. Another entry in the record, dated February 6, 1904, informs us of a report made by the Italian Consul General in Geneva that Mussolini had been denounced to him as an anarchist.

It seems that Mussolini spent most of January and the entire month of February 1904 at Annemasse, a French town near Geneva. Here he announced the publication of a bi-weekly review, *The New Times, a Periodical of International Socialist Culture*, to be edited by him and his friend Salvatore Donatini, but this periodical was never published.

In March, we hear of him at Geneva where he joined the local Italian socialist club which chose him as its representative to the congress of the Italian socialist party in Switzerland, held at Zurich on March 19–20, 1904. Among others at this congress were Angelo Oliviero Olivetti, who presided, Giacinto Menotti Serrati and Angelica Balabanoff. Mussolini's encounter with these three persons is of considerable interest. Olivetti, a native of Bologna and a practising lawyer at Lugano in the canton of Ticino, presented at the Zurich Congress a reformist resolution which was overwhelmingly defeated by Mussolini's revolutionary resolution. In 1906, he was one of the founders of a syndicalist review, *Pagine Libere*, in which he set forth extreme revolutionary views. Eventually this ex-reformist and ex-syndicalist became a rabid fascist and one of Mussolini's most faithful henchmen. His career is typical of many Italian syndicalists who ended up in the fascist ranks, thereby achieving a remarkable feat in moral and intellectual insincerity.

Throughout Mussolini's career as a socialist up to the autumn of 1914, his connections with Olivetti were of slight or no importance. On the other hand, Mussolini established close relations with Serrati and Madame Balabanoff. Some years later, both of them aided him considerably in attaining leadership of the Italian socialist party. Since many and confusing legends have grown up around the origin and early character of these relations, it might be well to mention certain facts which have too lightly been ignored. Serrati was a well-known figure among Italian socialists in Switzerland even before he went to the United States where he edited *Il Proletario*, an Italian socialist weekly. During Mussolini's stay in Switzerland in 1902 and 1903, Serrati was in the United States, and it is therefore obvious that they could not have met personally during these years. It is quite possible that they began to know each other by correspondence in the year 1903, when Mussolini contributed several articles to *Il Proletario*. Serrati did not return to Switzerland until January 1904, and I think it was sometime during this month that he made the personal acquaintance of Mussolini at Geneva. They met again at the Zurich Congress in March of that year, and they came to know each other very well at Lausanne. When Mussolini left his post as editor of the *Avanti!* in 1914 in order to advocate Italy's intervention in the Great War, he and Serrati became bitter personal and political enemies. During the post-war period, Serrati, as editor of the *Avanti!*, maintained close contacts with the Russian Bolsheviks and upheld the need for communism in Italy, while Mussolini, as editor of *Il Popolo d'Italia*, clamoured for the fascist seizure of power.

Angelica Balabanoff, a cultivated Russian exile, formed an acquaintance with Mussolini, which lasted up to the autumn of 1914. Equipped with an excellent formal education and a rare gift for languages, this child of a well-to-do Russian family started in her twenties to propagate the Marxist gospel with unusual fervour. She mastered Italian easily and began to address Italian socialists in Switzerland at least as early as 1903. She met Mussolini at the Zurich Congress of March 1904, and later during that year, she probably helped him translate a pamphlet of the famous German socialist Karl Kautsky. Mussolini praised her report at the congress on the exploitation of girls in religious institutions connected with industrial establishments and the campaign she was carrying on against this evil in a socialist paper addressed to Italian women. "After capitalistic exploitation", Mussolini observed, "monastic seclusion with all its infamies: this is the condition of those poor girls, the majority of whom are from the Ticino and northern Italy."

Madame Balabanoff was one of the many Russian revolutionists living in Switzerland, among whom was her comrade and acquaintance Lenin, who was writing for the Russian revolutionary paper *Iskra* (*Spark*) during part of the time that Mussolini spent in Switzerland. The future leader of the Bolshevik Revolution and the future leader of Italian fascism never met. Madame Balabanoff eventually identified herself closely with the Italian revolutionary movement, and she was made, together with Mussolini, a member of the Executive Committee of the Italian socialist party in July 1912. In December of that year, Mussolini became editor-in-chief, and Madame Balabanoff an assistant editor, of the *Avanti!* They parted company as bitter enemies when Mussolini became an interventionist. After playing a prominent rôle in the socialist anti-war movement during the Great War, she joined Lenin and Trotsky in revolutionary Russia and served as the first secretary of the Third International. For several years she has been living in Paris, where she edits the *Avanti!*, which was banished from Italy by its former editor and her former comrade.

At the Zürich Congress, Mussolini presented the report on the conditions of the socialist party in Italy and offered a resolution emphasizing the intransigent and revolutionary aims of the party. This resolution, which was overwhelmingly victorious over the reformist resolution offered by Olivetti, affirmed the necessity of revolutionary tactics in the struggle against the bourgeoisie, which possesses the means of production, and against their political institutions of defence; it regarded as "anti-socialistic the reformist affirmation of the co-operation between classes" and of the possible participation of socialists in a bourgeois ministry; and it maintained that reforms by the bourgeoisie were forced, partial and illusory concessions, intended to put off the day of its expropriation.

Finally, the resolution declared that "direct collaboration with the governing classes to obtain these reforms may form a part of the programme of radical-liberal parties, but not of the programme of the socialist party whose aim is eminently subversive and revolutionary: to abolish private property, the first cause of economic inequality, and the state—the instruments of class oppression".

Mussolini also made a proposal about the reorganization of the editorial board of the Italian socialist weekly paper in Switzerland, but this was almost unanimously voted down by the congress. The detail is worthy of note because I think it is the only recorded instance during Mussolini's socialist career from 1902 until 1913 that a proposal made by him to a socialist gathering was not accepted. As a socialist and as a fascist, he has been eminently successful in satisfying his domineering passion for having his own way.

Coupled with Mussolini's advanced revolutionary views were his extreme anti-religious beliefs. He zealously supported the anti-religious agitation carried on by the Italian socialists of Geneva and Lausanne. On March 25, 1904, there took place at the Maison du Peuple of Lausanne a debate between Mussolini and the evangelist preacher Alfredo Taglialatela on the subject: "God does not exist. In science, religion is an absurdity; in practice, it is immorality; and in men, it is a disease." The debate between the "atheist and the priest", held before more than five-hundred workers, was reported at length by Serrati: "Mussolini, a perfect master of his subject, was calm and serene" and delivered a "fine address". What Mussolini said was soon embodied in a pamphlet issued by the International Library of Rationalist Propaganda of Geneva under the title *Man and Divinity*.

Mussolini's stay in Geneva, like his stay at Bern, ended in a cantonal expulsion. In April 1904, he was expelled from the Canton of Geneva because he was using a falsified passport. About May 5, shortly after the socialist deputy Dr. Adrien Wyss had made an interpellation at the Grand Conseil relative to Mussolini's expulsion, Mussolini sent an interesting letter in French to Dr. Wyss, who permitted me to make a photostatic copy of it when I visited him at Geneva:

"ANNEMASSE,
"*Thursday night* [*May 5*(?), *1904*]
"DEAR COMRADE WYSS,

"I have just read in the *Genevois* [a Geneva daily] that you will interpellate the Grand Conseil about my expulsion. Odier has up to the present, maintained an alarming silence; perhaps he is preparing something surprising . . . At any rate, to avoid any trouble and to give you some information which you may need, here is my past:

"In Italy I attended the normal schools and I was graduated a teacher. I taught for some time, and afterwards, about July 1902, I came to Switzerland. Until last year, I worked and earned my living honestly at Lausanne. I returned to Italy and went to my mother. I stayed there for two months, after which I went to Annemasse where Donatini and I had planned the founding of an international periodical of socialist culture. The first of March, I came to Geneva where I thought of registering as a student or as an *auditeur* at the University.

"People will tell you that I am an 'anarchist'. Well, Comrade, nothing could be more false. During these last few years, I have written a good deal in the newspapers of our party. I have contributed—with compensation—to the *Proletario*, a daily in Italian which was published in New York. I have often written for *L'Avanguardia Socialista* of Milan and for *L'Avvenire del Lavoratore*. I defy any authority to find in a single article a single line or argument that could classify me among the anarchists. I have always been registered, both in Italy and Switzerland, in the socialist party. In our congress, held just recently at Zürich, I was the reporter on the famous question of 'tendencies', and I introduced a resolution which, while revolutionary, could never be interpreted as anarchistic. You can see it in the *compte-rendu* published in *L'Avvenire* of Bellinzona. I was in Geneva for 40 days, and I took very little part in political life. I spent almost all my time at the

Library. I spoke only on the commemoration of the Commune, and it was on this occasion that I had the pleasure of shaking your hand.

"My dossier is a pack of lies. A symptomatic thing is that it is joined to that of Donatini [also an expelled socialist]. I was 'despatched' without being given the time to return the key of my room, to ensure the safety of my diplomas, to greet some friends and my lawyers . . . In truth, like a mangy dog that could infect everybody . . . And to hide me from view, they lied to Maitre Zurlinden and to Victor Snell [lawyers for Mussolini] by telling them that I had left and had been taken to Annemasse while I was on the way to Chiasso. The rest you know, dear Comrade, and I shall not dwell upon it.

"I am very glad you are bringing the question before the Grand Conseil because my expulsion could cover with shame a democracy that wants to keep intact the holy traditions of Helvetic liberties and does not find a protest against these proceedings, unworthy even of a monarchy.

" Now I am going to Lausanne, to the University, and I hope to remain undisturbed there. I shall learn there the result of your interpellation. It will be difficult for Odier to justify his action. Afterwards I shall appeal to the Grand Conseil against my expulsion.

"My socialist greetings to you, dear Comrade.

"Yours truly,
"MUSSOLINI BENITO.
"POSTE RESTANTE, LAUSANNE."

Odier was the head of the Police and Justice Department of the Canton of Geneva. On May 11, at a session of the Grand Conseil of Geneva, he answered Dr. Wyss' interpellation and described at considerable length the steps leading to Mussolini's arrest, detention and expulsion. Some of his important remarks follow:

"What happened in Mussolini's case? On March 9 [1904], Mussolini went to the bureau of residence-permits to ask for a residence-permit. In support of his request, he presented a

French registration card, dated January 16, 1904, which indicated that he had used a passport. After the employee brought to his attention the fact that this card was not sufficient, he decided to produce a passport. This passport, at first glance, was recognized as irregular. It bore the following date: '31 December 1905', but it was evident, on sight, that there was a surcharge on the number five and that the number 3 was the real number and had been changed to five by the addition of a little curl on top of the number 3. After the employee had taken note of this change, a temporary permit was given to Mussolini and information about this passport was asked of the Italian Consul at Bellinzona. This official replied on March 11, 1904: 'In answer to your letter of the 9th instant, I hasten to inform you that the passport of the said Mussolini, Benito, was valid up to December 31, 1903. The date 1905 is therefore false. If you believe that you need not take any steps against this individual because of the falsification committed, I should be obliged to you if you would kindly send back this passport to me, as I shall inform the Italian authorities of what has just happened.'

"On April 9, Mussolini again went to the bureau for foreigners and asked to have his papers returned to him. In the interim, the Parquet had been notified, and by order of the police commissioner, Mussolini was arrested and taken to prison. When first questioned by the police commissioner, Mussolini answered as follows: 'I acknowledge that the year 1903 was falsified and changed to 1905, but I am not the author of this falsification. Nevertheless, I admit that I made use of my passport knowing that it had been falsified.'

"It is true that Mussolini later went back on his declarations. When questioned by the investigating judge who asked him if he confirmed the answers made before the commissioner, he replied: 'Yes, but I rectify them on one point: When I used my passport at Geneva to prove my identity, I had not noticed that it had been falsified by the change of the date from 1903 to 1905. This falsification must have been made in Italy when I left this passport in the hands of third parties. I do not know who did it.'

"This explanation did not appear sufficient, and the dossier of the matter, after this interrogation, was transmitted by the investigating judge to the Parquet of the Prosecutor-General. The Prosecutor-General then considered the question of finding out if it was expedient to prosecute Mussolini, and after examining the question, considering that Mussolini had already been in prison for seven days—since he had been arrested on April 9 and it was now April 15—and considering, in addition, that the expulsion of Mussolini had been decided upon in an administrative manner, the Prosecutor-General decided not to summon Mussolini to appear before a magistrate.***

"Now, gentlemen, a few words on the personality of Mussolini. He is a former Italian school teacher who is at present engaged in revolutionary socialist propaganda. He was arrested at Lausanne, for vagrancy, in July 1902; at Bern, in 1903, for a political offence, kept in prison until June 19 and expelled from the canton of Bern. He was pointed out to us as an anarchist in a circular of July 31, 1903, issued by the federal authorities. I believe that Mussolini protests against this description of him as an anarchist and that he is content with that of revolutionary socialist. It is, in fact, in this capacity that Mussolini has acted among us. Even before he appeared at the bureau for residence-permits to regularize his status, he was already playing a part in the sessions of the Italian revolutionary socialist club of Geneva. In a session which took place in the early days of March, Mussolini made a big speech, talking about the present political movement in Italy. He gave the history of the party, the birth of which is due to internationalism. He traced its different phases and the revolutions effected in the course of time. According to him, the movement has always been insurrectional and revolutionary.***

"Mussolini therefore frankly declared himself a partisan of the revolutionary group. Consequently, gentlemen, Mussolini, by very reason of his activity at Geneva, had placed himself in the position of being expelled like his friend and *alter ego* Donatini, who has been, as you know, likewise expelled from the canton [of Geneva] and whose appeal has been denied by the Council of State.

"Gentlemen, can we reproach the State for having asked Mussolini to cross the frontier when on the one hand, in order to establish himself among us, he sought to use dishonest means by falsifying a record of legitimation which was asked of him, and on the other hand, he spoke and displayed his activity in an essentially revolutionary milieu which seeks by all possible means to combat our institutions? I do not believe so, and I think that it is the duty of the State, as a simple matter of self-defence, to keep away from its territory men whom it must consider dangerous to our institutions. It was, above all, because he had tried to present false papers that Mussolini was arrested, that he was questioned and that his expulsion from our territory was decided upon. But, as you see from this information, it is not simply a question of an unfortunate foreigner who tried to procure for himself, even through dishonest ways, a means of legitimizing his request for a residence-permit, but a question of a man whose presence here is dangerous because of the ideas which he professes and, above all, because of the means which he preaches and of the activity which he tries to arouse among his Italian co-religionists and compatriots."

The socialist protest in what was then called the *affaire Mussolini* was directed particularly against the Genevan authorities for having attempted to "despatch" Mussolini to Chiasso, a frontier town in the Canton of Ticino, and turn him over to the Italian authorities. This would have meant his immediate arrest by the Italian police because he was a *réfractaire*; that is, a shirker, an evader or dodger from military service, one who had not responded in due time to the call of his class for compulsory military service in Italy. It was principally through the quick co-operation of the Geneva and Ticino socialists that this was averted. In the Ticino, the prominent benefactor on Mussolini's behalf was the socialist Giuseppe Rensi, now a well-known Italian philosopher, who at that time was practising law at Bellinzona. Since the Geneva police had no authority over Mussolini once he was in Ticinese territory, pressure was brought to bear on the Ticino authorities, which resulted in his being set free before he could be brought to Chiasso. This was consonant with the well-established international practice that a state should not send back a *réfractaire* to the country of his origin. After his release by the police, Mussolini enjoyed a night's hospitality at Rensi's home.

Under the heading "Number 2", Mussolini wrote an account of his expulsion from Geneva which, among other things, establishes definitely, on his own confession, that he was a *réfractaire*:

"In the brief turn of a year, it is already the second time that I have been hit by a cantonal expulsion with police escort. The judicial comedy that precedes the police measure exasperates me. Just as at Bern, so at Geneva, I am arrested under the charge of an ordinary misdemeanour. After the charge and detention, I choose a defender and await the trial. I want to go to the Court, refute the charge and show it to be a pretext to seize my person and expel me without even allowing me the choice of a frontier. I want to prove my innocence to the judges and tell them: 'You serve the police.' But no. After seven days of jail, the charge vanishes and there appears the red phantasm created by the phenomenal stupidity of the agents of order—the 'dangerous anarchist' who must be 'despatched' to the border of the country of his origin. The proofs of my anarchism are gathered together. The dossier that concerns me is voluminous and irrefutable. Like a package, I am 'despatched'. The Justice and Police Department at Geneva makes out a certificate of transport up to Chiasso. I am a *réfractaire* since March 27, but just to 'despatch me', the Genevan authorities have no scruples whatever about violating international treaties; and the cantonal expulsion becomes a 'disguised and arbitrary extradition'.

"If I am free to-day, if instead of being in jail in Italy, I find myself in another and more hospitable republican territory, I owe it to the work of the comrades of Geneva, to the efforts made by comrade Lawyer Rensi, and to the interpellation of Fusoni on account of which the cantonal government of the Ticino, by refusing complicity in this monstrous arbitrary act, had the good sense to set me free on federal territory.[1] My thanks to those who concerned themselves with my case. It remains a symptomatic sign of the reactionary storm that is raging at Geneva. In the city reformed by Calvin, that most repulsive type of inquisitor who can be seen at the 'Salle Ami Lullin' [at the Geneva Library], a government of 'direct democracy' with the attendant 'sovereign people' wages war against ideas that are freely and honestly professed. It is painful to see a 'sausage makers' democracy' that has never known how to find the road of protest and pretends to be unaware of its immense shame, believing perhaps that to perpetuate a tradition of liberty the apple of William Tell is sufficient."

After his expulsion from Geneva, Mussolini probably spent a few days at Annemasse with his friend Donatini. In the spring, we find him again at Lausanne where he remained most of the time until November or December 1904 when he left Switzerland permanently and went back to Italy. Mussolini delivered speeches at Uster in October and at Coire and St. Margrethen in November. On November 12, the Italian socialists of Lausanne, whose leader was Serrati, gave him a farewell party. A reporter tells us that in his speech on "Neo-Marxism", Mussolini intended to demonstrate "that contrary to what the revisionists affirm, the theory of Marx is neither dead nor antiquated; that, on the contrary, it is younger, more alive than ever; the facts year by year lend lustre to it and history shows it to be true. Some of the economic conclusions of Marxism may perhaps be erroneous, but the sociological conceptions are valid. Against the new theory of collaboration or compenetration of classes, there stands firm and unshaken in its Marxist foundation the theory of class struggle; there stands the concept of international struggle, the concept of the class union of the international proletariat, the concept of the revolutionary conquest of

[1] Fusoni was a radical member of the Grand Council of the Canton of Ticino.

public power. Mussolini was very much applauded and applauded still more when—after the affectionate greeting extended to him by comrade Serrati—he incited everyone to do his duty in the ranks of the party and for the socialist party." As a token of esteem, the workers gave him a fountain pen. Joined to the greeting of the Italian socialists at Lausanne was that of *L'Avvenire del Lavoratore* which remarked on Mussolini's "very intelligent propaganda work" among the Italian proletariat in Switzerland.

The most remarkable tribute paid to Mussolini during his Swiss sojourn appeared in a small news item of twenty-four lines sent from Geneva to *La Tribuna*, a conservative daily newspaper issued at Rome. The item, dated Geneva, April 17, 1904, and published on the first page of the *Tribuna*, April 18, was written by a Geneva correspondent who signed himself "Domino". Besides reporting Mussolini's expulsion from Geneva, this correspondent described him as a *réfractaire* and as an Italian socialist from the Romagna "who has been for some time the great duce of the local Italian socialist club [of Geneva]".

The discovery of this item was one of the most interesting results of our research. Mussolini was called a Duce, indeed a great Duce, for the first time when he was twenty years old! No tribute could be more flattering to him than to be called a Duce. Eventually, it became a matter of little moment to him whether he was called a Duce in connection with socialism or fascism. What has always mattered to him is that he be regarded as a leader. Looking at his socialist and fascist career as a whole, we find that his fidelity to a cause has always been secondary to his love of leadership.

I am convinced that Mussolini has never read the news item in the *Tribuna*, for I think it is inconceivable that he could have read it and then have forgotten to utilize it to his advantage especially after he became the Duce of the fascist state. Had he read it or known about it, he would certainly have brought it to the attention of the public either through his fascist press or through one of his many enthusiastic biographers.

While there can be no doubt that Mussolini's Italian socialist comrades at Geneva held him in high esteem, it is extremely doubtful that he had achieved the stature of a "great duce" in their eyes, even though they had selected him as their representative at the Zurich Congress of the Italian socialists in Switzerland in March 1904, where he had made an excellent showing as the exponent of a victorious resolution relating to revolutionary tactics. It must be remembered that Mussolini was called a "great duce", not by a fellow socialist, but by the correspondent of the *Tribuna*, a conservative and, from the socialist point of view, a reactionary newspaper. As a close observer of happenings in Italian immigrant circles in Switzerland, Domino doubtless took more than a passing interest in the activities of the Italian socialists who were steadily increasing in strength and numbers. During the months of March and April 1904, Domino probably became familiar with three facts about Mussolini: the notoriety connected with his debate on religion with Taglialatela, his prominent rôle at the Zurich Congress, and the wide publicity attending his expulsion from Geneva. All these occurrences may have impressed Domino so sharply that he was led to call Mussolini a "great duce". A possibility which should not be dismissed *a priori* is that Domino, as the correspondent of a "bourgeois" paper, used the term "great duce" in a sarcastic vein. In any case, whatever Domino's motives might have been, it is noteworthy that the man who was destined to be the acknowledged Duce of the Italian socialist movement and of the fascist movement was described as a Duce in his twentieth year.

Who is Domino? I have sought in vain to identify him. Although I have what I consider a good guess as to his identity, I think it best to hold it in abeyance for the present. Should Domino happen to read this book, we hope he will disclose his identity.

About two years after Mussolini became Italian Prime Minister in 1922, some of his enemies began to circulate the serious charge that he stole a watch while he was in Switzerland. One version has it that after stealing the watch, he asked forgiveness of the owner; another, that legal proceedings were begun against him but were not completed because the owner withdrew his charge; and still another, that he was sentenced by a Swiss court for stealing a watch, but after becoming Prime Minister, he persuaded the Swiss government to suppress all traces of the court sentence. All these and other vague versions are unsubstantiated. My researches on the origin and details of the serious charge against Mussolini lead me to conclude that it has no foundation whatsoever. In this connection, I have been able to consult a volume printed before the Great War, which was intended for the sole and exclusive use of the Swiss police. Public circulation of this volume was and is prohibited. The volume, entitled *Répertoire des signalements*, contains references to the police record of foreigners who have been in Switzerland. On page 192, Mussolini's name is listed, but there is no sign indicating that he was ever sentenced for the crime of theft in Switzerland.

An irresponsible charge was made in a pamphlet written in 1928 by an anti-fascist, Maria Rygier, who maintained that Mussolini was engaged as a spy by the French government while he was staying in the Upper Savoy section of France in 1904. This charge is lacking in any foundation whatsoever and should be dismissed as one of the many anti-fascist and anti-Mussolini legends which are as much a hindrance to the understanding of Mussolini's character and career as the fascist and pro-Mussolini legends.

3. THE SOCIALIST JOURNALIST

Throughout his stay in Switzerland, Mussolini was active as a journalist. He wrote most frequently for *L'Avvenire del Lavoratore* (*The Future of the Worker*), the weekly organ of the Italian socialists in Switzerland; he was a fairly regular contributor to *L'Avanguardia Socialista* (*The Socialist Vanguard*), a weekly paper of the revolutionary faction of the Italian socialist party, published at Milan and edited by Arturo Labriola and Walter Mocchi; he wrote several articles for *Il Proletario*, the New York weekly paper of the Italian socialists in the United States, and on one occasion, he sent a short notice to the *Avanti!*, the daily organ of the Italian socialist party, published at Rome.

What is, to my knowledge, the first published article bearing his signature appeared in the *Avvenire* on August 2, 1902, less than a month after his arrival in Switzerland. Entitled "A Fall", it compares the fall of the Armenian people with the fall of the campanile of Venice. In view of the recent conquest of Ethiopia, the reader would do well to substitute the word fascists for the word Kurds and the word Ethiopia for the word Armenia.

"A people falls. An entire people, good and forsaken, leaves every day its body, its liberty and its traditions in shreds on a bloody road of ruins. The telegraph daily announces the massacres consummated by the Kurds against the Armenians. None of them escapes slaughter. A few days ago, a Kurd chieftain, after having buried a village, ordered all the women to be tied, and then committed against them acts of incredible cruelty and made them die in horrible pain.

"Well then, these facts which, at the auspicious dawn of the twentieth century, should arouse in everyone a feeling of horror, pass completely or almost completely unobserved, like episodes of secondary importance, amid the farrago of daily news. A few isolated individuals raise their voice to protest in the name of the rights of peoples. But the public cannot interest itself in Armenia during the dog-days that drive everyone towards some sea-resort or some place in the mountains. And the papers deal with another fall: the fall of the campanile of Venice.

"Strange, however! For the tower that crumbles because it is powerless to sustain the weight of centuries, even diplomacy and the higher-ups in the more or less bureaucratic or financial circles bestir themselves; a chorus of protests and of supplications is raised in the name of art, of memories, of the fatherland, and even of humanity. For a people—still in its infancy—that falls, crushed by the moloch of blindly fanatical barbarism, no one gets excited. Europe, which shudders on account of a loss that is after all disputable even from an artistic point of view, does not find for this cause an outburst of generosity; it has no protests against those who could, if willing, prevent a region from becoming a cemetery.

"Oh! if a shrub could become an oak, defying a hurricane; oh! if the proletariat, by bringing together its ranks in a compact phalanx, could with its own hand, determine the course of justice, the massacres worthy of the times of Attila would cease. And the disappearance of the tyranny that one social class, with its economic privileges, exercises over another will also mark the end of every violence instigated by race fanaticism and hatred; and all men will be united by a bond of fraternal solidarity."

Mussolini's violent and ardent nature found expression in his writings against almost everything in his Swiss environment: the complacent and conservative temperament of the people, their democracy, their dull intellectual interests, their puritanical "Protestant canaille", their so-called liberal and republican institutions and particularly their socialist movement and leaders. By way of emphasizing the hotel keepers' mentality of the Swiss, he used the well-known jibe of referring to William Tell as William "Hotel". He had occasion to note the attempt to dismiss Professor Giulio Carrara from his post in a Swiss Gymnasium. Carrara, he wrote, was "a talented writer, noted for his libertarian views. The campaign was made by the despicable Protestant clergy which hates the irreligion of Carrara and fears the influence of modern

teachings on the minds of the youth. It is well to add, however, that the Committee on Studies has re-appointed the
distinguished professor to his post. None the less, the fact is
symptomatic and demonstrates how right Frederick II was in
declaring that 'among all the Jesuits, the Protestants were
the worst'. " The mobilization of troops by various cantonal
governments in order to repress strikes angered the young
Romagnuole emigrant. Where Italian strikers were involved,
such a measure was apparently taken without much ado. "It
is a matter anyhow of Italian flesh, already accustomed to
massacres."

Of course, Mussolini looked upon the so-called free institutions of Switzerland as a mockery. Excoriating the Swiss
authorities for their ruthless treatment of foreign revolutionists, he declared : "Revolutionists, the majority of whom
are Russians and Italians, are expelled from that land which
was painted to them as an oasis of liberty. The Swiss democracy shamefully keeps silent. At bottom, it approves these
reactionary measures.*** Never as in this year of grace, 1903,
have the republican rulers shown themselves to be so reactionary"—as evidenced by their repression of strikes at Bern,
Geneva, and other places. "It is the socialist party that
furnishes—painfully—the opium. I have made the acquaintance of this unworthy *camaraderie*.*** The English tourists,
the sowers of the sterling and the dollar, want to be tranquil . . . Why then do these socialist, anarchist and revolutionary foreigners come to disturb our slumbers?"

Mussolini reserved his bitterest scorn for the Swiss socialist
movement and, above all, its leaders. His expulsion from
Bern excited his ire against its indigenous socialists, whom he
condemned in a letter sent to the anarchist Bertoni and published in the latter's paper, *Il Risveglio*. After calling Bern an
old city where "the sellers of brandy and the priests of the
tepid social-democratic popery prosper", he attacked the
city's socialist leaders, these "eligibles for the red papacy"
and these "cozy, very cozy revolutionaries" for their refusal
to aid Italian strikers.

The reformism and the spirit of conciliation characterizing

the Swiss socialists repelled him, and he warned the Italian socialists not to follow their tactics. Their practice of "rancid patriotism under a proletarian mask" disgusted him. It was not as a patriotic Italian but as an anti-patriotic socialist and internationalist that he resented the reactionary and national-istic prejudice against foreigners on the part of the Swiss people in general and of the Swiss socialists in particular. Besides defining socialism in Switzerland as "a vague philo-sophy that vacillates between Luther and Calvin", Musso-lini asserted: "If by socialism is meant a Protestant democ-racy which, imbued with socialism, enacts reforms within its borders and charitably thinks that with the motto 'Liberty and the Fatherland' it can reconcile capitalism and the proletariat, then we can include in socialist literature even the bulls of Pope Pecci [Leo XIII] that summon the masters to their duties towards the workers.*** If by socialism, how-ever, is understood the goal and the movement (collective property, class struggle) of the majority of the expropriated (the proletarians) who aim at the expropriation of the holders of wealth (the capitalists) *** then only the blind cannot see that authentic socialism is yet to be born in this curious republic. And Swiss socialists may be sought for in vain, even if one is furnished with the already over-exploited lantern of the Cynic of Sinope [Diogenes]."

4. THE ANTI-MILITARIST

Throughout his stay in Switzerland, Mussolini was a confirmed anti-militarist. There is no better proof of this than his status as a *réfractaire*, which he himself admitted and which the Swiss as well as the Italian press noted after his expulsion from the Canton of Geneva. *Le Peuple de Genève*, a socialist semi-weekly, described him as a "réfractaire par conviction antimilitariste", and as a "victime de la tyrannie militaire". The Italian consular authorities carefully watched his movements. According to an entry dated April 28, 1904, in the secret police record of Mussolini's activities, kept at the Royal Prefecture of Forlì, "Benito Mussolini was on the tenth of April declared absent without justification when his class was called for army service". While in Italy in November and December 1903, he was, of course, aware of the fact that the men of the class of 1883, the year he was born, would soon be summoned to perform their military service. Since his original passport was valid until December 31, 1903, the change of date from 1903 to 1905 enabled him to use a falsified passport in order to leave Italy in January 1904.

Mussolini's position on anti-militarism was farther to the left than that of the reformist socialists, the revolutionary socialists, and even of many anarchists. His comparatively extreme stand is best indicated by his advocacy of desertion from the army even in times of peace. In February 1904, he wrote: "Militarism is in us, in our habits. It is we who fatten the evil beast when, with stupid resignation, we pay the taxes destined to its maintenance; it is the sons of the proletariat who populate the barracks; it is our powerlessness that fortifies jingoistic patriotism.*** There is indeed an infallible means of destroying from its foundation the infamous militarist constraint: Desertion!"

Mussolini's success in Ethiopia lends special interest to his former anti-war propaganda. He held up to the scorn of the Italian proletariat the grand manœuvres and all forms of military display, which now constitute one of the characteristic marks of the fascist state. As he put it, kings and the personages of their retinue with their loud and many-coloured uniforms, their chests bristling with crosses, decorations, and similar foreign and domestic hardware, surrounded by a picked guard and followed by a swarm of generals, ministers, and officials, pass on in parade, blinding the public with dust and flaunting in its face their impudent display. Mussolini was certain that if the caprice of a monarch or some crazy megalomaniac should plunge people into war, the proletariat would refuse to fight and would start a general strike:

"The time is now past when the caprice of a monarch can drive peoples to slaughter. To-day, bankers are above kings. The interests of the big banks explain many strange situations.*** Surely, without bankers a war cannot be waged. When, many years ago, it seemed that one of these bloody conflicts would break out, Madame Rothschild, on being interviewed, could answer that nothing would happen simply because her husband was not lending money.

"We dare add that another force—just come upon the scene of history, but already vibrating with a human ideal—will impose itself on kings with crowns and on kings of finance. This force, which finds its most beautiful and eloquent expression in the proletariat that rises to the enlightened aims of Justice, this force, which aspires to *humanize* the men of all the world, has already manifested itself as sentiment that brings about fraternity, as thought that justifies sacrifice, the daily work of solidarity.

"From bloody '71, from the day the workers of Paris spiritually shook hands with their comrades across the Rhine and above the heads of the soldiers proclaimed the Internationale; from that day, which like a ray of light cuts across those dark times, war, at least in Europe, has become impossible. And if there should appear a crazy megalomaniac, the proletariat would no longer lend itself, as a docile herd, to the holocaust. We are ready—Jules Guesde [the French socialist] has said—to set against the armies on the march the General Strike, beginner of the Social Revolution."

Mussolini did not have the slightest hesitancy in recalling the defeat of the Italians by the Ethiopians at Adowa (or Abba Garima), at Amba Alagi, and at Dogali. The history of the Italian monarchy since 1870, he cried out in 1904, was a shameful record. "Italy needed bread and she was bled white by an army and a navy. She needed to regenerate herself completely and she was plunged into colonial enterprises. The dream of a jingoistic minister [Francesco Crispi] and of an imperialist sovereign [King Humbert] was suffocated in the blood of Abba Garima, of Amba Alagi and of Dogali."

As everyone knows, Mussolini has surpassed Crispi in jingoism and has given the title of Emperor to King Victor Emmanuel III, the son of the "imperialist sovereign" King Humbert.

It appears that Mussolini left Switzerland and returned to Italy in November or December 1904, and it is certain that he was back in his native country not later than December of that year. But so long as he was a *réfractaire*, he stayed outside of Italy, for had he returned, he would have been subject to arrest and to special penalties for having failed to answer the army summons of his class. In September 1904, he was doubtless relieved by an event of prime importance to him. On September 17, King Victor Emmanuel, in anticipation of the birth of a successor to his throne (the present Crown Prince Humbert), issued a decree of amnesty to some categories of *réfractaires*, including those of the class of 1883 to which Mussolini belonged. This amnesty was to be applied only on certain conditions which provided for the eventual service of the *réfractaires* in the Italian army. By deciding to fulfil these conditions, Mussolini was free to return to Italy without fear of arrest or special penalties. In 1905 and 1906, he served his regular term in the army, as the following entries in the secret police record clearly indicate: "The thirty-first of December, 1904, having presented himself at the military district of Forlì, as inscribed in the first category of conscripts in arrears of the class of 1883, Mussolini is assigned to the tenth regiment of Bersaglieri stationed at Verona. On the eighth of January, 1905, left for Verona where the regiment is stationed.*** On the sixth of September, 1906, arrived at Predappio, released from the tenth regiment of Bersaglieri."

In February 1905, he was granted a short leave in order to see his mother, who died of meningitis on February 19 of that year. About two decades later, after Mussolini had become Prime Minister, it was alleged by fascists that on February 26, 1905, he had written the following letter from Predappio to a captain of his regiment at Verona, a certain Simonetti:

"MOST HONOURABLE CAPTAIN,

"In the name also of my father and my sister, I wish to thank you heartily and with you the officers and my comrades for the kind words sent to me. Of the dozens of letters which I have received in these days, many will go into the fire because they only repeated the usual and banal phrases for the occasion, but I shall keep yours, Captain, among the dearest memories of my life. Now, as you say, the only thing that remains is to follow the counsels of my mother and to honour her memory by fulfilling all my duties as a soldier and as a citizen. It becomes women to wail and weep, but it becomes strong men to suffer and die, in silence, and rather than shed tears, to work and work along the path of good and to honour the memories of the family and those more sacred of the Fatherland not with sterile lamentations, but with fine deeds. It is well to remember, to commemorate the heroes who, with their blood, cemented the unity of the Fatherland; but it is still better to prepare ourselves so that we may not be ignoble descendants and so that we may set up a sturdy bulwark of breasts in case the barbarians of the North should attempt to reduce Italy to a 'geographical expression'. These are my sentiments. Please accept, Captain, my respectful regards.

"Yours faithfully,

"BENITO MUSSOLINI."

The text of this alleged letter has been garbled and variously given by the apologetic biographers of Mussolini, among whom is Signora Sarfatti who presents, in her "official" biography of the "Dux", a text of the letter which does not correspond to other Italian texts which we have consulted. But we need not linger over these textual changes which are common when writers are careless and copy from one another. What is important to stress is that the letter has been exploited in order to make Mussolini appear an Italian patriot and nationalist as early as 1905. Signora Sarfatti waxes eloquent on this theme. Like other apologetic writers on Mussolini, she shows complete ignorance of or disregard for Mussolini's status as a *réfractaire* and his extreme anti-militarist views. Since these authors project in bold relief Mussolini's letter to his captain and gloss over his revolutionary activities, they give their readers a wholly distorted picture of his early career.

Despite repeated inquiries in several quarters, I have never been able to see the original letter. When I asked Signora Sarfatti if she could show it to me, she told me that it was in Mussolini's possession, and when I asked Mussolini himself for a photostatic copy, he refused to comply with my request. His refusal together with other considerations lead me to conclude that the letter is false.

Assuming that Mussolini did write the letter to Captain Simonetti in February 1905, we must then aver that the patriotic, indeed the nationalistic statements in it are in complete disharmony with his vociferous anti-militarism between 1902 and 1904. A few months after the *ex-réfractaire*, the revolutionary socialist and preacher of desertion from the army leaves Switzerland, he writes a nationalistic letter to his army captain. Was Mussolini, then, a hypocrite as early as 1905, saying one thing in his published writings and exactly the opposite in a private communication to his army captain? The question is a fair one and we leave it to the reader to answer it for himself.

One factor should be kept in mind: Since the Royal Prefecture of Forlì was keeping a secret police record of

Mussolini's activities as early as January 1, 1904, it is almost certain that the Forlì police informed the military authorities at Verona of his status as an *ex-réfractaire* and as an ardent socialist propagandist. This procedure was generally taken by the Italian police in such cases. It may be, therefore, that Mussolini, as a "red" member of the tenth regiment of the Bersaglieri, wrote his letter to Captain Simonetti in order to conceal his anti-militaristic views and to make a good impression on his military superiors. After all, his letter was a private communication to his captain and not a public statement. His socialist comrades in Switzerland before 1905 and in Italy after 1906 would have never dreamed of Mussolini's expressing in public the sentiments embodied in his private communication. Naturally, when he embraced nationalism and became the fascist Prime Minister of Italy, it was found convenient to publish the letter and thus make it appear that he was an old and stalwart patriot.

Mussolini's service in the Italian army in 1905 and 1906 in no way attenuated his hatred of militarism or deepened his love for the Italian fatherland. His later career as a socialist reveals his trenchant anti-militarist and anti-patriotic opinions. He preached a general strike and civil strife in case of a war. In 1910, he called the national flag "a rag to be planted on a dunghill", and in the following year, he was sentenced to a year of imprisonment for his violent agitation against the Turco-Italian War.

5. THE DEFAMER OF MONARCHY

Mussolini was a defamer of emperors, kings, and everything associated with monarchical institutions. This does not mean that he had any respect for republics. For example, he had nothing but contempt for the Swiss republic, this "monarchical republic" and "sausage-makers' democracy",[1] two cantons of which had expelled him from their borders. In his eyes, democratic and bourgeois republics as well as monarchies were bulwarks of capitalism and of human exploitation. Like his father, Alessandro, he was a republican only in the sense that he desired a socialist republic. It must not be thought for a moment that Mussolini's opposition to monarchy was merely a youthful sentiment, expressed only in his earliest years and during his stay in Switzerland. The fact is that he was a republican throughout his socialist career and his early fascist career, indeed up to several days before the fascist "March on Rome" in October 1922. His original fascist programme called for a republic in Italy.

During his Swiss sojourn between 1902 and 1904, he frequently attacked monarchies and their representatives in Italy and elsewhere. The German Kaiser, William II, who is now an admirer of Mussolini, was then "lousy William, the emperor of the Germans, the verbose and already ridiculous Attila of the twentieth century", who "delights in bragging"; the ex-Prince of Wales (King Edward VII of England) was a "libertine"; the members of the House of Savoy were "bigots and reactionaries"; Czar Nicholas II of Russia was the "hangman of the Neva". When it was announced that Czar Nicholas would make a state visit to Italy in October 1903, Mussolini joined the demand of many other Italian socialists that the Italian people receive the Czar with hisses. These hisses, he said, would demonstrate the solidarity between the Italian people and the "martyrs of Holy Russia", the victims of the Russian

[1] I am quite sure that he appropriated the latter phrase from Arturo Labriola, then a prominent Italian revolutionary socialist.

autocrat. "Psychology has shown that sentiments are the dynamic motives of human actions. The sentiment of solidarity for the victims of the Russian autocrat urges us on to an act of protest." The hissing of the Czar, continued Mussolini, would be a warning to the royal cousins, the Czar and the King of Italy, and it would constitute an outcry of execration against the massacres in Russia and in Italy. So widespread was the Italian popular protest against the visit of the Czar that the Russian ruler decided not to go to Italy at that time.

Of course, all socialists were opposed to the monarchical form of government and in favour of a socialist republic. But in order to appreciate Mussolini's position on this subject, it is necessary to make certain important distinctions. Since we cannot afford to discuss here the attitude of English and German socialists towards their respective monarchies, we shall centre our attention on the attitude of the Italian socialists towards the House of Savoy. Up to the year 1900, all Italian socialists, from the mildest reformist to the most violent revolutionist, were forceful in their demand for a republic in Italy. For them, the reign of King Humbert of Italy—who succeeded his father, Victor Emmanuel II, in 1878 and was assassinated in 1900—symbolized the worst form of reaction, characterized, as it was, by proletarian "massacres", brazen disregard for constitutional rights, persecution of the socialists, the ill-fated attempt to conquer Ethiopia, the severity against the Sicilian *fasci*, the bloody repression at Milan in 1898 and the ultrareactionary ministries of Crispi and Pelloux. For liberals, democrats, republicans, and socialists, Francesco Crispi personified the most reactionary ideals of any ministry that had governed the United Kingdom of Italy. During the first two decades of this century, the nationalists were the only organized group of men who praised the ideals and personality of Crispi. They argued that a "decadent", democratic, parliamentary Italy was incapable of appreciating Crispi's political genius and his aspirations for a greater Italy. After the Great War, Mussolini and his fascists joined the nationalists in holding up Crispi as an exemplary political figure. But when he was a socialist, Mussolini called Crispi a "jingoistic minister" and King Humbert an "imperialist sovereign". He praised Gaetano Bresci who had assassinated King Humbert; and to the shame of Crispi, King Humbert, the Italian nationalists and imperialists, he recalled the Italian defeats in Ethiopia.

The assassination of King Humbert in 1900 coincided with the end of the reactionary Italian governments. His son and successor, Victor Emmanuel III, made Emperor by Mussolini, appeared to be a liberal-minded man. In 1900, Italy entered upon a remarkable period of healthy and sane growth politically, economically and intellectually. The most conspicuous leader of the new liberal policies was Giovanni Giolitti who early distinguished himself as a supple statesman. The liberal outlook of the monarchy and the new ministries was such that the reformist socialists ceased to insist upon a republic for Italy. They regarded the institutional problem of whether Italy should be a monarchy or a republic as secondary so long as the monarchy respected the constitution and allowed the radical and socialist parties free scope in fighting for their demands. No longer did they attack the person of the King. In short, the reformists believed that the struggle for reforms could be carried on successfully in a monarchical regime.

On the other hand, a very small but articulate minority of revolutionary socialists kept the institutional problem in the forefront of its programme and actively agitated for a republic. Mussolini, who belonged to this minority, freely attacked monarchical institutions, but he went even farther than most revolutionary socialists and was more like the anarchists because he attacked also the person of the King, Victor Emmanuel, describing him by the fairly well-known and disparaging nickname *Spiombi*. The Italian word *piombo* means plumb-rule or plummet line. Since one of the King's legs is allegedly shorter than the other, he is said to be somewhat out of balance; hence the nickname *Spiombi*, which, I think, was first applied to him by certain Florentines when he was Crown Prince.

Mussolini looked upon the "a-monarchical" position of the reformist socialists as a sign of the degeneration of the revolutionary movement. He excoriated a socialist Chamber of Labour in an Italian town for paying its humble respects to the King instead of hissing him. The incident, Mussolini noted, revealed the unfortunate mentality of those socialists who believed in the co-operation or collaboration of classes instead of the class struggle. In the name of what socialist theory, he asked, did the Italian labour organization pay homage to the King who is "the supreme representative of the political interests of the bourgeoisie"? He would have none of that niggardly, utilitarian trade-union mentality which, he said, had been exported from England in order "to corrupt the workers' organizations of the Continent".

It would be interesting to present every word that Mussolini had to say about Victor Emmanuel III who is now one of his most intimate collaborators. By virtue of a royal decoration, Mussolini is a "cousin" of the Italian King. The Italian dictator regards the monarchy as one of the pillars of the fascist state. As a socialist, Mussolini denounced the King's civil list and spoke of the King's robbing the Italian people of more than a hundred lire a minute. One of his reasons for censuring the socialists who were "a-monarchical" was that the monarchy was becoming more powerful as a result of their indifference to the institutional question.

"Enjoy, O Spiombi, this nice transformation, and you, famished canaille, pay the civil list. The king is young, a numismatist and a 'chauffeur'; he has the beautiful and inviting Montenegrin; he is four feet eleven inches tall; he is the son of the 'good king' and the grandson of the *galantuomo* . . . Oh, by God, he deserves 107 lire a minute!"

The Montenegrin is Queen Elena of Italy, the "good" King is Humbert and the *Re Galantuomo* is Victor Emmanuel II. After the fascists came to power in 1922, the fascist and monarchical press spoke eloquently and tenderly about the relations between Mussolini and the Queen Mother, Margherita, the widow of King Humbert. In 1904, Mussolini called her that "bigot of a queen".

6. THE DEFAMER OF GOD AND OF RELIGION

Mussolini was best known to his Italian socialist comrades in Switzerland for his pronounced anti-religious and atheistic propaganda. He was opposed to all forms of belief in God whether in the shape of Catholicism, Protestantism, or deism. He was more than an agnostic. Like his father, Alessandro, and like the majority of Romagnuole socialists, he was an atheist. During the movement for Italian unification, his native Romagna had been the home of the most ardent anti-clericals and anti-Catholics in the peninsula; this was largely due to the fact that the Romagna, as a part of the Papal States, had found papal rule insufferable. In the nineteenth century and in the present century, at least up to the Great War, no district in Italy counted as many atheists as the Romagna.

On the subject of religion, Mussolini went much farther than most socialists in Italy and in the rest of Europe. His ideas were more like those of the anarchists than of the socialists. The official socialist position had been stated in the German socialist congresses at Gotha (1875) and Erfurt (1891) as follows: "Religion is a private affair." In practice, this meant that the European socialist parties, while demanding the complete separation of Church and State, were not concerned with the private religious opinion of a socialist, his conception of God and his mode of worship. Since these were regarded as matters of conscience for the individual, the socialist parties avoided giving offence to the religious sentiments of their members. Most of the official socialist leaders felt that the gradual and eventful realization of socialism would lead to the disappearance of organized religion and to the triumph of free thought.

Mussolini disagreed with the official socialist position on the grounds of principle and tactics. For him, any religious belief was incompatible with a professed belief in socialism. Instead of showing respect for religious sentiments, he scorned and ridiculed them. Religion was an arm of reaction, the

servant of the capitalist class and the enemy of every movement for human emancipation and progress. He exhorted
the workers to keep away from churches and to fight for the
destruction of religious dogma and for the triumph of human
reason. He was as bitter in his denunciation of Evangelists
and Protestants as he was of Catholics. Indeed, he thought
that Evangelical and other Protestant sects were more
dangerous to the people than Catholicism, "this religion
par excellence", because they gave a social veneer to their
faith and tried to appear advanced and modern in their
social outlook. He was suspicious of those so-called great
men who professed to be atheists and yet believed that the
people needed the idea of a God in order to bear their
distress and poverty with resignation. "These men are
generally reactionaries, and their god is the god of the social
status quo. An example is Gaetano Negri, an atheist who
as Mayor of Milan, had made religious teaching obligatory
in the primary schools." This is precisely what Mussolini
did on a national scale when he became Duce of fascist
Italy.

As a socialist, Mussolini insisted upon the close identity
between socialism and atheism: "When the German socialists defined religion as a private affair, they understood
religion as a matter of individual belief and not as a political
and class institution. But it would be absurd to repeat the
motto of the German comrades, now that religion has fully
revealed itself as an institution aiming towards political
power in order to perpetuate the exploitation and the ignorance of the people. The socialist philosophy is essentially
atheistic. If it were not so, socialism would be ridiculous."

Mussolini made a similar declaration on the atheistic
character of socialism in a much romanticized incident between him and Émile Vandervelde, the prominent reformist
socialist who later became Foreign Minister of Belgium, and
not Jaurès, as was said by some of Mussolini's biographers,
like the ignorant Beltramelli who naturally built up a fantastic picture of the incident. Other apologetic biographers
of Mussolini, like Signora Sarfatti, although they speak

of Vandervelde, not Jaurès, also present utterly untrustworthy narratives of the incident, simply imagining what took place, without any reliable authority for their statements. All of them fail to mention Mussolini's atheistic opinions. Signora Sarfatti, after explicitly telling us that the truthful historian must face painful duties in destroying certain legends, proceeds glibly to erect a legend about the Mussolini–Vandervelde incident.

Our account of this incident is based on a contemporary report written by G. M. Serrati, which has never been used. In June 1904, Vandervelde delivered three lectures at Lausanne, one of which dealt with socialism and religion. The Belgian sustained the thesis of the German socialist congresses of Gotha and Erfurt that religion is a private affair; asserted that socialists must fight for the separation of Church and State and guard against the substitution of a Church despotism by a state despotism; and extolled liberty of thought, of religious conviction and of tolerance for all, maintaining the point that socialists must open their arms to all those convinced of the necessity of destroying the capitalist regime. As Serrati noted in his report: "This speech was followed by an interesting debate with comrade Mussolini who upheld the necessity of the socialist party's proclaiming itself atheistic." This is all that I have been able to find about what Mussolini said. When I wrote to M. Vandervelde asking him several questions about this debate, he replied that he had no recollection whatever of it.

Mussolini's anti-religious views are elaborated in the first pamphlet bearing his name. Entitled "Man and Divinity, a debate with the evangelist pastor Alfredo Taglialatela *** at Lausanne", it was published at Lugano in the summer of 1904 under the auspices of the International Library of Rationalist Propaganda, of which he and Serrati were the principal organizers. It is forty-seven pages long and contains only the arguments advanced by Mussolini. In his preface, he states that "with this pamphlet the 'International Library of Rationalist Propaganda' begins its publications, confident to meet with the favour of the working element and happy to contribute with its work to the general movement for human emancipation. The fight against the religious absurdity is more than ever necessary to-day. Religion has revealed its essence in the full light of day. Still to delude one's self would be cowardly. The adaptations of the Church to the new and insurmountable necessities of the times do not deceive us. They are attempts, generally vain, to raise the stock of the 'divine bank', which is already on the road to bankruptcy. Confronted with the spread of Free Thought, Pope Sarto [Pius X], trembling over the fate of his domain, cries out: 'Faithful ones, the Anti-Christ is born!' The 'Anti-Christ' is human reason which rebels against dogma and destroys god."

The pamphlet is replete with conventional rationalist and materialist arguments against religion. While there is nothing original in its contents, it is an important document in Mussolini's biography. The allusions to all sorts of writers who expressed themselves on religion bear witness to the wide range of his discursive reading and to his facile and extraordinary power of assimilation. The style of the pamphlet, which Mussolini wrote in his twentieth year, shows a marked improvement in clarity over his earlier writings in 1902 and 1903.

In the name of reason, science, evolution, and atheistic materialism, Mussolini devoted the first part of his pamphlet to his thesis that "God does not exist". With every discovery in the scientific world, he said, a dogma falls, a section of the old religious edifice crumbles into ruins. "The steady advance of the natural sciences goes on dispersing, from the cities to the country, the dark shadows of the Middle Ages; and the multitudes desert the churches where for generations and generations they dragged themselves to pray to a god— a monstrosity born of the ignorance of mankind.*** The fantastic and supremely ridiculous god of all the theological schools serves to hold back philosophical investigation and is a barrier obstructing the progress of the human mind." After ridiculing the deists as well as the theologians of revealed religion and after quoting Marx's dictum that

"Religion is the opium of the people", Mussolini proceeded to argue that religion is immoral, that it serves the forces of reaction and that it is a disease, a psychopathic phenomenon. "The gospel and the so-called Christian morality are two corpses", he declared as he inveighed against religious, authoritarian, dogmatic morality.

While many deists, rationalists, agnostics, atheists, socialists, and anarchists had no use for organized religion, they respected Jesus Christ as a man and as a teacher of a higher morality. At first, Mussolini was also inclined to pay homage to Christ as a man, teacher, apostle, and humanity's martyr who had been betrayed by priests and churchmen. In an article on the Christmas celebration of 1902, he exclaimed: "Ah! good Jesus, your martyrdom has not been futile, just as the sacrifice of Socrates, Servetus and Bruno has not been futile." But this attitude of respect for Christ was indeed short-lived, for in 1904, he carried his atheism to the point of disparaging Christ and his teachings from every point of view. He questioned the mortal existence of Christ and noted the "mania" of so many persons in exalting him. "Christ the redeemer, the apostle, the humanitarian, the socialist, the anarchist has already done his time."

Mussolini went on to say that from the point of view of morality, Christ originated nothing. "About seven hundred years before Christ, Buddha had spent forty-five years of his life in India, preaching fraternity, benevolence and love of one's neighbour. Before this colossus of charity, how small and insignificant Christ seems to us, Christ who preached for two years in small villages and succeeded in convincing a dozen ignorant vagabonds—the scum of the plebe of Palestine! It is an inconceivable absurdity to make of Christ the originator and the propagator of any morality whatsoever. The famous Sermon on the Mount is copied almost literally from Hebrew books. As for the few precepts of morality that would constitute a Christian ethic, they are nothing but counsels of subjection, of resignation, of cowardice. Christ is supposed to have said: 'Blessed are the poor in spirit, for theirs is the Kingdom of Heaven.' And we say: 'Wretched are those poor who do not know how to gain their kingdom on this earth!' Christ is supposed to have counselled: 'Whosoever shall smite thee on thy right cheek, turn to him the other also.' We say: 'Repay in kind the provokers; oppose force with force, violence with violence . . . Whoever lets his own person be trampled upon without reacting is not a man!' Christ said: 'Resign yourselves!' We say: 'Rebel!' The 'Christian brotherhood' was a brotherhood that was passive before the supreme judge—god. The brotherhood *** of socialism is a human, active, beneficent brotherhood that effaces injustice, destroys classes and creates a great family of free men. The morality of Christ leads to brutishness and cowardice and perpetuates misery."

During his stay in Switzerland, Mussolini translated from the French J. H. Malot's *The Black Charlatans!*, an antireligious writing containing twenty-seven pages of text and five pages of a preface by the French socialist deputy Maurice Allard. In a few notes of his own, Mussolini attacked the so-called anti-clericals who marry in church and have their children baptized; he alluded to the crimes of the popes, especially those of Pope Alexander VI (Borgia), the "prototype of the born criminal"; he cited instances of priests who abused children in their care; and he expressed the hope that the concordat between France and the Vatican would be abrogated. Mussolini's translation of Malot, published in 1904, was the third pamphlet issued by the International Library of Rationalist Propaganda.

The revelation of the harsh discipline imposed on girls in certain French convents led Mussolini to expatiate on the "horrors" of the convent: "The walls of the convents conceal a gangrenous sore. They defend the Bastilles of religion. And as such they should be razed to the ground ***. In Europe, the religious Middle Ages have disappeared from the public squares to lurk in the convent. The processions of a former time are no longer seen. If the pagan conception of life is about to triumph in modern times, it is due to socialism which has combated the Christian idea of the 'valley of tears'. If reason will prevail over the infamies of convents, it will be a further merit of the socialist and democratic press, not of official Freemasonry which has mourned the death of the Pope [Leo XIII]. In order that the conscience of humanity may make impossible the aberrations of seclusion, it is necessary to better the economic conditions of the sacrificed classes and to diffuse new ideas among them. It is necessary to free the hands, but it is also urgent to liberate the minds from the religious absurdity."

While Mussolini was in Switzerland, the struggle between Church and State dominated the political scene in France. He could not understand why French officials like Loubet, the President of the Republic, Combes, the Prime Minister, Delcassé, the Minister of Foreign Affairs, and Rouvier, the Minister of Finance, had sent or were about to send their sons to church to receive Holy Communion. What right had these fathers to impose a cult on children who could not possibly grasp the import of certain religious acts? How could the republican ministers send their sons to the "pestiferous dens of immorality" while the struggle against the clergy was at its height? Were they not hypocrites? In preaching one thing in public and practising another in their homes, were they not guilty of that "Jesuitism" and lack of "political courage" that were so characteristic of the times?

7. THE REVOLUTIONARY SOCIALIST

When in Switzerland where he first became an articulate propagandist, Mussolini elaborated his beliefs on a variety of questions—violence, religion, militarism, the monarchy. With respect to all these issues, he was in complete disagreement with the reformist socialists and in some instances his opinions were similar to those of the anarchists.

He was never a reformist, but always an extreme left or revolutionary socialist. The Italian socialist party, dominated by Filippo Turati, Leonida Bissolati, Camillo Prampolini and Claudio Treves, was conspicuously reformist in its outlook. After the period of reaction towards the end of the last century, the party entered upon a period of vigorous political activity and soon became one of the most powerful political organizations in Italy. The accession of Victor Emmanuel III to the throne and the advent of liberal ministries witnessed a fresh beginning in liberal and democratic governmental policy. This policy, which was best personified by Giolitti, made it possible for the socialist party to grow rapidly in strength and convinced the reformists that they had ample scope for their propaganda. So overwhelmed were they with fear lest a reactionary government should again be established, that they helped by their votes in parliament to keep the liberal ministries in power. Further to insure respect for constitutional liberties, the radical, the republican and the socialist deputies constituted a parliamentary group known as the Extreme Left.

The tactic of the reformist socialist deputies, consisting of frequent, though not regular, support of liberal ministries, was predicated on the idea that a liberal government was infinitely preferable to a reactionary government. This tactic, known as ministerialism, was the principal cause for a feud between two factions in the party, the reformist faction and the revolutionary faction, a feud which was characterized not only by doctrinal differences but also by bitter personal animosity. From 1900 until 1915, when Italy entered the Great War, the debates between these two factions centred around ministerialism and the activity of the Socialist Parliamentary Group. The most prominent spokesman of the revolutionists' demand for energetic anti-ministerialist action was Enrico Ferri, whose writings on criminology, great oratorical ability, handsome physical features and apparent disinterestedness had won for him much popularity in socialist circles. Ferri had the vanity of a prima donna and was indeed the diva of that verbose socialist current which claimed to be revolutionary but was, in reality, reformist. In a few years, he recanted socialism and ended up, supreme political charlatan that he was, in embracing fascism and in writing what is probably the most idiotic book ever written on the fascist Duce. But in the first years of this century, Ferri, the socialist, was taken quite seriously.

Another representative of the revolutionary socialist faction was the remarkably brilliant writer and fiery orator Arturo Labriola who, better than any one else, set forth the criticism of the reformists from a revolutionary standpoint. Although Ferri and Labriola, as representatives of two distinct groups in the revolutionary faction, differed widely in their views of what a revolutionary policy should be, they temporarily joined their forces in opposing the reformism of Turati, Bissolati, and Treves. For some years, Labriola exercised such a great hold on the minds of young revolutionary socialists that they generally regarded him as their foremost intellectual leader, worthy of emulation. Mussolini was one of his admirers, closely following and frequently alluding to his prolific writings. In so many ways did Mussolini seem to be responsive to the direction of Labriola's thought that we are strongly inclined to think that Labriola had more influence in giving an intellectual veneer to his youthful writings than any other revolutionary propagandist. After an interlude of revolutionary syndicalism, Labriola became a member of the Italian Parliament as an independent socialist, favoured war on the side of the Allies and served as Minister of Labour in Giolitti's post-war Cabinet. Fascist persecution forced him into exile where he defamed fascism and all its works, writing extensively while in France and Belgium and editing for a short time a New York anti-fascist paper. His constitutional instability led him to return to Italy in order to support Mussolini's war against Ethiopia, apparently on the ground that since the national interest was involved, he had to support his country, even though it was internally ruled by a government which he had denounced as infamous. Labriola's career offers an excellent example of the glaring moral and intellectual contradictions that have characterized so many men, including Mussolini of course, who started out to redeem the world from the "capitalist scourge".

From the beginning of his socialist career, Mussolini was an adherent of the revolutionary faction, and by virtue of his accentuated censure of parliamentarism, his exaltation of violence and his anti-monarchical views, he was decidedly more sympathetic to the Labriolans than to the Ferrians.

Between 1902 and 1904, the Ferrians became more moderate in their outlook and tried to form a centre between reformists like Turati on one side and revolutionists like Labriola on the other. During this same period, Labriola, Walter Mocchi, and others assailed both the reformists and the Ferrians and thus laid the groundwork for the Italian syndicalist movement. In December 1902, Labriola and Mocchi founded *L'Avanguardia Socialista* (*The Socialist Vanguard*), a weekly published at Milan. Together with others of lesser fame, they sought to stress the proletarian basis of the socialist movement, to emphasize the revolutionary value of the general strike as an instrument for the workers' redemption and to combat what they regarded as the degeneration of the socialist party, reflected in the excessive reliance on parliamentary methods which, they claimed, threatened to make the socialist party a group in the bourgeois governmental majority. It was they who championed the general strike of 1904.

Mussolini's principal writings during his sojourn in Switzerland were published in *L'Avvenire del Lavoratore* and in *L'Avanguardia Socialista*. While *L'Avanguardia* called itself the organ of the revolutionary faction, it would be more accurate to describe it as a syndicalist paper. As a contributor to *L'Avanguardia*, Mussolini was a revolutionary socialist with strong syndicalist sympathies. Although he wrote a few articles for this paper and for a time was its regular correspondent from Switzerland, he was in no sense one of the important contributors to it.

The chief target for the youthful and obscure agitator was the reformist socialists and the Socialist Parliamentary Group. According to him, the reformists' "ministerial" tendencies and "mania" for social legislation and reforms had diverted the socialists from their real aim which was not reform, but the expropriation of the bourgeoisie and the abolition of private property. He would get rid of all traces of Utopian and what he called political or reformist socialism. Since reformist policies served the bourgeoisie, not the proletariat, they could only weaken the revolutionary ardour of the workers. Mussolini advocated a consistent and combative anti-ministerialist policy on the part of the socialist deputies; under no circumstances should they vote for a bourgeois ministry. He decried the sophistical "alibis" that the reformists employed to justify their collaborationist and ministerial tactics. The liberalism of the government was a legend. Giolitti, by his insincere promises, was succeeding in "domesticating" the socialists. Ever since the party had entered upon the "slippery road of opportunism", it was no longer feared by the bourgeoisie. It was becoming too parliamentary, innocuous and pacific; its methods of combat were becoming too respectable.

The fear of a return to reaction, insisted Mussolini, did not justify the socialist support of liberal ministries. He preferred brazen reaction to rule by so-called liberals. As for fighting the possible recurrence of reaction, he placed his trust in revolt and direct action. Thus, he agreed with the bitter attacks on the compromises and parliamentary manœuvres of the reformists by the extreme revolutionists and syndicalists, among whom was Costantino Lazzari whose name we mention here because he was later to have a decisive influence on Mussolini's rapid rise to leadership in the Italian socialist party.

Especially in the year 1904, Mussolini championed such pronounced syndicalist opinions that he almost embraced the view that a definite split between the revolutionists and the reformists would be desirable. It may be said that from 1904 until 1909, he was a syndicalist sympathizer, but since he did not take an active and militant part in the Italian syndicalist movement, he should not be described as a syndicalist. After he left Switzerland in the winter of 1904, he took a very negligible part in the doings of the Italian socialist party until 1910. Meanwhile, the long duel between the syndicalists and the reformists culminated in the withdrawal or expulsion of the former from the party by the year 1908. Still remaining in the party was a small group of revolutionists like Lazzari, which gained control of the party organization in 1912, with Mussolini as its outstanding spokesman.

Although Mussolini was always an adherent of authoritarian socialism and at no time an anarchist, he followed the anarchist movement and literature with great interest. In the fall of 1903, it was announced that he would speak at weekly meetings of Italian socialists in Switzerland on "the difference between the socialists and the anarchists, their tactics and their ends", but, unfortunately, there is no record of these speeches. An illuminating hint on his point of view is given in his report of a speech at Lausanne by the French anarchist Sebastin Faure. Mussolini described Faure as an "anarchist" or "libertarian communist" and described himself as an "authoritarian communist".

Mussolini did not disdain the use of anarchist writings and arguments in order to buttress his denunciation of the reformists. In the spring of 1904, while he was translating into Italian the *Paroles d'un Révolté*, the work of the distinguished anarchist Prince Kropotkin, he wrote an article in which he emphasized Kropotkin's criticism of the degeneration of socialism and its compromises: "Twenty years have passed [since the publication of the book], but the *Paroles* seem to be of yesterday, so much are they alive with present-day interest. On reading them, one has a first impression that grips one, quite apart from the theories enunciated. They overflow with a great love for oppressed mankind and with infinite kindness.*** What a sense of profound discouragement pervades the mind, as we think about the matrix idea of socialism and the degeneration to which it has been brought by exiles of the bourgeoisie, who have infiltrated themselves in the movement to corrupt it and retard it! But socialism, sooner or later, will return to what it was in its beginnings: proletarian and revolutionary. Only in this case will it be able to attain its goal. As for the reformist multitude, it will have already disappeared on the day of the Social Revolution."

8. THE APOLOGIST OF VIOLENCE

It is impossible to understand Mussolini unless it is constantly borne in mind that the core of his political philosophy and an abiding characteristic of his socialist and fascist career is his faith in the necessity and efficacy of violence as an instrument of social change. The entire life of this voluptuary of activism has been a hymn to the nobility of violence, extolled first for socialist and later for fascist purposes. Bullets are more important than ballots, barricades more urgent than electoral majorities, machine-guns more effective than resolutions by the League of Nations. He abhors deliberation and discussion.

The predominant source of his exaltation of violence is his rebellious and belligerent temperament. His native Romagna had responded enthusiastically to the republican, Mazzinian "theory of the dagger" and to the anarchist theory of "propaganda by deed" so that from his earliest years he moved in a "red" environment. His temperament and home surroundings would seem sufficient to indicate why he had little or nothing to learn from "literary" apologists of violence or force like Nietzsche and Sorel. If he read such men with enthusiasm, it was because they served to give an intellectual structure to his love of violence.

While in Switzerland between 1902 and 1904, Mussolini went much farther to the left in his evaluation of violence than the reformist socialists. He praised what they so frequently condemned: insurrectionism, the "rabble", the *teppa* or "hooliganism"; and by apt references to such events in the French Revolution as the fall of the Bastille and the "August Days", he emphasized the need for violent action in bringing about the expropriation of the bourgeoisie. This expropriation "will be accompanied by a more or less long period of acts of violence", and there will take place "a bloody duel between the forces of conservatism and those of the future—an insurrectional tempest, the preliminary episode of that profound transformation of human society which will be realized with the advent of socialism".

An event which thrilled Mussolini and the extreme Italian revolutionists was the Italian general strike of September 1904, probably the first large-scale general strike in any European country. Some of its ardent supporters hailed it as the first experiment in proletarian dictatorship. About ten years later, in June 1914, Mussolini was one of the leading protagonists of the "Red Week", the most famous and most serious strike in pre-war Italy. Speaking of the 1904 strike, twenty-one year old Mussolini expressed the hope that in analogous cases, the strike committees would keep the 100,000 Italians in Switzerland better informed of the course of events "so that it may be possible for us to utilize our energies for the coming revolution". The strike, according to him, showed two things of capital importance: "It has demonstrated, notwithstanding the desertion of the railwaymen, the possibility of an improvised and simultaneous mobilization of the proletarian forces; it has definitely buried reformism and the reformists. I hope that this strike will *** be the strategic prelude to the coming and supreme battle."

Although Mussolini had some reservations about individual acts of violence as a steady tactic, this did not prevent him from appreciating their revolutionary value in special circumstances. "However much the killing of one man by another is profoundly repugnant to my convictions, I find, nevertheless, that violence from below in response to violence from above, although regrettable, is sometimes necessary. When all the roads are closed, it is necessary to open a passage, even at the cost of blood. Sometimes, vengeance for continued acts of infamy that have been suffered is holy. Thus, I admire the obscure heroes and martyrs of the *Boseraja Organization* of Russia, and I bow before Michael Angiolillo [the assassin of the Spanish Minister, Canovas del Castillo] and Gaetano Bresci [the assassin of King Humbert of Italy]. It may also be that at a given moment, the individual act may have consequences of great importance and may mark a revolution in the political life of a nation.***

When we say that—as an affirmation of principle—the individual act is useless, we do not obey a pacifist or quietist sentiment. We, called the *catastrophic ones* by the Italic reformist group, do not preclude a future epoch of bloody conflicts in which we will be forced to the painful necessity of violence. The arrogant demeanour of the classes in power shows that they prefer death under ruins to a long, slow and inglorious agony. Violence then will be useful, fruitful and decisive. After the tempest of the revolutionary period is over, the socialist revolution will be a great practical consecration of respect for the human being. We will not kill individuals unless we are forced to. Even the former professional military men will become producers. We will take the sword from them and put them to the plough."

Perhaps the revolutionary tradition which appealed most to Mussolini is embodied in the word Blanquism, after the famous French revolutionist Louis Auguste Blanqui (1805–1881). In 1903, Mussolini published in *L'Avvenire del Lavoratore* an enthusiastic sonnet on the principal forerunner of the Blanquists, François Noël Babeuf, the French revolutionist who was executed in 1797. The essential belief of the Blanquists was that a small, resolute and well-prepared revolutionary minority of armed men should be ready at the opportune moment to overthrow the dominance of the bourgeoisie, seize political power and maintain it by dictatorial force in the interest of the proletariat. Once dictatorship was established, steps would be taken to organize society along communistic lines. The necessity of insurrection, *coups d'état*, minority action and authoritarian rule were integral parts of the Blanquist credo. Since the spirit of Blanquism was reflected in some of the early writings of Karl Marx, revolutionary socialists like Mussolini appealed to the early Marx when they censured the reformist socialists, those "smug and serious people", as Mussolini called them, who disdained Blanquist methods and emphasized the careful preparation of a political and economic mass movement which would rely on democratic and parliamentary methods. As a subscriber to the chief tenets of Blanquism,

Mussolini was interested more in the development of pugnacious vanguards of revolutionists than in the development
of trade-union organizations, more in direct action, general
strikes and the like than in parliamentary action and electoral victories. As the Duce of the Italian socialist party
between 1912 and 1914, his writings and activities were
characterized chiefly by a Blanquist outlook. As the proud
Duce of the fascists who had succeeded in seizing power,
he has often chided the Italian communists for not having
taken to heart the lessons in Blanquism which he had given
in his socialist days.

9. THE "SOCIALIST INTELLECTUAL"

Mussolini's stay in Switzerland between 1902 and 1904 served to expand his intellectual horizon. From his nineteenth to his twenty-first year, he travelled in various parts of the French, Italian, and German sections of the Helvetic Republic, observing and coming into contact with all sorts of people and doctrines, perfecting his French, learning the rudiments of German and translating works from both languages. Incidentally, he has always had a predilection for French; the study of this language helped him to develop a capacity for forceful, direct, and laconic statement, which, unusual as it is among Italian orators and journalists—even revolutionary ones—was to serve him in good stead in his exhortations to the masses. Besides translating from the French Malot's *Black Charlatans!* and Kropotkin's *Paroles d'un Révolté*, he translated from the German Karl Kautsky's *Am Tage nach der Sozialen Revolution (On the Morrow of the Social Revolution)*. While Mussolini's name appears as the translator of Malot and Kautsky, his name does not appear as the translator of Kropotkin.

With the exception of two chapters of the *Paroles*, namely, "To Young Men" and "The Spirit of Rebellion", which had previously been published in Italian, Mussolini translated gratis the whole of Kropotkin's work under the auspices of the noted anarchist of Geneva, Luigi Bertoni, who published it in the summer of 1904. Although he did not know Bertoni very well, he admired him and closely followed his writings and activities. A few years later, Bertoni paid him three hundred Swiss francs for translating a considerable part of Kropotkin's *French Revolution*. In 1920 when Mussolini was at the nadir of his political fortunes, with adversity and indifference besetting his incipient fascist movement, he exalted the anarchist ideal and recalled the above translations of Kropotkin. Of course, Mussolini's "spiritual communion", as he put it, and his early acquaintance with Kropotkin widened his knowledge of anarchist thought as presented by one of its greatest exponents.

For his translation of Kautsky's pamphlet, which *L'Avanguardia Socialista* published in instalments, Mussolini probably received about fifty francs. The first instalment appeared in September 1904, but owing to lack of space, instalments did not reappear until 1905. It is questionable if Mussolini had acquired a sufficient knowledge of German to translate the Marxist scholar by himself. He was probably aided by Angelica Balabanoff, and it is not unlikely that he found serviceable the French translation of Kautsky's essay which had been published in instalments in the year 1903 by the French revolutionary socialist or syndicalist review *Le Mouvement Socialiste*.

Mussolini had one distinct advantage over the vast majority of Italian emigrants in Switzerland. He was a normal school graduate and had been an elementary school teacher. His diploma and teaching experience immediately set him apart as an "intellectual" among his socialist comrades who were engaged in manual work. Socialist workers, however humble and uneducated, have great respect for the schooled individual, like Mussolini, who devotes himself to socialist propaganda. The Italian socialist workers in Switzerland knew Mussolini as a secretary of labour organizations, as a public speaker, as a writer on socialist papers, and as a specialist in anti-clerical and anti-religious propaganda. His greatest "intellectual" achievement during his Swiss sojourn was his pamphlet on "Man and Divinity".

Mussolini has always been an omnivorous reader of newspapers and periodicals, and while in Switzerland, he built up his "socialist culture". In calling him a "socialist intellectual" and in speaking of his "socialist culture", we mean to suggest not only that he was essentially a propagandist rather than a manual worker but also that he was familiar with the conventional and stock theses known to all socialist agitators. Our long review of his propaganda has illustrated this.

Of course, he was conversant with what passed as the

essential tenets of Marxism and with the arguments over Neo-Marxism, revisionism and orthodoxy, anarchism and socialism, etc. There was such a vast output of books, pamphlets, periodicals, and newspapers dealing with these subjects that it was easy for a literate and intelligent young man like Mussolini, who wanted a new socialist order, to be well versed in them. It was not difficult then, as it is not now, for a professional socialist agitator to acquire a fair knowledge of problems pertaining to Marxism without having read or even seen the book covers of a work by Marx. One of the books discussing Marx, which Mussolini read when he was in Switzerland and from which he probably learned a good deal, was *Socialism and the Social Movement in the Nineteenth Century* by the eminent German economic historian Werner Sombart. Although a "bourgeois thinker" in the socialist sense of the term, Sombart was highly regarded in socialist circles. His aforementioned work had been translated into Italian and French, and in 1903, Mussolini wrote a résumé of it.

It cannot be repeated too often that Mussolini did not come from the bourgeoisie. While the chief leaders of the pre-war Italian socialist movement, Turati, Prampolini, Bissolati, Treves, Ferri, and others came from the bourgeois class, Mussolini was the son of a poor blacksmith—an ardent socialist who reared him on socialist ideas. Moreover, he was the first editor of the *Avanti!* and the first distinguished leader of the Italian socialist party who was the son of a socialist.

There was nothing in his culture that distinguished him from hundreds of other propagandists and journalists engaged in the vulgarization of socialist ideas. If it were feasible for us to present in this book a detailed history of socialist intellectual currents in Italy and an extensive review of the writings of numerous Italian propagandists, it would be easier to appreciate how his writings on socialism were mere echoes of widely circulated ideas. While many of his contemporaries achieved a certain prominence through their books and articles, he came to be known to his comrades because of his abilities as a man of action. His career is the record of a gifted revolutionary man of action, not of a speculative thinker or theorist, and this is amply illustrated not only by his leadership of the fascist movement, but also by his leadership of the Italian socialist movement between 1912 and 1914.

The fascist and apologetic biographers of Mussolini have built up a veritable legend about their hero's student days in Switzerland. Signora Sarfatti's official *Life of Benito Mussolini* contains a chapter entitled "Mussolini as University Student at Geneva", but since Mussolini was never a student at the University of Geneva, it follows that the tales about his student days there are fictitious.

On the other hand, it can be affirmed that Mussolini was a registered student and an *étudiant* in the 1904 summer session of the University of Lausanne, which lasted from April 8 to July 25. With his application for admission, he presented his high school and normal school diplomas. On May 9, he expressed the wish to enroll in the *École des Sciences Sociales*, a branch of the Law School. On May 17, 18, he registered in and was admitted to the following courses: (1) a three-hour course in Political Economy given by the celebrated economist and sociologist Marquis Vilfredo Pareto and his assistant Signor Boninsegni; (2) a one-hour course in Sociology given by Pareto; (3) a two-hour course in General Philosophy given by Professor Millioud. By registering on May 17, he could attend the University at most for about nine weeks out of more than one hundred weeks which he spent in Switzerland. Therefore it cannot be said, as some writers would have us believe, that he passed the larger part of his time in Switzerland as a student.

How regularly Mussolini attended Pareto's and Millioud's courses—if he attended them at all—and how much he may have derived from them cannot be definitely established. Since he did not and was not obliged to take any examinations, he was not granted a diploma or a certificate by the University. Nowhere have I seen any reliable evidence showing that Pareto and Mussolini knew each other personally during Mussolini's sojourn in Switzerland. It seems that at no time during his socialist career did Mussolini make any allusion to studying under Pareto. It also appears that Pareto never recalled having had Mussolini as a student.

Nevertheless, it may be appropriate at this point to discuss Mussolini's intellectual relationship to Pareto, especially in view of the growing and, for the most part, irresponsible literature on this subject. It should be emphasized that this relationship can be adequately understood only in the light of Pareto's and Mussolini's connection with the revolutionary socialist movement in the early part of this century. Mussolini's antagonism to reformist socialism, which we have amply considered, was fed not only by anarchists, who were at the extreme left of the revolutionary movement, but also by certain non-Marxian and non-socialist writers like Pareto. In the first years of this century, Pareto was such a severe critic of the bourgeoisie and of the democratic, parliamentary, and humanitarian brand of socialism that many syndicalists and revolutionary socialists regarded him with favour. Pareto further endeared himself to many revolutionists by his conviction that the bourgeois ruling class was decadent and that the victorious advent to power of a new ruling class or aristocracy, emerging from the proletariat, was very probable and almost inevitable. For him, the outcome of the battle between the old bourgeois aristocracy and the rising proletarian aristocracy could not be doubtful because the former was worn out, weak, and cowardly, while the latter was young, vigorous, and courageous.

It is not surprising, therefore, to see the revolutionary socialist Mussolini appealing to the authority of Pareto in order to buttress his attacks on reformist socialism. By relying on hitherto unrevealed sources of information, we can reconstruct, in some measure, Mussolini's early impressions of Pareto. In 1904, when he was twenty-one years old, he praised the work and style of Pareto, the "distinguished author of *Les Systèmes Socialistes*" (1902–1903), whose works were characterized by "precision", "clarity", and "frankness". The young Romagnuole agitator found that the "bourgeois economist" taught "us socialists two things: the first relates to the 'unity' and the second to the 'tactics' of the [socialist] party". After noting Pareto's penetrating analysis and denial of the so-called moral, intellectual, political, and religious "unity" of society, whose refrain was being sung by many reformers, Mussolini applied this Paretan point of view to the talk of unity among socialists by declaring that an honest separation of the diverse parts of the socialist organization was preferable to an adulterous marriage between them. As a revolutionary socialist, he was also comforted by Pareto's insistence on the differences in the interests of various parts of the social aggregate because it supported his belief in the class struggle, which had been forsworn by so many reformists: "It is from these differences of interests among the different parts of the social aggregate—in our case Bourgeoisie and Proletariat—that the class struggle has its natural genesis. And it is probable that this struggle, instead of assuming temperate forms, will continuously become more and more acute, as one part and the other become conscious of the unalterable diversity of interests."

These comments by Mussolini, occasioned not by his attendance at Pareto's lectures (to which he does not even make any reference), but by his acquaintance with one of Pareto's briefer sociological writings, furnish another example of his remarkable faculty for assimilating any current of thought that would reinforce his own political beliefs—in this case, his revolutionary conception of socialism and of socialist tactics. By making Pareto an instrument of his propaganda against the reformist socialists, he was echoing a general tendency among syndicalists and revolutionary socialists who viewed Pareto as something of an ally in the diffusion of their ideas. Since he moved in a revolutionary milieu, he probably knew of Pareto's hospitality and friendly attitude towards several Italian revolutionists who had fled to Switzerland after the Italian government's repression of the Milan riots in 1898.

The Pareto whom Mussolini cited was the Pareto of the first decade of this century when he enjoyed a considerable vogue among syndicalists and revolutionary socialists, who were quite fervent in their encomiums of the social thinker. One of the by-products of this vogue was that these revolutionists popularized for their political purposes the Paretan theory of the *élite*, according to which history is a record of the succession of dominant minorities (or aristocracies) varying in their composition and ideology throughout the course of human experience. An organized minority always constitutes the ruling class of a given people. Since the contemporary European bourgeois *élite* or aristocracy was proving to be very disappointing to Pareto, he began to view sympathetically the rise of a new *élite* or aristocracy from the proletarian class, thus ingratiating himself with many revolutionary writers. At the same time, an Italian group of extreme nationalists—the ideological precursors of fascism, whom Mussolini then despised—applauded Pareto's ideas about the *élite* and utilized them for its particular ends.

If we may, for the moment, abandon our chronological order, we shall refer to some of Mussolini's observations in the year 1908, in so far as they relate to the *élite*, and we shall find that he too, again echoing a general opinion in syndicalist circles, translated the Paretan conception of the *élite* into revolutionary terms. Naturally, he appeared to be fully convinced that in the struggle between two worlds and two classes, represented respectively by the bourgeoisie and the proletariat, the latter would ultimately be victorious. As he expressed it, the bourgeois world "will be 'transcended' by the proletarian civilization, just as the bourgeoisie 'transcended' the clergy and the nobility during the French Revolution. Do you recall the theory of the *élites* of Vilfredo Pareto? It is probably the most extraordinary sociological conception of modern times. History is nothing but a succession of dominant *élites*. Just as the bourgeoisie took the place of the clergy and the nobility in the possession of wealth and political power, so the bourgeoisie will be replaced by the proletariat, the new social *élite* that is now forming, in its trade unions, leagues and chambers of labour, the nuclei of future economic organization on a communist basis. While the bourgeois revolution has maintained the classes, the proletarian revolution will abolish them."

Obviously, Mussolini, like many other revolutionists, paraphrased the Paretan concept of the *élite* to bolster his faith in the future accession to power of the proletarian *élite*, of which he considered himself a member. And in the course of his commonplace remarks on the proletariat's succeeding the bourgeoisie, he found it convenient to insert Pareto's theory of *élites*. Later on, when he gave up his socialist faith, he began to talk about fascism in terms of the *élite*. The varied meanings which Mussolini placed on the word *élite* throughout his entire career illustrate how differently the word could be interpreted. As presented by Pareto, the concept of the *élite* was intended to serve as a helpful instrument in the interpretation of history, a new tool in the methodology of history, and yet, as we have seen, it could easily be manipulated by various political groups for different political objectives.

While we cannot afford to discuss in detail the complicated history and implications of the concept of the *élite*, we should at least observe that it was not originated by Pareto. The importance of minorities in history is a theme that runs through the writings of socialists like Fourier, Blanqui, and Marx, of anarchists like Kropotkin, of historians like Taine, and of sociologists like Gumplowicz and Ammon, all of whom wrote independently of Pareto. In our opinion, the writer who, several years before Pareto, gave the most brilliant and systematic elaboration of the theory of minorities as governing classes is Gaetano Mosca in his great work *Elementi di scienza politica* (1896) and also in an earlier work *Teorica dei governi e governo parlamentare* (1884). It is high time that the scholarly world recognize Mosca's precedence over Pareto with respect to the theory of the political class, as Mosca calls it, or the *élite*, as Pareto calls it.

To make these assertions implies no derogation of Pareto, whose contributions to economics and sociology no one will deny. Rather, they are designed to place in proper perspective

Mussolini's sententious remark that Pareto's theory of the *élites* was probably the most extraordinary sociological conception of modern times. This remark, if taken by itself, *in vacuo*, independently of the intellectual climate of Europe in the first decade of this century, could be grossly exaggerated by those who enjoy establishing affinities between Mussolini and a host of "great thinkers".

The name of Pareto has recently been made familiar to the English-speaking public by the excellent Livingston translation and edition of his *magnum opus*, *Trattato di sociologia generale*, which originally appeared in 1916 and which was translated under the title *The Mind and Society*. While many of those who have talked about Pareto and Mussolini have glibly expressed themselves with glittering generalities regarding the possible influence of this book on Mussolini's intellectual and political evolution, they have been ignorant of or they have failed to understand the character of Mussolini's earlier contacts with Pareto. These contacts were perfectly compatible with Mussolini's revolutionary socialist philosophy and appear to have had nothing to do with his shift to fascism. Although there is every reason to doubt that Mussolini ever read or pondered Pareto's *Trattato*, we have definitely seen his awareness of Pareto's ideas and vogue as early as 1904. Eventually Pareto, who once so scornfully derided the "decadent", humanitarian and democratic bourgeoisie, enthusiastically hailed the advent of a vigorous bourgeoisie in the form of fascism, the anti-democratic movement *par excellence*. Was it not appropriate for Mussolini, as the Duce of fascism, to propose him for membership in the Italian Senate?

CHAPTER IV

THE "TRUE HERETIC"

1. A Quiet Interlude—2. The Professor—3. To the Flames with the Law!—4. Nietzsche and Others

1. A QUIET INTERLUDE

SOMETIME in November or December 1904, Mussolini left Switzerland and returned to Italy. Under circumstances which we have already described, he reported for his military service and was assigned to the tenth regiment of Bersaglieri stationed at Verona where he discharged his legal duty as a soldier from January 1905 to September 1906.

Owing to the grave illness of his mother, he was granted a furlough. Her death on February 19, 1905, caused him great sorrow, as is attested by contemporaries who knew his family. She is, by the way, one of the few human beings whom he has ever sincerely respected. While on this leave of absence from his regiment, Mussolini had an interview with a republican deputy from Forlì, which was published in *L'Avanguardia Socialista* on March 11, 1905. Although the deputy is not named, he is doubtless Giuseppe Gaudenzi, the editor of *Il Pensiero Romagnolo*, to which Mussolini's father had been a contributor. Mussolini cited the remarks of Gaudenzi in support of the thesis that the efficacy and importance of socialist action in parliament should not be over-emphasized. In this way, he concluded, the worker would not be imbued with "ridiculous and absurd hopes" that would distract him "from the use of that real force which he possesses not as a citizen, but as the 'sole producer' of social wealth". Occasionally, during the year 1905, his name appeared in *L'Avanguardia* as the translator of an essay by Kautsky.

After completing his military service, Mussolini returned to his home at Predappio, and shortly thereafter he went to Tolmezzo, a small town situated in the mountainous Friuli section of north-eastern Italy, where he taught second grade boys during the scholastic year 1906–1907. When he proceeded to Tolmezzo in November 1906, the Forlì police authorities sent a copy of their secret biographical record of him to the Prefecture of Udine, the provincial centre near Tolmezzo, and informed the Prefecture of the "necessity for vigilance".

On February 17, 1907, Mussolini joined the socialists and anti-clericals of Tolmezzo in commemorating the martyrdom of Giordano Bruno, the Italian friar and philosopher who was born at Nola and was burned at the stake in Rome on February 17, 1600. The anniversary of Bruno's death, one of the great days in the Italian socialist calendar, was the occasion for yearly anti-clerical demonstrations throughout Italy. According to the best contemporary report of the Tolmezzo meeting in honour of Bruno, the presiding officer asked Mussolini, the "school teacher", to speak. In his extemporaneous address, which lasted about three quarters of an hour and received great applause, he brought out the rebellious and combative spirit of Bruno and described him as the "greatest innovator of his time and the precursor of free thought". After others had spoken, all those present at the meeting paraded to the vicarage, singing the workers' anthem, and when they got there, they shouted: "Long live anti-clerical France!" "Long live the martyr of Nola!" A Tolmezzo correspondent of a clerical paper published at Udine was indignant that a teacher, who was being paid by the town, had participated in such a meeting. During the scholastic year, protests were made to the effect that a certain teacher was swearing in his classes; and while I cannot definitely say that the teacher was Mussolini, I am quite certain that it was he.

Meanwhile, whether or not he was perfecting his mastery of blasphemous language, he was probably improving his knowledge of French. In April 1907, the University of

Bologna granted him a diploma qualifying him to teach French in high schools.

Mussolini returned to Predappio from Tolmezzo in September 1907, and as the secret police record tells us, he was "being adequately watched".

2. THE PROFESSOR

Mussolini found another teaching post at Oneglia where he went in March 1908 to teach French in a private Technical School connected with the Ulisse Calvi College, a private preparatory institution for boys. Oneglia is a small town on the Italian Riviera, a few miles north of Genoa. As early as 1893 a socialist weekly, *La Lima* (*The File*), was founded there as the organ of an active and growing local socialist movement which was essentially reformist in its outlook. Among the young leaders of this movement, before he went to Switzerland and New York, was G. M. Serrati. Although it cannot be ascertained definitely, it was probably through Serrati's influence that Mussolini received his teaching appointment at Oneglia. The Ulisse Calvi school no longer exists, and since its records are not available, little can be learned about Mussolini's teaching duties; but it can safely be surmised that he taught French grammar and composition to boys between eleven and fourteen years of age. Henceforth, he came to be known as a professor, a title which was then, as it is now, loosely applied in Italy and elsewhere to all sorts of instructors: those who teach in elementary schools, high schools, and universities as well as those who give private lessons in dancing, fencing, and music. Mussolini himself seems to have become proud of the title, for in 1909, when a judge asked him his profession, he replied: Professor of French language and literature!

Teaching, however, was never attractive to him, and he doubtless took it up because it was the most convenient and most respectable means at his disposal to earn a livelihood. More appealing to him was socialist journalism and propaganda. But the position of teacher and the high-sounding title of professor proved to be an excellent introduction to journalistic circles and to proletarian groups which felt the need of educated men for "enlightenment" and leadership. The *Lima* seemed to be in need of writers, and within a few days after his arrival at Oneglia,

Mussolini became one of its regular and most important contributors.

His first article in the paper, published on March 14, 1908, was occasioned by the death of one of Italy's most popular authors, Edmondo De Amicis (1846–1908), who, touched by the plight of the poor and humble classes in Italy, had embraced socialism as a new gospel of redemption and progress. De Amicis was mourned all over Italy, particularly by the socialists. Oneglia was his birthplace, and *La Lima* paid tribute to him through the pen of Mussolini. Although Mussolini did not share and was not sympathetic to the sentimental, humanitarian, "evangelical" brand of socialism that was so dear to De Amicis, he wrote an enthusiastic obituary on the Italian author, the conclusion of which has a lyrical strain: "De Amicis is not dead! He continues to live in us; his memory will be perpetuated. As long as men have the cult of art, as long as men are capable of cherishing a hope, of feeling a faith, of fighting for an idea, the name of De Amicis will not be forgotten. And in case the minds of men should be completely conquered by stupid and shopkeepers' commercialism, in case life, in a more or less near future, should have no other aim but the satisfaction of material needs, we—last pilgrims of the ideal—will go to a distant solitary place to guard there, in the solitude and the silence of unbounded deserts, our final hopes, our supreme illusions, and the memories of our dead."

In the columns of the *Lima*, Mussolini attacked at considerable length the Catholic Church and religion as well as reformist and parliamentary socialism. To him, both religion and the gradualist type of socialism were "illusions", and by way of emphasizing his aversion to them, he assumed the somewhat arrogant pseudonym of *Vero Eretico* (*True Heretic*). We have so amply considered the sources and character of his censure of religion and of reformist socialism that we need not devote too much space to an analysis of his opinions on these subjects as expressed in the *Lima*. It is desirable, however, to present his most characteristic thoughts in order to show how certain ideas were deeply rooted in his mind.

The greater part of socialist activity in small Italian towns was given over to anti-clerical and anti-religious propaganda because the Church was so powerful in the small provincial centres that it was considered the most formidable enemy of a new social order. Locally, at Oneglia, the socialist weekly *La Lima* and the Catholic weekly *Il Giornale Ligure* were in constant polemic with each other. In his fiery denunciation of Holy Communion, the Easter holiday, and Christianity, Mussolini went much farther than the reformist socialists and frequently made use of banal and vulgar arguments. For example, in speaking of Holy Communion, which he termed "religious conscription", he was sure of shocking the local Catholics with his sacrilegious words when he wrote:

"Every year, at the time when the good Jesus, somewhat drowsy after the Lenten rest, is about to reawaken and rise again, the priests conscript all the children of religious families and lead them to the holy balustrades to perform the most solemn of ceremonies—communion. The child knows nothing about it: he is too unreflective to understand the symbol, and he does not explain to himself nor does he even ask himself why his soul must be purified by swallowing a farinaceous host. The parents, then, arbitrarily and tyrannically exercise their right of spiritual *patria potestas*, substituting, as they do, their own convictions for those that might be embraced by the child when he becomes a man. The good faithful ones have none of the scruples that a freethinker has. With the first communion ends the Catholic initiation. The child who has eaten Christ is now considered a sheep of the fold. And now, we wish to pose a nice question to the theologians, the priests and the believers: How do you explain the fact that notwithstanding the first and successive communions, a man can become an unbeliever, a heretic, an atheist, and, even worse, a malefactor? Yet Christ has entered him, has cleansed him of the foul scoriae of sin and has made him worthy of the favour of God for the day when the trumpets of the Apocalypse will gather together humanity in the valley of Josephat . . .

"You answer: After communion, he has again sinned. And I say in rebuttal: But how could he have sinned, if he had the son of God within him? One of the two: Either Christ is always present and man cannot sin, or Christ has . . . *evacuated*, in which case he is a food that passes through the canal of ordinary foods. Blasphemy, heresy, mystery! If communion is a sort of wash for the sins committed and not for those to be committed, it is better then to give hospitality to Christ when one is on the verge of death and make at a single time the wash for his entire life . . . Sacrilege . . . sacrilege!***

"It is painful that a good part of humanity, believed to be intelligent, refuses even to-day to reason about divine things, but if progress is not a lie and if history does not deceive us, there is coming upon you a lethargy that will have no awakening. Your whole structure will be thrown into the refuse heap, and if you *** threaten us with the beyond, we will cheerfully answer you: your paradise frightens us, your inferno makes us laugh."

Mussolini charged the Catholics with hypocrisy for invoking the principle of liberty in their demand for religious instruction in schools. "Black liberty" he called it. "The Catholics invoke the liberty . . . to kill liberty. They ask that the State authorize them to poison the children of the people with Christian teachings.*** We must recognize that the Catholic phalanxes lack modesty, not audacity. But your parabola is now completed, O black microbes who are as fatal to mankind as tuberculosis germs. History condemns you! You are the pale shadows of the Middle Ages. Do not profane the word liberty, you who have lit the pyres. Do not talk to us of Christianity. The monotonous Christian sing-song does not move us any more. We are decidedly anti-Christian, and we consider Christianity as humanity's immortal stigma of opprobrium."

In June 1908, the *Lima* announced the forthcoming publication of a pamphlet by the "True Heretic" on the

"Mission of the Priest" in relation to schools, women, children, and the workers' movement; but apparently such a pamphlet was never published.

Mussolini regarded himself as a true heretic not only with respect to religion but also with respect to reformist socialism. It was a serious mistake, he maintained, to confuse socialism with the socialist parties. His writings for the *Lima*, like those in Switzerland, reveal the revolutionary socialist with syndicalist leanings which become more pronounced because by 1908 the reformists had gained almost complete control of the Italian socialist party. He was thoroughly disgusted with reformist socialism—its emphasis on political, parliamentary action, its "mania for legislation" and its fear of violence and the general strike. Was it not ridiculous to look to the Italian Parliament, "that assembly of old fossils", as an instrument of social revolution? He demanded war, violent war between classes, not collaboration between classes, and greater reliance on the socialist worker than on the socialist deputy. In deploring the factional dissensions among those who labelled themselves reformists, intransigents, revolutionaries, syndicalists, and integralists, he attacked particularly the "imbeciles" who called themselves Turatians or Ferrians and thus conceived of socialism in terms of personal leaders such as Turati and Ferri. He refused to think that the gradualists could monopolize the spirit, the heritage, and the mission of socialism. Above all, he hastened to explain to non-socialist writers, to defamers of socialism and to "superficial hackwriters" who interpreted the factional fights among socialist groups as a sign of the decline of the socialist ideal, that socialism was still a great living force. "Those who do not distinguish between socialism and the socialist party reveal a phenomenal ingenuousness. The socialist party may die or at least change the forms of its present organization, but socialism cannot die. Men pass, not ideas. And a movement of ideas, which has its bases in the conditions of contemporary society and represents in its negations a superior stage of civilization, a movement of ideas, which for its extension and profundity can be compared only to Christianity, will always find militants, apostles and propagators up to the day when it will have accomplished its liberating mission."

Where, asked Mussolini, was there a movement comparable to socialism? Certainly, he argued, neither Protestantism, Freemasonry, the French encyclopaedic movement, liberalism, democracy, nor the national-patriotic movements were as universal in their appeal as socialism. "We can affirm that after Christianity, socialism is the only universal movement of ideas. Socialism has spread among all the peoples of the world; it is the soul of contemporary thought in all its finest philosophical and artistic manifestations; it has found its way in books, in the theatre, in the public squares; it has rehabilitated man, substituting for the evangelical idea of renunciation the revolutionary idea of conquest, and substituting for the principle of the struggle for life the principle of harmony in life; it has demolished the idea of an ultramundane 'providence' and of earthly 'privilege'. Socialism is the inevitable negation of the bourgeoisie. It is the Anti-Christ for Pope Sarto [Pius X], the hidden threat for Disraeli, the preoccupation of governments, and the sole, the great, the luminous hope of all the oppressed! O innumerable writers of the entire reactionary press, how you seem microbes when you speak to us about the end of socialism!"

Mussolini could not understand revolution and social change except in terms of violence. He was familiar with the literature of violent revolt that circulated in anarchist, syndicalist, and revolutionary socialist circles. Georges Sorel, the French theoretician of revolutionary syndicalism, was extolling the necessity for violence, and Mussolini quoted him at length as an authority who was corroborating his own views on this subject.[1] Praising the efficacy of physical and, as he put it, "muscular" violence, and insisting that violence is necessary and inevitable, for in it resides "the principle, the logic, the necessity of life", the "True Heretic" maintained that ideas are not abstract entities, but physical

---

[1] On Mussolini and Sorel, see below, pp. 228–245.

forces which cannot leave their impress on history unless they are armed with violence. He applauded two famous strikes in Italy: the general strike of 1904 and the widespread agrarian strike in the province of Parma in 1908, both of which had been brought about by the syndicalist and revolutionary elements in the socialist movement. The 1904 strike, he said, "illumines the dark sky of Italy like a great fire. But it was hardly ended when it was calumniated in the presence of adversaries who had been frightened by it; it was depreciated and disparaged in the presence of comrades in the name of that creature of ambiguous sex that is called the philosophy of history." The current Parma strike was proof of the "colossal failure of the 'co-operation of classes' that the charlatans of reformism intended to substitute for the class struggle. You, O workers of the Parma region, maintain that it is impossible to 'co-operate' with the delinquents recruited by the landowners. You prove to us instead, that only with a struggle without quarter are the partial conquests of to-day and the final victory of to-morrow made possible. May victory smile upon you!"

Infuriated by another *eccidio* or proletarian "massacre" at Rome in April 1908, Mussolini showered scorn on the timid reformists who believed in legal methods, who frowned on violence and who regarded it as the expression of base instincts. He maintained that "verbal protests are not enough, and we repeat the hope that the men who misgovern us may choke in their own blood. The hymns to pacification leave us sceptical. Those who believe in the possibility of eliminating bloody clashes between the proletariat and the defenders of the bourgeoisie through a series of administrative reforms deceive themselves. We believe that the suppression of violence is impossible in a society divided into classes that have antagonistic interests and in which one class oppresses the other 'with violence'. We have a different concept of *ideas*. For us, ideas are not abstract entities, but physical forces. When an idea wishes to assume concrete form in the world, it does so through nervous, muscular, physical manifestations. Opposing ideas will be historically concretized by way of antithesis, by way of conflict; and this process will be violent because the practical agent of an idea is material."

Just as the revolutionary ideas of the encyclopaedists ultimately led to the violent explosion against the *ancien régime* and to the destruction of the Bastille by the "muscular fury of its assailants", just as the spread of Christianity was attended by the gigantic military expeditions of the crusades and a long period of wars, so "the socialist idea, that is, the new form of social life based on a radical change of present property relations, will be realized through violent, revolutionary manifestations.*** The new society cannot get out of the involucrum of the old society, except by smashing it to pieces; two conceptions, two classes, two worlds will contend for primacy, and only force will compel the weaker to disappear. For this reason, we socialists of the first school, Marxists and catastrophic, if you wish, explain to ourselves the partial violence of to-day and the violence of to-morrow. For this reason, instead of arguing and instead of deluding the proletariat with rosy illusions about the possibility of a triumph through the peaceful means of legality, we say to the proletariat and to our comrades that they should prepare themselves in order to be able to endure the most difficult trials and the most painful sacrifices. The bodies of those who have been killed by bourgeois lead are signposts of our march forward . . .; they are the victims that every renovating movement demands. It is through death that humanity reaches the summits of the ideal."

Mussolini continued to argue that in the struggle between two conceptions, two classes and two worlds, represented respectively by the bourgeoisie and the proletariat, the former would prove the weaker of the two. If the proletariat is to succeed, it must be prepared to use effective force or violence: "Do not call us prophets of massacre if we present the possibility that the socialist revolution will have insurrectional episodes. It is puerile to think that such a radical displacement of interests, such a profound transformation of habits can be accomplished without violent conflicts.

The bourgeoisie has made a revolution with blood. Read the first volume of *L'Histoire Socialiste* by Jean Jaurès, and you will see from which class came the demolishers of the Bastille, the demonstrators of Paris and the members of the revolutionary clubs ***."

Mussolini despised the Italian ruling class and its chief representative, Premier Giolitti—"the most astute actor of the third Italy and worthy head of the government of what the English, in a characteristic phrase, call the *carnival-nation*". The "True Heretic" had this to say: "We can explain to ourselves the infinite poverty of initiative that characterizes our ruling classes when we think of the political composition of the Italian state, of this *Caesarian democracy*, as Arturo Labriola has somewhere defined it. Italy is not one. There are different peoples badly amalgamated by an administration that is fiercely unitary and centralizing.[1] The moral ties which unite a Piedmontese with a Sicilian are questionable. The racial ties are even more questionable. From this there follows different evaluations of the same fact. A large part of Sicily is Nasian [after Nunzio Nasi, deputy from Sicily who, as Minister of Public Instruction, was implicated in a financial scandal] and regards the ex-Minister of Public Instruction as a victim, a martyr, a hero. For us Northerners, Nasi is a vulgar swindler. Italy is still in chips as in the time of Giusti. There are regional, not national problems and politics."

As an incentive to more effective socialist action, Mussolini emphasized the value of culture, although in doing so he painted a dark but exaggerated and untruthful picture of the state of Italian socialist culture. "The absolute or almost absolute lack of socialist culture explains to us the superficiality of our conduct as a party. The 'practical persons' who do not attribute any importance to the theoretical, doctrinal element in the life of socialism delude themselves. It is culture; it is its greatest diffusion that must prepare the new spirit; it is culture that will give us the *'human element'*

---

[1] Of course, the most fiercely centralizing and unitary administration in the history of united Italy is Mussolini's fascist government.

capable of rising above bestial everyday life, capable of understanding the beauty of an idea and of interesting itself in great problems." Hence he described as a new mania the diffidence of certain socialist "manual" workers towards the "intellectuals" in the socialist movement. "The stupid campaign begun in several socialist circles against the intellectuals has no *raison d'être*. The dangerous persons for the socialist movement are not the intellectuals, but those who are *not convinced* of socialism and all those who call themselves socialists without knowing why they are socialists."

Throughout his stay at Oneglia, the "True Heretic" engaged in lively controversies with the local Catholic weekly *Il Giornale Ligure*. Weekly publications representing divergent views, such as the *Giornale Ligure* and the *Lima*, while trying at first to appear as "friendly neighbours", usually ended up with vituperative campaigns against each other. Though both sides seemed "offended" and tried to appear to be above petty squabbles, they none the less indulged in and enjoyed them. Mussolini was particularly piqued when accused of being showy, of being a "poseur" and of making pretensions to culture: "I do not give myself the air of being a philosopher, nor have I ever 'posed' as a philosopher. I am simply a seeker of knowledge; friends and adversaries know it." Among other things, the writers of the *Giornale Ligure* probably had in mind Mussolini's quotations from or references to such writers as Weishaupt —the founder of an obscure sect, Ibsen, Stecchetti—the satirist, Bovio—the popular philosopher, Carducci—the famous poet, and Max Nordau—the brilliant sociologist who enjoyed a considerable vogue among socialist intellectuals.

With the exception of two or three articles, which he signed with his full name, Mussolini wrote all his articles in the *Lima* under the pseudonym *Vero Eretico* or its initials. It is probable that he used a pseudonym in order to avoid reprisals by the police of Oneglia, who, apparently from the moment he went there, were acquainted with his "revolutionary past" and regarded him as a "suspect" person. It is likely that they received information from his "reactionary" enemies at Oneglia and from the Royal Prefecture of Forlì. At the end of the academic term in June 1908, the "True Heretic" felt free to use his real name for an attack on the official authorities in an "open letter to the command of the Royal Carabineers of Oneglia, to the Police Commissioner and through them, to Di Rovasenda, the Prefect. The circumspection that personal reasons and school duties imposed upon me has ended with the closing of the academic year. Now I can speak and submit to the judgment of all honest men the conduct of the police authorities towards me. What I relate cannot be contradicted.

"In the first days of last March, I came to Oneglia as a teacher of French in the private Technical School connected with the Ulisse Calvi College. I had not yet opened my bags when the carabineers went to the Directorate of the College to obtain and give information about me. The Directorate did not lend itself to the oblique police manœuvre. I was simply told of this and nothing more. Several days later, the carabineers again came to the College and after portraying me in very black colours, asked the Directorate for *my immediate dismissal*. The Directorate did not comply, and for this it should be praised. Now, may I be permitted to ask a simple question: Is not the attempt to take away bread from an individual criminal? If the Directorate, by yielding to the insistent pressure of these egregious guardians of order, had dismissed me, would I not have probably found myself on the streets? Why did not the police proceed through administrative means to my expulsion from Oneglia, and why did they prefer instead to have an act of brutal political reaction done by others? Finally, is not this persecution of ideas sincerely professed revolting?

"O tools of all the police departments of Italy, know once and for all that, in the exercise of your functions, I detest you, and that, as citizens, I dislike you. All that you have done and will do henceforth will have no effect whatever in swerving me from the road which I have freely resolved to pursue. I am going within a few days, and in order that you might be able to '*mark me*', I leave you my exact address.

House located on the provincial road of the [River] Rabbi, at 15 kilometres [from the provincial capital], village of Dovia, commune of Predappio, province of Forlì. Take note of this and study . . . if it is possible to force me to leave even my own house."

On the eve of his departure from Oneglia, about June 30, 1908, Professor Mussolini was tendered a farewell banquet by about thirty of his comrades. The *Lima* informs us that the socialist lawyer Bruno who, I think, was Mayor of Oneglia at this time, spoke of "his own devotion and that of the socialists of Oneglia for him who had been able to sustain for about six months the noble journalistic battle against the adversaries. He expressed the wish of again having him among us soon and concluded by extolling socialism. The guest answered him in sincere and heartfelt language."

3. TO THE FLAMES WITH THE LAW!

In July 1908, we find Mussolini back home at Predappio, one of the centres of the serious agrarian troubles then agitating the Romagna region. The following month, he wrote: "I have lived for some weeks in an atmosphere saturated with revolt. I have participated wholeheartedly in the struggle that marks another signpost in the forward march of the agricultural masses of Italy."

The dominant form of land tenure in the Romagna was the *mezzadria* or *métayage* system in which the tenant, the cultivator—the *mezzadro* or the *métayer*—divided his crop with the landlord who had given him a plot of land to live on and to cultivate. This form of share-tenancy goes back to feudal times and survives to this day in the Romagna and in other parts of Italy as well as in some parts of France.

In addition to the *mezzadri* or share-tenants, there was the large mass of *braccianti* or day-labourers who had no land. When they were not engaged in public works, they worked for the share-tenants, especially during harvest time, and received the miserable compensation of two lire and fifty centimes to three lire for ten hours' work. Since they were exposed to long and frequent periods of unemployment and since they were almost completely dependent on the labour demand of the share-tenants, dire poverty was their usual lot. They organized themselves into co-operatives, generally under the leadership of the socialists, so that they might gain a greater share and a more regular participation in agricultural production. One of the chief demands of these co-operatives was that they furnish the personnel for working the threshing machines. In order not to be dependent on the day-labourers, the share-tenants, urged on by the land-lords, retaliated by resorting to the practice of the exchange of labour among themselves. When the day-labourers insisted on the abolition of this practice, there arose between them and the share-tenants conflicts which were often accompanied by strikes, violence, and bloodshed.

Mussolini censured the "agrarian feudalism" in the Romagna and characterized the share-tenants as men perverted by the ideas of landlords and priests. The aim of the day-labourers, he said, was the abolition of the share-tenant system and the elimination of the landlord. If the share-tenants could understand that they should co-operate with the day-labourers, not with the landlords, there would remain only two classes—the workers of the land and the proprietors—and between them there would be waged the final battle which, of course, would culminate in the abolition of private property.

Professor Mussolini would show in his home town that he was a good Romagnuole socialist and that his soul was with the workers. On July 18, he was arrested on the charge of having threatened to strike with a cane a certain Emilio Rolli, a "scab" organizer. In an article entitled *Ti Svirgolo*[1]—*I will crack you down*—he describes his arrest and trial:

"This is the phrase, indeed the verbal locution for which I have been sentenced to three months' imprisonment. Friends, be calm! The story is exhilarating and would deserve to be versified in the Latin of the immortal Folengo or Cocaio [a pseudonym of the Italian poet Folengo].

"On the afternoon of July 18, 1908, the animals, the plants, the fields and the waves exhibited nothing out of the ordinary. I do not fix exactly the hour. We savages look at the sun during the day, and at night we are guided by the crowing of the rooster. The astronomers who initiated me into the science certify that a miscalculation is never more than two hours out of the way. It might, therefore, have been four o'clock. I happened to be on the roadway while a well-known monopolizer and organizer of *scabs* was apostrophizing a group of day-labourers. When he passed near me, I said to him: *Ti svirgolo!* I had a cane, but I did not raise it because the *scab* said nothing and continued on his way.

[1] It is difficult to translate this Romagnuole phrase. It is a strong term of threat and may also be translated, "I'll give you a beating" or "I'll beat you up".

In the evening, I was arrested and taken to Forlì with an escort of half a squadron of cavalrymen! This extraordinary eagerness for my personal safety 'touched' me. The nocturnal cavalcade had something romantic about it. It seemed to me that I had suddenly become famous and—may the great Jupiter pardon me—I compared myself to that quasi-namesake of mine, the Calabrian who studies Greek at Portolongone.[1] At a certain point, we stopped. A strange noise was heard. It was the bridge of Calanca that laughed, laughed, laughed . . . The stamping of the horses awakened the good Forlivese. From doors and windows, noses appeared and then eyes were sharpened 'Like an old tailor at his needle's eye [Dante]'.

"Second Act. An immediate session of the Court.

"The prosecutor declares that I am enough of a malefactor and demands six months of imprisonment, a fine of 1,000 lire, damages and costs. The Court sentences me to *three* months of imprisonment, damages and costs, orders restitution of the confiscated cane, and denies me a suspended sentence. The Court of Appeals of Bologna grants—subject to bail—my request for provisional liberty, and after a vacation of fifteen days, I leave the prison.

"Moral: The sentence of the Forlì Court has 'amazed' even the adversaries. The huge police set-up wanted to have a penal sanction and attained its aim. I am happy about it. For me, for us heretics, prison is a 'comma'. At all times and in many places, the heretics have known the caresses of the masters. A Russian proverb says that a man can call himself a man only after 6 years in a gymnasium, 4 years in a university and 2 in a prison. I am happy about the sentence because it shows again the sinister cohabitation between the police and the judiciary. No, justice is not as poets and painters—incorrigible little rogues—represent it. She is not the beautiful Themis of the pagans; she is an

---

[1] Mussolini refers to the notorious Italian brigand from Calabria, Musolino, who was then in the famous Italian prison of Portolongone where criminals sentenced to long terms of imprisonment were usually sent.

old idler who prostitutes herself to the first one who comes along, provided he belongs to the police, to this ignoble collection of hirelings. To the flames with the law!"

Among the left-wing papers which paid tribute to Mussolini as they denounced his arrest and the verdict were the *Avanti!*, the daily organ of the Italian socialist party, the *Pensiero Romagnolo*, the Forlì republican weekly, and the *Lima*. The *Avanti!* referred to "Professor Mussolini" as an "intelligent young man"; the *Pensiero* described the professor as a "young man of lively intelligence and an autodidact, frank and sincere"; and the *Lima* spoke of "comrade" Mussolini, its "keen, alert and cultured *Vero Eretico*", and the police reaction that "was scheming its revenge in secret. Benito Mussolini belongs to those men who do not enjoy excessive favour with the low-down Italian police ***. We, who had him as a brother in arms in recent battles, hold dear the memory of his mild and refined character, his clear and lively intelligence."

On the other hand, the Catholic *Giornale Ligure*, after noting the disagreement of the Forlì judges with Mussolini's thesis that violence was inevitable and necessary in political and economic revolutions, offered the following comment: "While we profoundly regret the disagreeable incident which has befallen our worthy adversary, we express the hope, now that he has been taught a lesson by cruel experience, that he will be able to add much water to his wine and to confine his ideals always within the pure and innocuous field of theory."

After spending about fifteen days in jail, Mussolini was granted provisional liberty by the Court of Appeals of Bologna. When this court heard his appeal in November 1908, it reduced the sentence to 12 days' imprisonment (which he had already served) and it also decreed that the judgment of conviction should not be recorded in the registry of those sentenced for a criminal offence. The moderate and, from the socialist point of view, the reactionary daily newspaper of Bologna *Il Resto del Carlino* sarcastically commented that since Professor Mussolini was free, "he could, from now on, better appreciate the benefits of a school vacation".

But the young agitator continued to get into trouble with the police. In September 1908, he was sentenced to a fine of 100 lire for making a public speech without authorization at Meldola, a town near Predappio.[1] In November 1908, the following item was entered in the secret police record of Mussolini's activities: "November 12, 1908. N.P. [File Number] 3041. November 12, 1908, removed residence to Forlì, Via Mazzini 27. Is adequately watched, the more because he is a fervent anti-militarist."

[1] For his failure to pay this fine, he was arrested and imprisoned for ten days in November 1909.

4. NIETZSCHE AND OTHERS

After his release from prison in July 1908, Mussolini did some writing for *Il Pensiero Romagnolo*, the Forlì republican weekly. His most striking contribution was a long essay dealing with Nietzsche and entitled "The Philosophy of Force. Marginal Notes to the Speech by the Hon. Treves". Mussolini doubtless heard the speech on Nietzsche, which the brilliant reformist socialist deputy had delivered at Forlì in November 1908. When I met Treves at Paris in June 1933—several years after he had been forced to flee from fascist Italy and two days before his untimely death—and told him how his speech had apparently prompted Mussolini's essay on the German thinker, he showed considerable surprise, for he had had no idea of his connection with it.

Although the essay is more a description and exposition of Nietzsche's principal ideas than a candid confession of his own personal reactions to them, it is a revealing document in showing not only that Mussolini was aware of many of the principal intellectual currents in contemporary Europe but also that he was responsive especially to those currents which appealed to his Romagnuole temperament and reinforced his own predilections. He regarded Nietzsche as the "most extraordinary mind of the last quarter of the last century"; the "most discussed man of our day"; the recognized leader of the *homines novi*, the new men who would live beyond good and evil; the Anti-Christ, the enemy of the Christian morality of renunciation, compassion, pity, resignation, and love of one's neighbour; the hater of the herd, the common run of people, the weak and the mediocre who are incapable of "willing strongly"; the pitiless critic of democracy and equality; the champion of the rights of the strong, "hard" men, the new species of "free spirits" fortified in war, solitude, and great danger; the creator of the superman, the hero, possessed of an irrepressible "will to power". The superb conception of the "superman", said Mussolini, is Nietzsche's "great creation", suggested perhaps by the "*tedium vitae* . . . of our life, of life as it goes on in contemporary civilized societies where irremediable mediocrity triumphs at the expense of plant-man".

However inviting it may be to speculate at length about the possible affinities between Nietzsche and Mussolini the revolutionary socialist—this would lead us too far astray at this point—we shall limit ourselves to a few observations. Above all, it must be stressed that in the first decade of this century, Nietzsche enjoyed a considerable vogue among certain anarchists, certain socialists of the extreme left like Mussolini and other kinds of revolutionists, all of whom saw in the philosopher such an uncompromising enemy of the contemporary bourgeois order that they contributed greatly to the diffusion of his ideas in such a manner as to make of him an ally in their struggle to overthrow the bourgeois system. Even the conception of the superman, which at first glance might seem to be repugnant to revolutionary ideals, was interpreted to symbolize the type of man who could emerge only if the false philanthropic, gregarious, humanitarian, sentimental, and mediocre bourgeois mentality were destroyed.

Nietzsche is one of those writers who easily lend themselves to a variety of meanings on the part of men upholding different moral, political, and social ideals. Hence it is possible to read in him and in Mussolini's essay an anticipation of fascism. After the fascist "March on Rome", Nietzsche's sister, Elizabeth, the high priestess of a Nietzschean cult, acclaimed the fascist Duce as the embodiment of her brother's ideal of the superman. And yet in the year 1908, we submit, Mussolini, like many other Italian revolutionists, found in Nietzsche a source of inspiration for his subversive aims.

Nietzsche's restless spirit of activism, his audacious unrestraint, his glorification of violence were as appealing to syndicalists as to royalists, as appealing to some rebels as to some capitalists, as appealing to Mussolini the socialist as to Mussolini the fascist. In many ways, these elements in Nietzsche found expression in the person of Mussolini who, from the socialist activist that he was to the fascist activist that

he became, eventually lost or gave up any social ideal whatsoever, unless he could utilize such an ideal, be it socialism
or fascism, be it internationalism or nationalism, as a mask
to glorify and satiate his ardent passion for action and power.

When he was a socialist, Mussolini responded with enthusiasm not only to Nietzsche but also to such men as the
anarchist Kropotkin and the brilliant French thinker Guyau.
In exalting the spirit of solidarity, both Kropotkin and Guyau
urged men to a life of action, and although their respective
philosophies were fundamentally different from Nietzsche's
philosophy, the young Romagnuole agitator frequently
quoted them because they too were teachers of action and
stimulated his activist nature.

An interesting detail in connection with Mussolini's
essay on Nietzsche is his use of the German edition of the
philosopher's works, thus revealing a thorough knowledge
of German which he had begun to study in 1904 when
he was in Switzerland. Almost contemporaneously with
the appearance of his writing on Nietzsche, Mussolini published in the Italian syndicalist review *Pagine Libere*, a brief
study on "The Poetry of Klopstock from 1789 to 1795". He
took this occasion to draw a revolutionary moral as he
presented the following observations about poets and so-
called "great men":

"His [Klopstock's] attitude towards the French Revolution shows us that poets in general are not able to
understand and judge historical events. Klopstock who
exalts the Revolution, Klopstock who defames the Revolution: this contradiction in the Klopstockian conscience
brings us to a consideration of the psychology of 'great
men'. Great men are, at bottom, reactionary conservatives.
Their talent, their style, their being at a given moment the
most elect representatives of a nation are factors that lead
them to give a sort of prophetic or dogmatic and categorical
tone to the expressions of their minds. They sketch the lines
of the future development of peoples and they fix the limits
beyond which they must not go; and when peoples go beyond that point, there is a downpour of anathemas, maledic-

tions and calumnies. How else can the harsh judgment of
Mazzini on the Paris Commune be explained? . . . O anonymous and obscure crowd who live at the bottom, very much
at the bottom, of the so-called social pyramid, you are great,
strong and courageous, as long as you heed the counsels of
your wise spiritual rectors, but when you dare break down
the fences that provident shepherds had placed around you,
then you are no longer the 'sun of the earth', but the un-
governable canaille 'without moral ideas'. . . ."

Could not this passage by Mussolini serve well as a description of his own evolution from socialist to fascist ideals?

Besides his essay on Nietzsche, Mussolini contributed a
few more articles to the *Pensiero Romagnuolo* in the second
half of the year 1908 and in the first month of the following
year. Reviewing Giuseppe Forastieri's *Prepariamo l'avvenire
d'Italia* (*Let us Prepare the Future of Italy*), a book stressing
the need for various reforms, Mussolini emphasized his own
lack of faith in legislation and parliamentary rule: "I am an
incorrigible pessimist concerning the value of all laws,
especially in the economic field, and I share the opinion
of Buckle who declared that 'a law is good only when it
destroys another law'." While Mussolini highly praised Aldo
Spallicci's sonnets in Romagnuole dialect, he sarcastically
criticized Antonia Beltramelli's *I canti di Faunus*: the "Bel-
tramellian prose", the "mountain of phrases" and the
"tropical abundance of adjectives" of "this chevalier of
the House of Savoy". Mussolini's view of this work is of
special interest because Beltramelli, beginning as an extreme
nationalist and ending up as a devout fascist, wrote in 1923
the first lengthy apologetic biography of the fascist Duce
under the title *L'uomo nuovo*, embodying, he said, an "act
of faith", an "act of devotion to the Man of our destiny".
This book could hardly be better characterized than in
the terms that Mussolini used in his review of the *Canti
di Faunus*. Of course, Beltramelli made no mention of this
review and of the most important facts in the life of the Duce.
In 1929, Mussolini made this third-rate novelist and syco-
phantic biographer a member of the Royal Italian Academy.

CHAPTER V

AUSTRIA-HUNGARY

1. AMONG IRREDENTISTS AT TRENT

TOWARDS the end of 1908, the Secretariat of Labour in the Trentino, one of the great centres of Italian irredentism in Austria-Hungary, asked Mussolini to serve as its secretary and as the editor of its weekly paper. This post had been held for a time by the socialist propagandist Domenico Gasperini. It seems certain that Gasperini had asked Serrati to recommend someone for the post and that Serrati had suggested Mussolini.

On January 22, 1909, *L'Avvenire del Lavoratore* (*The Future of the Worker*), the weekly organ of the local secretariat of labour and socialist party, which was published at Trent, announced the choice of Mussolini: "The selection could not be better, for Benito Mussolini, besides being a proved fighter, is a fervent propagandist, versed especially in the subject of anti-clericalism. He is a cultured young man, and to the great advantage of our movement, he has a thorough knowledge of the German language."

The Trentino environment was pre-eminently unsuited to Mussolini's temperament and ideas. The conservative and passive nature of its people made him often remark that what they needed was some of the spirit and blood of the Romagna, a "battalion of Romagnuole blood". The city of Trent and its outlying section, the Trentino, were not sufficiently developed economically and industrially to be adapted to the revolutionary Marxian type of propaganda. Socialism in the Trentino, emphasizing the gradual economic betterment of the working classes rather than a bitter class war spirit, was at once reformist and patriotic. This outlook was best embodied in the person of Cesare Battisti, the distinguished leader of the Trentino socialists and an heroic champion of irredentism, who attained martyrdom in the Great War. His love of the Italian fatherland and his devotion to the cause of social betterment, motivated by lofty humanitarian impulses, were aspects of his ideal of a better-ordered society. The liberal traditions of the Risorgimento were cherished in the Trentino where men like Battisti were imbued with the same passionate love of country that animated Mazzini. The socialists, as much as any other group in the Trentino, harboured fervid hopes for the deliverance of the "lost provinces" from feudal and reactionary Austria-Hungary which offended their social aspirations and national consciousness. To them, socialism meant not only social reform but also the liberation of oppressed peoples from a foreign yoke. So vital was the irredentist problem that the economic disagreements between different social classes were frequently obscured, with the result that socialism in the Trentino assumed the character of a temperate reform movement, hopefully striving for the autonomy of the Trentino within the Austro-Hungarian Empire until the day when it could be united with Italy.

There was little opportunity to stir the economic class struggle at Trent, and Mussolini realized how little he could accomplish there. He was a revolutionary socialist, a "syndicalist" among reformists, an extreme anti-patriot and internationalist among irredentists. He stressed the teachings of Marx, not those of Mazzini. On almost every question, he was sure to maintain a position much more extreme and revolutionary, much more to the left than the position taken by any of his Trentino comrades.

That he was not at all happy in his new position is made clear in a letter he wrote to his close Romagnoule acquaintance Torquato Nanni on February 26, 1909, about three weeks after his arrival at Trent.[1] "As for my future, I have no fixed plans. I am living, as always, from hand to

[1] Incidentally, Nanni is the author of the first biographical sketch of Mussolini; it is twenty-three pages long and was published in 1915.

mouth.*** I have put advertisements in the newspapers, offering myself as a private teacher of French. If I succeed in living by this means, I shall give up the secretaryship immediately". Although he foresaw the danger of his expulsion, which would be "demanded" by the Trentino clericals, he had a higher opinion of the Austrian than of the Italian police. As one who had been expelled from two cantons of Switzerland, that "very free republic of sausage-makers", he could not as yet complain of the "blood-thirsty, Catholic and feudal Austrian Empire". One thing he did like about Trent was the city library and other cultural facilities which permitted him to read foreign periodicals and newspapers as well as the latest works of foreign authors, such as *L'Oiseau blessé* by Alfred Capus. These facilities were much better than those at Forlì, "the city of dealers in hogs and hay".

And yet, despite his dislike for the new stopping-place, Mussolini brought great enthusiasm to his work. His stay in Trent enriched his experience, for besides reading extensively, he lectured a good deal before workers' groups; he developed his literary talents by writing short stories, character sketches and feature articles; and he perfected his mastery of violent and abusive language. "Professor" Mussolini was the "intellectual" of the Chamber of Labour and overawed his hearers by what appeared to them profound learning. He played the violin and had the reputation of being an omnivorous reader, a first-rate speaker and writer, and a proud "proletarian". With his small salary of one hundred and twenty crowns or twenty-four dollars a month, he contented himself with living in a room in the poorest section of the town, with a daily fare of beans and polenta, and with clothes that were almost threadbare. When his comrades gave him a new hat and a new suit of clothes, he crumpled the hat and the suit in order not to look like a "bourgeois." His unconventional attitude was summed up in the motto over his bed: *Viver liberi.*

Mussolini's passion for journalism was amply satisfied at Trent. Besides editing the *Avvenire*, he contributed frequently

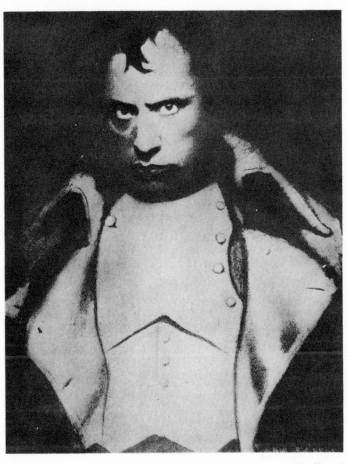

(*Harlingue*)

THEIR NAPOLEON.

to a socialist daily, *Il Popolo*, and to an illustrated weekly, *La Vita Trentina*, both owned and edited by Cesare Battisti. After he had been at Trent for about six months, Battisti made him managing editor of the *Popolo*, a post that he held for little more than a month. On August 2, 1909, the *Popolo*, doubtless through the pen of Battisti, announced the new appointment to its staff: "We do not think a long introduction is necessary. He is known to our readers as an agile, incisive writer, as a vigorous polemist and as an upright man who is able to bring to his journalistic work all the exuberance of sentiment and all the pride of the Romagnuole character, tempered by a varied and up-to-date culture. For these reasons, we are sure that the greeting which we extend to him to-day for his coming among us well interprets the sentiment of our friends and comrades and all our readers, even those who do not fully share his views but are able to appreciate the frankness and the loyalty with which he upholds them."

During his eight months' stay at Trent, Mussolini wrote numerous editorials and feature articles on a variety of themes suggested by contemporary events, by his extensive reading of periodical literature and by famous anniversaries in the socialist calendar. Some of the topics were the Paris Commune, the Clubs in Paris and their rôle in the Commune, Giordano Bruno, socialist activities in various countries, the responsibility of the current "decadent" morality for infanticides, the spread of Neo-Malthusianism in a bourgeois society, the relationship between Darwinism and socialism, the degeneration of May Day as a revolutionary holiday and the aviation exploits of Latham and Bleriot.

The exaltation of the Paris Commune was the theme of one of his early articles in the *Avvenire*. After an historical review and an interpretation of this event, which usually assumed almost mythical proportions in the minds of extreme revolutionary propagandists, he concluded in language uncommon among the moderate Trentino socialists: "The Commune died in blood, fecund blood, blood that is sacred to us. The best way to commemorate the Commune is to take up its teachings, to keep alive its historical significance, and to demonstrate that, in spite of the petty acts of cowardice of to-day, we desire that the 36,000 workers who fell defending it shall not remain unavenged."

Austria-Hungary's desire for more armaments, despite the severity of the economic crisis, called forth an attack on militarism: "The millions that should go for the relief of the people are instead swallowed by the army under the guise of military preparation. Militarism! Here is the monstrous polyp with a thousand viscous tentacles that sucks unceasingly the blood and best energies of peoples! Here is a goal for our struggle! Destroy this relic of barbarism; cry out that the army is to-day the organized school of criminality and that it serves solely to protect the capital and income of the bourgeoisie; and be not afraid to affirm that we internationalist socialists have no borders, no flags and that we detest any weapon, any institution that serves to kill men, to dissipate energy and to suffocate the forward movement of the working class. Against militaristic parasitism, we raise the old cry: 'Down with arms and up with the flags of humanity!' "

Commenting on the acquittal of fifty-seven socialists who had been in an Italian prison for almost a year because of their alleged participation in the Parma agrarian troubles, Mussolini excoriated the "criminal" landowners' agrarian association: "Woe to you, O delinquents of the Agrarian Association, you who protest against your bourgeois justice because it did not have the courage to write out at any cost a sentence of conviction, woe to you! The day when you will have to implore mercy, 'our' mercy, is probably not as far off as you suppose. Then, we shall apply the good natural law which decreed: an eye for an eye, a tooth for a tooth!"

In a series of articles on "Men of the Day", Mussolini familiarized his readers with the revelations of the Russians Bakai and Burtzeff and with the deeds of the Indian student Dhingra. The "dry prose" of Bakai, an ex-Czarist police official who had turned against the Czarist regime, served "the cause of the Russian revolution in the same way and as much as the prose of Stepniak, Dostoevski, Tolstoy, and Gorky". The memoirs that Burtzeff, a former professor

in Russia, was publishing in the French socialist paper
L'Humanité constituted "a formidable indictment. The Czar
will not find defence lawyers; he will probably resort to a
hired assassin in order to suppress the free voice of Burtzeff
with blood. It is the weapon of all tyrants. But every new life
that is sacrificed brings nearer the ruin of the system."

Of Dhingra, the Indian student who was hanged in London
for the murder of Sir W. H. Curzon Wyllie and Dr. Lalcaca
in 1909, Mussolini remarked: "The social vendetta is therefore accomplished, and the prodigal metropolis throws a
corpse to the colony where people are dying of hunger.
Dhingra died like a hero. No trembling at the announcement
of the sentence; no wavering in walking with a solemn air
towards the horrible scaffold; not a word of remorse. As he
put his neck to the slender noose of black silk, Dhingra knew
that he was representing his unhappy fatherland, mysterious
India, cradle of a very ancient civilization; India, rich and
plundered by English capitalists***. Why did Dhingra kill?
In order to protest against England, the robber.*** He has
killed. The law has condemned him. But the law deludes
itself; but London deludes itself if it thinks that it has controlled the causes of Indian discontent by committing
Dhingra to the hangman. The body, stark and hanging from
the gibbet, will become a symbol of revolt."

Writing of Marx, Mussolini stressed his greatness as a man
of action. For the benefit of the lukewarm, the discouraged,
and the weaklings who believed in the collaboration of
classes, he quoted the stirring concluding passage from
Marx's *Poverty of Philosophy*, which, he said, "resounds in our
ears and hearts like a fanfare of war and a herald of resurrec-
tion. This page and innumerable others give us evidence of
the profundity, the versatility and the intellectual acumen
of the man whom the socialists the world over recognize as
their father and teacher. Karl Marx—the comrades should
remember this well—was, above all, a man of action. The
last of his theses on Ludwig Feuerbach is at once a fine re-
buke and an inspiration: it is no longer a matter of studying
the world but of changing it! We do not deny that certain

parts—the secondary ones—of the Marxist economic doctrine are weak, but the basic concepts of Marxism are still intact, and criticism has tried in vain to contradict them."

Like many journalists, Mussolini tried his hand at literature and literary criticism. His most ambitious effort was a novel, *Claudia Particella*, published in serial form in the *Popolo* and translated into English in 1928 under the title *The Cardinal's Mistress*. The best of his four short stories, bearing the title suggested by the Nietzschean phrase *Nothing is true, everything is permitted*, deals with the morbid feelings of two lovers after the suicide of the woman's husband. *Notturno in "Re" Minore* contains jibes against the Austrian police made in the course of his imaginary walk through Trent with the sixteenth-century sculptor Alessandro Vittoria. Another imaginary experience, with the Trent police, is sarcastically related in what he describes as a *Terrifying Story à la Edgar Poe*. In *Convegno Supremo*, he fancies himself meeting a number of masqueraders, under whose masks are hidden several types of so-called respectable people, such as the judge, the usurer, the journalist, the politician, the professor, the military officer, the priest, and the unfaithful wife. A short article *How One Becomes a Tramp* recalls a prison stay in Switzerland, during which he met a professional tramp who told him about his life. Mussolini was planning to publish several short stories *à la Poe* and then to bring them together in a small volume which he thought of entitling *Perverse Short Stories*, but he never carried out this project.

Mussolini reveals his uncanny faculty to read motives and character in a series of "bourgeois medallions" wherein he portrays with ironic touches various bourgeois types—the speculator, the usurer, the judge, the serious man, the respectable woman, the *viveur*, and the nobleman. Some parts of these "medallions" were considered so offensive that they were censored.

Among Mussolini's attempts at literary criticism was an essay on the women in Schiller's *William Tell*, which he announced would be incorporated, along with his study on the poetry of Klopstock, in a volume of *Critical Studies in*

German Literature, but this volume never appeared.[1] While discussing Verhaeren's poem *Les Villes Tentaculaires*, he introduced his impressions of poems by Baudelaire and by Petöfi.

The Trent journals for which Mussolini wrote contained his translations from French and German writings. His translation of *My Youth*, the anonymous memoirs of a German working woman, was published in instalments in the *Avvenire*. He translated the preface of the famous work on *L'Homme et la Terre* by Reclus; a dialogue between two workmen by Paul Lafargue; *The Last Human Couple* by Edmond Harancourt; *The Spectre* by Fritz Sänger; *The Good Horses* by Erbert Nadler; and in addition, he rendered into rhyme Robert Seidel's *Hymn to Liberty* and Ernest Raynaud's *Elegy*. He also intended to translate "a very funny short story" by Mark Twain, apparently from a French version, since he did not know English at that time. I have found no trace of this translation, and it is idle to guess which story by Twain he had in mind.[2] Sometime in the autumn of 1909, after his expulsion from Austria-Hungary, Mussolini stated that he was translating Schopenhauer's critique of the ethics of Kant, but there is no evidence that such a translation was ever published.

Mussolini's duties at Trent enabled him to develop his oratorical powers as well as his journalistic and literary talents. He was probably the founder of the socialist League for Social Culture at Trent, the purpose of which was to stimulate the intellectual interests of the workers. Among the topics discussed at its "weekly conversations", in which he usually took a leading part, were "The Communist Manifesto", "Christianity and Socialism", and "Has the proletariat an interest in the preservation of the present-day fatherlands?" Mussolini made a deep impression on his Italian socialist audiences in speeches at Trent, Rovereto, and

[1] In July 1909, the *Popolo* published Mussolini's article on August von Platen and his love for Italy. Mussolini's essay on "Platen and Italy" was published in 1910 in *Le Cronache Letterarie*, a periodical edited by Vincenzo Morello (Rastignac).

[2] Incidentally, Mussolini is now the Honorary President of the International Mark Twain Society.

other small centres in the Trentino, and at Bozen (now Bolzano) and Innsbruck in the German-speaking Tyrol. A report of his first speech at Trent, on the anniversary of Giordano Bruno's martyrdom, said: "The first meeting of Mussolini with our workers could not have been more pleasant and could not have achieved greater success. He was heard with the greatest attention, and he knew how to make himself immediately understood by his listeners who perceived that they had before them not only an excellent speaker and a persuasive propagandist, but also—and above all—a scholar, a man of firm beliefs, an enthusiast who was able to bring to his truly fine speech the results of his serious studies, the force of his convictions and the fervour of a man who has a faith which he upholds and wishes to inculcate in others." Moreover, we are told that his May Day speech at Trent, "as every other speech by Mussolini, not only was eloquent, straightforward and distinguished, but also reflected all the faith, hope and ardour of his cultured, meditative, candid and proud attitude of mind. If, we repeat, our young students could have been present *en masse* at this speech, how much more good—besides the great deal it has done among the workers—it could have done! How much faith would have been aroused among the doubtful, how many fertile thoughts would have been sowed, how many acolytes would have been called forth, and how many capable leaders would have matured!"

Mussolini's talents as a speaker, as a journalist, and as a labour leader were at various times recognized by his Trentino comrades. After his expulsion from Austria-Hungary in September 1909, Battisti paid tribute to his "Romagnuole pride", his "lively intelligence", and his "solid culture": "If his being expelled was for us a misfortune, for him it was an honour; his being forcibly taken away from us is reason for greater friendship and closer fraternal ties." Another distinguished leader of the Trentino socialists, the lawyer Antonio Piscel, described him as "a young man of great intelligence and very broad culture, a facile writer, a very talented polemist, and a proud, indomitable character".

2. THE INTERNATIONALIST

While he was at Trent, Mussolini viewed Italian political life with cynical indifference. He noted the lack of excitement over the Italian general elections of 1909, observing that "the Italian people are sceptical, like all the peoples of the South, hence fatalistic and inclined to quick outbursts of enthusiasm and to unjustified and sudden expressions of diffidence." The programme of many parties was wanting in sincerity. "Zero sums up the programme, the mentality and the attitude of the illiterate mercenaries who are at least 300 out of the 508 in the Italian Chamber. And yet, the rudder of the political ship will be entrusted to them, and on them the Savoy monarchy will rely! Nothing surprising in a country where the government sells the prefect and buys the deputy."

In reiterating his distrust of parliamentary methods, his censure of reformist socialism, and his faith in direct action, Mussolini found himself almost alone among the Trentino reformist socialists. "The electoral struggle is an incident, an episode in our [socialist] party life. Whoever expects a social revolution from an assembly of deputies deceives himself. Instead, it is the working mass that will bring about 'its' social revolution as soon as it has acquired the necessary strength to overthrow the economic, political and moral institutions of bourgeois civilization." And "in case legal means should prove to be insufficient to renew the governmental system of the Savoy dynasty, the Italian people that to-day rushes to the polls, to-morrow will occupy the squares, will suspend national life, will strike the sources of bourgeois wealth with the proclamation of a general strike and will say to the men at the head of institutions: Either renovation or death!"

These comments indicate how rooted in his mind were certain conceptions of revolutionary socialism. The internationalist had come to Trent where the socialists were not only reformists but also Italian patriots. He was in the heart of a strong Italian irredentist region and he was in contact with

Cesare Battisti. Did the new environment have any effect on his internationalism?

Throughout his stay at Trent, Mussolini stressed the anti-patriotic, internationalist note, not the patriotic, irredentist note, concentrating his efforts on preaching civil and class war and on orienting the minds of the workers towards the socialist international rather than the Italian fatherland. He placed class solidarity above nationality, not nationality above class solidarity, as his apologists try to make it appear. He was anti-patriotic and insisted that the proletariat was anti-patriotic by definition and by necessity because he regarded patriotism and nationalism as masks for the rapacious militarism and capitalism of the bourgeoisie. His anti-clerical, anti-religious, and anti-patriotic sentiments were fundamental aspects of his hatred of the bourgeois order.

By way of answering the charge of Italian nationalists that the Italian socialists in the unredeemed provinces were renegades to the Italian fatherland, Mussolini presented his position in an introductory comment to a worker's article on patriotism and internationalism: "The bourgeois nationalists of Italy—to-day nationalism is in style, just as, ten years ago, free thought, the republic, and Masonry were in style—affirm that the German socialists are patriots and that the Italian socialists subject to Austria betray the nation to which they belong by virtue of ancestry, language and customs. All this is false. The Italian socialists subject to Austria, the socialists of all civilized nations do not renounce the language, the history, the customs and the traditions of the ethnic group in which they were born and of which they form a part, but they deny the bourgeois fatherland which reveals itself in the form of standing armies designed to make easy the existence of a caste of parasites and to save capitalist wealth. To love one's own nationality does not mean that other nationalities must be hated. Harmonious development and fraternization of all nations—that is the socialist ideal. In this sense, the article that we are publishing, written by a worker who lives far away from his fatherland, has a great moral significance and gives the lie to the exploiters of nationalism, who desire to

cover up their defence of privileges and of the riches of all
exploiters with their empty patriotecring ideology."

Particularly repulsive to Mussolini was any display of
nationalism among workers in the Trentino and the Tyrol.
In his eyes, this constituted a capital offence against the true
spirit of the socialist international. After noting manifestations of nationalism on the part of German-speaking workers
at the expense of the more internationally-minded Italian
workers, he observed: "We are divesting ourselves always
more and more of nationalism, and we leave it to the bosses
to practise it. The German-Austrian workers cannot free
themselves of it. This condition of things should be noted in
order to attest our superiority with respect to the socialist
ideal.*** We hope that the cry of Karl Marx, 'workers of the
world, unite!', will find a practical application. Certain
exclusive attitudes have no reason to exist. In a meeting of
workers, the use of all languages must be permitted. I have
attended meetings at Geneva, Bern, Milan and elsewhere, in
which speeches were made in four languages. Dear, very dear
German comrades, do not, therefore, practise Pan-German-
ism or, worse, linguistic imperialism! Even Italian, the much-
despised Italian, has the right of citizenship in the meetings
of workers and civilized people." And, unable to restrain his
irritation, he concluded: "For Italian, the much-despised
Italian, was consecrated by a universal poet [Dante] a long
time before Klopstock wrote his *Messiah* and Goethe his
Faust. Then, as for the great Austrian national poet, I offer a
little florin as a tip to anyone who can show him to me."

That he did not mean to be misunderstood is shown by the
statement that "no language is contemptible, not even that
spoken by the Zulus. Every language is the expression of the
needs, the attitudes and the spirituality of a given people.
For this reason, every language has a right to existence and to
the respect of everyone."

In contrast to the nationalistic manifestations of some
Austrian workers, Mussolini applauded the demonstration of
international solidarity given by a group of Croat workers
who had been brought into the Trentino by an "Italian

renegade" in order to break a strike. The Croats refused to become "scabs" and to betray their "Italian brothers". At a meeting of the Chamber of Labour at Trent, which they attended before returning home, Mussolini tells us that "the soul of the multitude vibrated with sentiment of universal solidarity that does not efface the fatherlands but encompasses them in a greater vision of brotherhood and of love. Yes! Twenty centuries after the preaching of the meek apostle of Galilee, an understanding between peoples of different races and languages is finally possible. A word, an interjection, a gesture is enough! The old nationalist hatreds are disappearing. The proletariat feels itself 'one' in its internationalism of economic interests and ideal finalities."

Worthy of special note are Mussolini's references to the internationalism of Christ. The internationalist agitator had a tactical reason for joining the name of Christ to that of Marx in his anti-patriotic propaganda. The clericals constituted the most powerful Italian group in the Trentino; and since a large number of workers in this region came under their influence, Mussolini found it desirable to impress them by invoking the internationalist teachings of Christ. Thus, he had occasion to say that the founder of the religion which the clericals defended was "a genuine internationalist. He frustrated the Hebrew people's expectation of a Messiah because instead of turning to his own countrymen and exclusively to them, he broke the narrow circle of Jewish chauvinism and preached the gospel for all men, whatever the nation to which they belonged, whatever the language that they spoke. And here, perhaps, is the fundamental reason why Jesus experienced the agony of Gethsemane and the martyrdom of the cross.***

"*The proletariat is anti-patriotic by definition and by necessity.**** Christianity also has been anti-patriotic by definition and by necessity. Christ *** did not have any fatherland, but sent out his disciples to preach the gospel the world over. The sacred writings clearly prove that Christ severed all relations that might bind him to the old institutions. Christ renounces even the family. He asks: Who is my mother? Who are my brothers? Thus, Christianity was and is anti-patriotic in its theological essence and in its morality."

Notwithstanding the strong current of irredentist sentiment which pervaded the Trentino socialist movement, Mussolini took special pains to point out that patriotism, like parliamentarism, was a bourgeois fetish, and to insist that in case of a war, the socialists had only one duty: War at the frontier must be the signal for a general strike, for insurrection and for civil war at home.

Obviously, Mussolini's chief concern was social revolution, not irredentism. His thesis was that socialists should take advantage of war in order to provoke civil war, spread the "revolutionary lues" and overthrow the bourgeois system. While socialist-irredentists like Battisti and Piscel were intensely interested in the union of the unredeemed provinces with Italy, Mussolini was indifferent to this cause. Misunderstanding and confusion might easily arise if one fails properly to interpret his view that socialists did not renounce the language, customs, and cultural traditions of the ethnic group in which they were born and of which they formed a part. This should not be construed to mean that he was a patriot or a nationalist, for it did not belie, but rather accompanied his revolutionary socialism. It is not hazardous to say that even the most extreme revolutionists, including the anarchists, would subscribe to such a view. For example, they would actively oppose any attempt to deprive a people of its native tongue, but in so doing they would be far from considering the continued use of a given language as a manifestation of triumphant nationalism. This explains the compatibility between Mussolini's anti-patriotic and anti-nationalist propaganda and his interest in upholding the linguistic Italianity of the Trentino. He would allow each ethnic or national group to preserve its language and customs and to cherish a certain predilection for and even a strong pride in its physical home, literature and traditions. This is evidenced in his article on Platen's love for Italy in which he rhapsodically praised Italy's past glory and its great promise for the future. All these considerations were subordinate, in his mind, to the idea that each group should constitute a part of a socialist, international, and class-less society, stripped of all artificial boundaries and of all traces of militarism, bourgeois-patriotic prejudice, and nationalism.

Despite the overwhelming evidence showing the anti-nationalist and anti-patriotic stand of Mussolini, his fascist biographers, writing after his shift from revolutionary socialism and internationalism to fascism and nationalism, have had the effrontery to insist that he was strongly imbued with patriotic, and even irredentist, sentiments during his stay at Trent. By disregarding every line that we have quoted on this subject—none of them studied at first hand the Trent phase of Mussolini's life—by clever and tendentious juxtaposition of certain phrases which they attribute to Mussolini, by tearing sentences from their context and presenting them in such a fashion as to confuse the reader and by perverting the character of Mussolini's relationship to Battisti in order to buttress their nationalistic interpretation of his early life, they have constructed a formidable legend which has no basis whatever in fact. It has been so widely circulated that even some of Mussolini's detractors—who in turn have never made a first-hand study of this phase of his life—have accepted certain parts of it. The cumulative effect of the irresponsible literature on Mussolini has been to fortify the belief that he was expelled from Austria-Hungary because he was an irredentist.

The legend about Mussolini's patriotism was easy to construct on the basis of his acquaintance with Battisti whose career lent itself to misinterpretation and exploitation on the part of fascists and nationalists. When the Great War broke out, Battisti, then a socialist deputy in the Austrian Parliament, fled to Italy where he engaged in an intensive campaign urging Italy's intervention in order that she might achieve, among other aims, the liberation of the lost provinces. During August and September 1914, when the fight for and against neutrality was raging in Italy, Mussolini, then the leader of the Italian socialist party and the editor of its daily, the *Avanti!*, vigorously supported a policy of absolute neutrality and was deaf to the arguments and pleas of Battisti that Italy should participate in the war. When, in October–November 1914, Mussolini abandoned the *Avanti!* and the policy of absolute neutrality and founded *Il Popolo d'Italia* to advocate Italy's entrance into the war, he did so primarily for revolutionary reasons, not for patriotic or irredentist reasons. In 1916, Battisti, who was a soldier on the Italian front, was captured by the Austrians, taken to Trent and hanged. Thereafter he was one of Italy's national heroes, a symbol of the irredentist faith of the Trentini and a martyr to the cause of patriotism and social democracy.

Although the fascists and the nationalists championed principles and methods that were repugnant to the entire philosophy of Battisti, they did not hesitate to exploit the apotheosis of Battisti for their own ends, and many writers began to place an exaggerated emphasis on Mussolini's relationship with Battisti in 1909 in order to show that the fascist Duce had always been an Italian patriot. But it is a serious mistake to say that Battisti and Mussolini, in 1909, cherished an ardent irredentist faith in common. Their personal relations were cordial, but they were never intimate or close friends. Although their aptitudes, temperaments, and conceptions of socialism and patriotism were widely dissimilar, they respected each other. Mussolini was not the conventional secretary of a labour organization or the conventional editor of a workers' weekly, and he was one of the few men performing these functions at Trent who was asked to contribute extensively to the *Popolo*. He was a member of the staff of this newspaper for little more than a month, but his connection with it was secondary to his duties as secretary of the Trentino Secretariat of Labour and as editor-in-chief of the *Avvenire*.

The writers favourable to Mussolini stress his relationship with Battisti, but underestimate, misrepresent, or totally ignore the importance of his work on the *Avvenire*. We shall give special attention to Signora Sarfatti's biography of Mussolini because it is regarded as official and because it was doubtless written with the Duce's intimate collaboration.

In her irresponsible treatment of Mussolini's stay at Trent, Signora Sarfatti tells us that Battisti's "new colleague, the Secretary of the Chamber of Labour, ignorant as to how things stood, had at first attached himself as a matter of course to the *Avvenire* of Trent, the journal of the Socialists, who were more in sympathy with Austria and who took their tone from Vienna, but it was not long before he discovered the ugly side of things and then he joined the *Popolo*, of which Battisti was founder and editor". She also asserts that the *Avvenire* was Austrophile.

Such writing, although inaccurate, misleading, and clever, fortifies the legend and the implications growing out of Mussolini's connection with Battisti. It is absolutely incorrect to call the *Avvenire* Austrophile. In fact, it was one of the most courageous and effective organs of Italianity in the Trentino. Mussolini had given it, if anything, a more extreme tone in the direction of revolutionary socialism, with emphasis on internationalism. From the very beginning of his stay at Trent in February 1909 to the very end of his stay in September 1909, Mussolini's principal activity was directing the affairs of the Secretariat of Labour and editing its weekly, the *Avvenire*. He did this work with great zeal. What was secondary was his writing for the *Popolo*. That he was made managing editor of the *Popolo* on August 2 was probably accidental as Battisti needed more time for his scientific geographical studies. Accidental or not, Battisti chose Mussolini as managing editor because he valued his abilities as a journalist; not in any sense did he choose him because there were differences between Mussolini and the *Avvenire*. Neither the socialists at Trent nor the *Avvenire* took their tone from Vienna. Mussolini was never in the slightest degree hampered in the performance of his work on the *Avvenire* by any conceivable Austrophile sentiment emanating from the headquarters of the Austrian socialist party at Vienna. There was nothing "ugly" about the men who supported the *Avvenire*. They were enthusiastic in their collaboration with Mussolini whom they respected and admired; they once paid his fine of one hundred crowns lest he be kept longer in prison; and they participated in the warm greeting extended to him at the frontier after his expulsion. It is unjust to cast aspersions on a generation of humble and honest men who were ardent Italian patriots, who remained faithful to Italy under trying conditions and who showed their faith when the Great War came. It is safe to say that the only genuine extreme internationalist in their midst in 1909 was Mussolini.

That the aspersions on the *Avvenire* and its supporters are a travesty on truth may also be shown by invoking again the authority of Mussolini himself. In 1911, about a year and a half after his expulsion from Austria-Hungary, there was published, under the auspices of the lively Florentine review *La Voce*, a book by Mussolini entitled *Il Trentino veduto da un socialista. Note e notizie* (*The Trentino Seen by a Socialist. Observations and Data*). This book of one hundred and four pages is one of the most intelligent studies on the irredentist question. Besides discussing the Pan-German movement, Mussolini presents an illuminating analysis of the linguistic, economic, and political situation in the Trentino. Years later, after the fascist seizure of power, his apologists offered distorted interpretations of the book in order to strengthen their thesis about his patriotism. Among them was, of course, Signora Sarfatti, who tears sentences out of their context to suit her convenience, but it is of little use at this point to follow her and other writers in their numerous gross misrepresentations of the book's substance and spirit which are neither patriotic nor irredentist. In describing the Trentino socialist movement, Mussolini asserts that the "finest page in the history of the Trentino socialist party" is the campaign in favour of the political and administrative autonomy of the Trentino (as distinct from the Tyrol). This campaign "is the merit of a single party: the socialist". Implicit in these remarks is his recognition of the valuable contribution in favour of autonomy that was being made by the two socialist papers of Trent, the *Avvenire* and the *Popolo*. In no manner or form does he reproach the *Avvenire* for being Austrophile and anti-Italian. On the contrary, he speaks of its work in maintaining linguistic Italianity among Italians in various parts of Austria-Hungary.

The degree to which Mussolini's heart and mind were set on world revolution, not on irredentism, is amply illustrated by his activity following his expulsion from Austria-Hungary in September 1909. Between 1910 and 1912, as editor-in-chief of the *Lotta di Classe* (*The Class Struggle*), the weekly organ of the socialists of Forlì, he frequently referred to the irredentist problem in the course of his militant anti-patriotic and anti-militarist campaign. His articles in the *Lotta* make unmistakably clear his pride in having combated the influence of the clericals at Trent, his growing enthusiasm for the Austrian socialists, his hope that through a socialist Austria, a peaceful settlement of the disputes between Italy and Austria might be obtained, and his condemnation of the irredentist "comedy" that was being played by various parties in Italy. They confirm our conclusion that the clericals were chiefly responsible for his expulsion, and they contradict the fascist legend that he was a patriot and an irredentist. At Forlì, Mussolini was perfectly free to say what he liked about the irredentist problem, but not once did he utter a word that could in any way be interpreted as sympathetic or favourable to the irredentist cause.

Instead, he called the national flag a rag to be planted on a dunghill, and he heaped vituperation on those groups in Italy who talked about irredentism—the Freemasons, the republicans, the nationalists, and others. He opposed the Turco-Italian War with such vehemence that he was sentenced to a year in prison. In March 1911, he wrote the following abusive attack on those who played up the irredentist issue in the Italian Chamber of Deputies: "From time to time, the Italian Chamber—that is, the most stupid Parliament in the world—enjoys itself in playing the irredentist comedy. Three or four years ago, the comedy in question was occasioned by a speech of Alessandro Fortis; the other day, it was occasioned by a speech of the republican Eugenio Chiesa *** [who] presented an interpellation to find out the reasons that had caused the Prefect of Florence to prohibit the production of *Romanticismo*, a patriotic play by Rovetta. We agree that any illiberal action whatsoever should be denounced from the parliamentary platform, and Chiesa did well. But the irredentist comedy that Chiesa, willingly or unwillingly, evoked, was disgusting. By now, we should have the courage to abandon the poses and the 1848 phraseology of Austrophobe irredentism. That is, unless one wants to provoke a war. In which case, O irredentists, you will re-live Lissa and Custoza: defeat and shame!"

This significant passage, in which Mussolini does not hesitate to remind the irredentists that in case of war with Austria, Italy would again suffer shameful defeats as she had in her war with Austria in 1866, is eloquent testimony to our contention that he had no faith in the irredentist cause, and it is an unanswerable indictment against the later fascist fabrications about his patriotic and irredentist sentiments.

During his stay at Trent in 1909, Mussolini stood out among his socialist comrades because of his extreme internationalist views. None of them regarded him as an irredentist. His activity, therefore, must not be confused with that of Trentino socialist-patriots like Battisti, Piscel, and Augusto Avancini, the socialist deputy in the Austrian Parliament. The Austrian government officials who ordered Mussolini's expulsion did not think of him as an irredentist agitator, but rather as an insolent and thoroughly obnoxious revolutionary agitator. The true reasons for his expulsion must be sought not in his alleged connection with irredentism, as his apologists try to make us believe, but in his violent polemics with the clericals and the government authorities.

3. EXPULSION

Mussolini, who was introduced to the Trentino workers as one especially versed in the subject of anti-clericalism, found ample scope for his anti-clerical and anti-religious feelings, for in no region where Italian was spoken was the Catholic clergy as influential as it was in the Trentino. The social and economic organizations, the banks, and the co-operatives of the Trentino clericals were extremely powerful, and their daily newspaper *Il Trentino* had by far the largest circulation of all the dailies published at Trent. They were not irredentists, but distinctly Austrophile, and they had never reconciled themselves to the abolition of the temporal power of the popes.

With Mussolini on the Trentino scene, the bitter polemics that had always characterized the struggles between the socialists and the clericals reached their highest point of verbal violence. His contentious nature, his bile, and his hatred of the established order were fully expressed in his tirades against the clericals. If the controversies between him and the clericals were replete with invective, innuendo, vulgar terms and banalities, it was not the merit or fault of Mussolini alone, but the merit or fault of both Mussolini and the clericals, all of whom were experts in the use of abusive and undignified language.

Of course, each side levelled the charge of insincerity against the other, and both deplored the personal character of the polemics, but since each of them always found a pretext to provoke the other, the asperity of the polemics continued unabated until the clericals had the satisfaction of seeing Mussolini expelled from Austria-Hungary. For example, in referring to the writers of the *Trentino*, Mussolini declared: "But I who know them—and the land where I was born is still fresh with the blood of papal massacres—I know that one cannot be proper and temperate with this band of freebooters.*** Again we say: 'Woe to the merciful!' We are ready to meet on the ground of ideas, but if instead, the adversaries prefer deceitful, personal, anonymous attacks, we shall accept the challenge. We shall continue the fight up to the point of ennui, up to the point of exasperation."

When the *Trentino* attacked the *Avvenire*, it usually had in mind the person of Mussolini. To the clerical paper, the *Avvenire* was a "bloodthirsty" and "cannibalistically anti-religious" organ, and the men associated with the socialist paper and Chamber of Labour were "desperadoes", "anarchists", and "thugs". To which Mussolini replied: "We are the 'anarchists' and the 'desperadoes'; but even to the patricians of pagan Rome, the humble folk—who at the word of Christ, vibrated with hope and faith—were 'desperadoes'. And yet, the meek apostle of Galilee said to the 'desperadoes': You are the salt of the earth." As for violence, "in us it is an 'episode'; in you it is the 'system' in life and in history".

Mussolini was naturally furious when the *Trentino* indulged in innuendo about his prison record. Attributing this particular slur to Don Giovanni Chelodi, a priest and one of the editors of the *Trentino*, he burst out: "And now, Signor Chelodi, I give you five days to declare in your newspaper that 'your' assertion *** is false. Write or have someone write to the prosecutor's office at Forlì. If then, you will not have the decency to make a correction, I promise myself and I promise you that before going away from Trent, I shall leave on your sacerdotal head a not easily removable sign of my hands." A few days later, he repeated his demand: "Answer, you microbe!" In his disputes with the clericals, he would reserve to himself the right to apply, if necessary, "the good, wise, and natural law of the desert: an eye for an eye, a tooth for a tooth".

Don Chelodi answered the first threat as follows: "To Signor Mussolini. Everyone does things in his own way. You threaten to use your fists against me; I make use of the law against you. You probably find that your system is ideal; to me, it seems to belong to barbaric times or, if you please, to the enlightened times of the sun of the future [socialism]. You can go to the Romagna to practise certain brutal impositions; here we call them acts of bravado. The Trentino is not a place where the D'Artagnans prosper nor am I such a man who loses his calm because of a rowdy phrase." Don Chelodi brought suit against Mussolini for the latter's threats, but because of a technicality in the law relating to threats, Mussolini was absolved by the court.

Mussolini vigorously combated the influence of the local clergy in the schools and among the workers, and vilified the Catholic church, that "big corpse", and the Vatican, that "den of intolerance and of a gang of robbers". In a speech occasioned by a victorious carpenters' strike, he rose to considerable heights of eloquence as he attacked the clericals and extolled the revolutionary tradition of his family: "The working class of Trent is faithful to the Chamber of Labour; that is the reason for the sinister hatred of the clericals. We must not preoccupy ourselves with these powerless people. They bring actions against me for libellous statements, and they commit me to the courts. Small and petty means that arouse in my mind a sense of pity for those who use them. I have had other adversaries much more to be feared. I have fought other and more difficult battles. I have come out of struggles and police persecutions more vigorous, more hardened and surer in my convictions. A prison does not frighten me, nor should it frighten us.*** I think that a prison is an excellent school for moral discipline that fortifies the will and strengthens the soul. My grandfather has known the papal prisons; my father has known those of the Savoy monarchy; and I have known those of a republic [Switzerland] and of a monarchy [Italy]. I shall also know those of the [Austro-Hungarian] Empire, and meanwhile, the sacred family tradition will not be broken. We do not ask of you to-night an act of protest against the criminals of the Trentino Vatican; but hold yourselves ready because if the foul campaign against the Chamber of Labour does not stop, we shall call you to action. And now, O comrades, let us think of the sacred duty which calls us to better ourselves and the environment in which we live. Let us solemnly promise ourselves that we shall struggle day by day, indefatigably, until economic miseries, political privileges and ultramontane superstitions disappear. In our hands is strength, in our idea is the future!"

When the *Trentino* seized upon the phrase relating to Mussolini's sacred family tradition, he retaliated: "If in the family of the usual anonymous writer, there is lacking that tradition to which I alluded with my words, this means that from his great-grandfather to his grandfather, to his father, and to the children who will come, there has been, there is, and there will be that tradition according to which it is a wise and moral rule to be cowards, Jesuits and spies just in order to avoid the prisons of the pope and of the other 'anointed' of God."

The *Trentino* censured and ridiculed the appointment of Mussolini as managing editor of the *Popolo* and the manner in which the "furibund Romagnuole" and "clown" had begun his new duties with attacks on the clericals: "For us, he has ceased to exist as a *man*; eventually, we will confute his ideas and arguments . . . if he has any."

This gave Mussolini an excellent opportunity to rage, to present his claims to ideas and culture, to express his disgust for the "nauseating stench" that emanated from the writings of the clericals, and to continue his defamation of Don Chelodi, this "trapper" of cigar butts, whom he held responsible for the *Trentino's* attacks. After reminding the clericals of the inquisition, the night of St. Bartholomew, the deportation and the execution of anti-papal Italian patriots, he asked: "Must I then again defecate under your nose the Carduccian imprecation against the 'old ravenous Vatican she-wolf'?" As for ideas and arguments, he retorted that while he could not call himself a very learned man, he had demonstrated, even to his adversaries, his culture and, above all, his right to a broader culture. For the special benefit of Don Chelodi, he pointed with pride to his writings in various journals and periodicals—polemical articles, short stories, critical literary studies, and translations from French and German—and finally, he told "sweet Chelodi" not to forget a little pamphlet in which he had documented and described the turpitude of one of Don Chelodi's colleagues. The pamph-

let consisted of an interview which Mussolini had had with a
certain Rosa Broll, the so-called "Saint" of Susà, a small
town near Trent. To conceal his illicit relations with this
woman, which had resulted in the birth of two children, Don
Prudel, a priest, tried to make it appear that since she was a
"saint", it was unnecessary for her to have relations with
a man in order to become a mother. Mussolini's interview,
which created a sensation in the Trentino, was published
first in the *Popolo* and then as a pamphlet. The *Popolo*
announced its publication in the following terms: "It is a
page of history. The experiences of this poor woman who,
after becoming a mother by a priest, was abandoned in
poverty, are told in that concise and curious style—with
vivid tone colours—which we recognize in Mussolini. It is a
human document."

Besides attacking Don Chelodi, Mussolini called Don
Barra, an Italian priest in Innsbruck, a "hydrophobic dog"
who should be turned over to a dog-catcher, and he directed
the following tirade against Don Dallabrida, a priest and an
editor of a Trent Catholic weekly: "To this tonsured illiterate
fool who takes from our newspaper the anti-religious phrases
that escape Signor Tranquillini [a prosecutor], doing this in
order to bring us to the attention of the police; to this priest
with the small and befuddled mentality of a Kaffir, I shall
never give the satisfaction of a polemic. In my capacity as
editor of a *dirty little sheet* of the Chamber of Labour, I say to
Don Dallabrida: You jackass, go to a school or to a vestry!"

For this and additional slurs on priests, Mussolini was sued
for libel, and more than once he had to pay a fine or spend
several days in the town jail. He received these sentences with
mingled feelings of indifference and pride, which perhaps
cloaked the satisfaction of his vanity in appearing as an *enfant
terrible*, a "man unafraid" of any consequences in his persistent devotion to the "cause". "There is now no doubt", he
wrote, "that during my sojourn in Austria, I shall break the
'record' for trials.*** There is no need to add that I am glad
to tramp so often into the sacred halls of sacrosanct Justice,
not to obtain a sort of martyr's crown, but simply to offer to

the judges a reason for a request for promotion.   At the end
of the year, the judges of Trent will be able to say: 'Authorities on high! Reward us in some way. Mussolini has made us
work very hard!' And every special effort merits—naturally—an adequate reward."

It is of interest to note that among the writers for the
Trentino whom Mussolini bitterly assailed was Alcide De
Gasperi, an active figure in the Trentino Catholic movement.
After the Great War, De Gasperi played a prominent rôle in
the Italian Popular Party, the powerful political organiza-
tion of the Catholics, and he became a deputy in the Italian
Parliament. He was one of the men whom Mussolini hated
the most after the advent of fascism to power. The animosity
between these men had its origin in the polemics between the
Trentino and the *Avvenire*.

That the clericals of the Trentino despised Mussolini and
would gladly have seen him expelled from Austria-Hungary
requires no elaboration. Their natural allies were the Austrian imperial officials and police authorities. While the
clericals were disgusted with Mussolini's truculent anti-
clericalism, the governing officials kept a watch on him as an
extreme revolutionist. Since he was a foreigner and a *regnicolo*
—that is, a subject of the Kingdom of Italy—he could be
expelled from Austria-Hungary without much ado and
merely by an administrative order from the proper officials.

As early as February 26, about three weeks after his
arrival at Trent, he realized that there was danger of his
expulsion, which would be "demanded" by the clericals. On
April 8, in a violent article declaring war on the clericals,
he said: "Woe to those who in civil war play the part of
romantic lambs; they will experience the sharp teeth of
wolves. Then, as for the possibility of my expulsion, I declare
openly that I don't give a damn!" On August 9, he asked
the following question about the clericals' motive in malign-
ing him: "Is it probably in order to effect my expulsion?"

The Austrian authorities never hesitated to censor any
articles or phrases in the press which they thought objection-
able. Of course, the socialist papers suffered most, and several

editions of the *Avvenire* appeared with blank spaces marked
with the word "censored". As often as the censorship was
exercised, there were protests. In reproaching Signor Tranquillini, the prosecutor at Trent who kept his eye on the
press, Mussolini referred to the "systematic persecution of
the socialist press—persecution *urged and desired by the clericals
and particularly by the Bishop of Trent*", and expressed the hope
that the "Parliamentary Union would rise like one man to
make respected that right to freedom of thought which is one
of the most glorious conquests of civilization". His articles
against the clericals emphasized their anxiety to bring the
Avvenire to the attention of the authorities. Convinced of
the futility of mass meetings and resolutions, he declared
that the best way to protest against the censorship was
to continue to be censored. Obviously, he was determined to do everything in his power to provoke both the
clericals and the government officials.

The zealous assistant prosecutor at Trent, Signor Pio
Tessadri, was a special enemy of the socialists. On July 14,
an article appeared in the *Avvenire* entitled "O Inquisitor, O
Idiot!" and signed by ten socialists. The contents of the article
were not published; and the blank spaces in their place were
marked "censored". The "inquisitor", the "idiot" was
doubtless Tessadri. Later in the month, a group of socialists
proceeded to his residence and staged a demonstration
against his "mania" for censorship by whistling and shouting.
Among those who were held responsible for this demonstration were Avancini, Battisti, and "Professor Mussolini", each
of whom was sentenced to spend three days in jail or pay a
fine of thirty crowns.

In May 1909, Mussolini was sentenced to pay a fine of
thirty crowns or spend three days in jail for insulting Don
Dallabrida; in June, he was sentenced to three days in jail
for unjustified interference with the functions of the police
when they were engaged in confiscating a censored number
of the *Avvenire*; in July, he was sentenced in connection with
the anti-Tessadri demonstration; and in August, he received
a jail sentence as a result of the suit brought by Don Barra.

On August 25, the *Popolo*, speaking of this last-named sentence, noted rumours to the effect that a decree for the expulsion of Mussolini would be ready upon his discharge from jail. "We hope that the police will not become an accomplice in such an unjustified measure of reaction. Meanwhile, these rumours and the arrest of Mussolini [to serve his sentence] have already produced some agitation in the workers' class which is on the watch and will not let pass any attempt at the destruction of liberty by the superior authorities without a general protest."

On August 31, Mussolini was sentenced to a fine of one hundred crowns for violations of the press law. About this time, the Trentino became the scene of troublesome events. On August 29, Emperor Franz Josef went to Innsbruck to preside over the celebration in honour of Andreas Hofer, the famous Tyrolese patriot. The officials of the Austrian government exerted pressure on the Trentino Italian population so that an impressive number of Italians could be sent to Innsbruck to pay homage to the Emperor. Only the Italian clericals were well represented. The socialists, of course, would not participate. The Italian liberals, most of whom were irredentists at heart, were placed in an embarrassing situation. The habit of being ruled by the Hapsburgs and the apparent hopelessness of a possible union with Italy in view of Italy's membership in the Triple Alliance had discouraged them and had made their position seem equivocal on many occasions. At the Hofer centenary, the Italian liberal deputies in the Austrian Parliament took part in the dinner given to Franz Josef. Almost contemporaneously, however, the Trent liberal daily *L'Alto Adige* carried a large picture of Garibaldi on the first page in order to manifest its patriotic sentiment and its disapproval of the participation of Italians in the Hofer commemoration. This edition of September 1 was censored, and the newspaper appeared without the picture. At Trent, an effigy of Hofer was found hanging on the statue of Dante, and the imperial coat of arms on many public buildings as well as the sign of the clerical paper *Il Trentino* was smeared with black paint; this was probably done mostly by socialists although some liberals had a share in it.

The indignant Austrian government started to seek the authors of these "insults". Confusion began when on the afternoon of August 30, the public and the government were stunned by the robbery of about three hundred thousand crowns from the Banca Cooperativa of Trent. For this crime, which was soon interpreted as part of a concerted plan to begin an armed irredentist movement, an employee of the bank, Giuseppe Colpi, was immediately arrested. The city was virtually placed under martial law; the homes of many reputable citizens, who were not socialists, were searched, and about twenty of them were arrested; and the irredentist Society of Trentino Students was dissolved a few days after it had held its twelfth congress at Rovereto on September 12. The government was really carrying on two searching inquiries: one relating to the robbery, and the other relating to a so-called political plot. They were distinct from each other, and it was due to a fortuitous circumstance that Colpi was made the centre of both of them.

Although there was no proof that Mussolini was in any way connected with the robbery or the plot, his position as an alien, as an extreme revolutionist and as a defiant critic of powerful government officials and clericals gave rise to considerable suspicion on the part of the police. If the Austrian police could arrest with impunity men with none of his "disabilities", why should they not also seize him? After the police had made a thorough search of his drawer at the *Popolo*, of his lodgings and of the Chamber of Labour, he was arrested on September 10. At the Chamber of Labour, all his personal papers, letters, and books as well as the books and records of the Chamber and of the League for Social Culture were confiscated; and at his lodgings, almost everything belonging to him was ransacked, confiscated, and placed in a basket as though it were garbage. A drama which he had just completed and which had cost him much time and labour was also confiscated and thrown in the basket. Even his music sheets were confiscated. Only his clothes, his watch, and his violin were left in the room. Handcuffed like a common criminal and accompanied by a considerable police escort, he was brought to the jail of the nearby town of Rovereto. His transfer here was doubtless due to the fear that his presence in the Trent prison might cause a demonstration.

This arbitrary arrest and mode of procedure were not explained by the police, and for a few days it was impossible to ascertain definitely the charges against him, but in view of the rather large number of arrests and the continual violation of constitutional rights that had taken place, it is not surprising that the police were so ruthless in Mussolini's case. On September 15, while he was still in custody, the *Popolo* published the following interesting news: "Concerning the inquest that is being continued with regard to him [Mussolini], we are informed that at Mezzolombardo, four gendarmes have searched the residence of comrade Cesare Berti, secretary of the Social Culture Club." The search, the *Popolo* went on to say, was fruitless.

This brief reference to Berti, a socialist carpenter and a warm admirer of Mussolini, yields what we consider an important clue to the police investigation of Mussolini. Taken in conjunction with many other details which we have ascertained, there is the strongest evidence that Mussolini was contemplating the use of dynamite against the Austrian authorities. In 1923 after the advent of Mussolini to power, Berti, who in the meantime had become a fascist, granted an interview to an obscure provincial fascist paper, in which he made some significant revelations as he proudly recalled his early acquaintance with the fascist Duce. Berti told his interviewer about the exasperation of many persons at Trent in 1909, the planning of conspiracies and the desire to blow up the police headquarters of Trent, the "wicked nest of the persecutors". After Berti had succeeded in carrying away some dynamite from a store-house at Mezzolombardo, the dynamite was distributed and, as Berti related to his interviewer, "the last six kilograms fall to Mussolini. Berti who arouses suspicion is searched in vain, but he is nevertheless arrested. The plan failed . . ."

The dots after the word "failed" signify that there is much more to the "dynamite story" than Berti was disposed to tell. After making searching inquiries bearing on this incident, I was able to establish satisfactorily the fact that the six kilograms of dynamite allotted to Mussolini and deposited at the Chamber of Labour were got rid of before the police could find any trace of them. My conclusion is that the news item in the *Popolo* in 1909 together with the recollections of Berti in 1923 and my own researches point clearly to a conspiracy between Berti and Mussolini and possibly a third or more parties to blow up the police headquarters or the offices of the *Trentino* at Trent in order to incite agitation against the reactionary acts of the Austrian government.[1]

That the Austrian government in September 1909 did not expect to bother about a formal trial for any charges which they might have had in mind against Mussolini and that they intended to expel him without much ado is shown by the fact that on September 14, while Mussolini was in jail, the Austrian government authorities notified him of his expulsion from Austria-Hungary. Immediately, the Hon. Augusto Avancini, the Italian socialist deputy representing Trent in the Austrian Parliament, sent a vigorous protest to the Austrian Minister of the Interior demanding the suspension of the order and Mussolini's release from prison until the Minister could make a thorough investigation; the socialist deputies,

---

[1] Berti, who lived in Mezzolombardo, a small town near Trent, was so deeply impressed with Mussolini in 1909 that he followed closely his later activities. About 1911, he left the Trentino and settled at Forlì in order to be near Mussolini, who was then editing the socialist weekly *The Class Struggle*. In 1914, after Mussolini had begun to preach Italy's intervention in the Great War, Berti helped to form at Forlì a *fascio* favouring Mussolini's pro-war stand. After the fascist "March on Rome", Berti enjoyed considerable prestige in certain fascist circles, and he acquired considerable wealth. Although I have not been able to trace his movements in detail, I have good reason to believe that he lost favour with the fascists and was exiled to an island by the Mussolini government. All this is worthy of note because I think Berti deserves to be called the first "Mussolinian", that is, the first man who was so captivated by Mussolini's personality as to remain devoted to him and ready to follow him irrespective of all his doctrinal divagations.

Adler and Pittoni, protested personally to the Minister of the Interior; and the Trent Chamber of Labour threatened a general strike. It was doubtless due to these protests and threats that the authorities suspended the order of expulsion. But they did not rescind it. Mussolini was not released from prison, as was expected, and it was announced that he would be tried before the Rovereto court on specific charges.

He was finally brought to trial on two charges: one, for inciting violence against the authorities of the state in a private letter to Mario Scotoni, the editor of *L'Alto Adige*; and the other, for sending with the letter a number of *L'Avvenire del Lavoratore* which had been legally confiscated. Both the letter and the confiscated number of the paper had been found by the police while searching the offices of *L'Alto Adige* in the early part of September when their preoccupation about a vast political plot was at its height.

In his letter to Scotoni, Mussolini had protested against the arbitrary censorship of the *Avvenire*, had asserted that Tessadri deserved the attacks of the socialists, and had asked Scotoni to refer to the acts of violence against the socialists. The confiscated number of the *Avvenire* was probably the original edition of the paper containing the article "O Inquisitor, O Idiot!" which was aimed at Tessadri.

The trial, which lasted about three hours on Friday morning, September 24, was held in an atmosphere of secrecy and behind closed doors. In his defence, Mussolini declared that by sending his letter to Scotoni, he had meant simply to ask for an expression of solidarity with respect to the censorship and that he had had no thought of urging Scotoni or anyone else to any acts of violence. Mussolini's lawyer, Piscel, dealt very ably with the legal aspects of the case. Since certain prerequisites for the commission of the acts charged to Mussolini were lacking, he was acquitted.

Despite the insistent demands of his counsel and the agitation of the socialists, his acquittal did not result in his release from prison. After applauding the decision of the Rovereto court, the *Popolo* made it quite clear that Mussolini's detention was due to the influence of "the black hand"—that is, the clericals. Ostensibly, one of the reasons for Mussolini's detention was that the prosecutor had appealed the judgment of the Rovereto court, and it seems that according to Austrian law, an alien like Mussolini could be kept in prison until the outcome of the appeal. Another reason for keeping Mussolini in custody was that he had failed to pay the fine of one hundred crowns imposed upon him for infractions of the press law in a trial held at the end of August. When asked to pay the fine, he is said to have replied: "Let me leave the prison, and I shall pay." This retort was interpreted as a refusal to pay, and the police proceeded directly to seize his effects. At noon on Saturday, September 25, he went on a hunger strike and refused to eat until he was set free. Meanwhile, the sale of his goods yielded virtually nothing, and he was informed that he would have to work out the fine by ten days' imprisonment. When this was learned by his comrades, the Secretariat of Labour immediately paid the fine.

None the less, Mussolini was detained. About two o'clock on the afternoon of Sunday, September 26, without any notice to the public, the Austrian police accompanied him to the Italian border. The order for his expulsion was carried out, and his sojourn in Austria-Hungary came to an end.

On the following day, the Trentino socialists, exasperated by the arbitrary infringement of the constitutional rights of several citizens and by the ruthless treatment of Mussolini, held a general strike as a warning to the government that it could not trample upon fundamental liberties with impunity. For a few days, Mussolini spent his time between Verona and Milan in northern Italy. On Sunday, October 3, a week after his expulsion, he went to Peri, an Italian town near the Austrian border, where a group of socialists who had come from the Trentino offered him a banquet as a last token of greeting and good fortune. Among those present were Piscel and his wife. An interesting incident occurred when the gathering proceeded to the stone which marked the frontier line between Italy and Austria. Mussolini, standing on the Italian side, shook hands with Mario Todeschini, who was on the Austrian side. The latter was a former socialist deputy in the Italian Parliament, who temporarily took over some of Mussolini's duties at Trent. The rare photograph facing page 176 is a memento of the meeting.

In his farewell speech to his comrades, Mussolini thanked them for their spirit of solidarity and exhorted them to continue the work for freedom from spiritual and economic servitude and towards an ideal of human redemption. What is most important, he made it plain that the "only ones" who were responsible for his expulsion were the clericals.

Mussolini had so many "disqualifications" that he was an easy target for expulsion on the ground that he was an "undesirable alien". He had done all he could to irritate and insult the most powerful people in the Trentino—the clericals and the government officials, especially assistant prosecutor Tessadri, prosecutors Tranquillini and Angelini, and judge Schumacher. His truculence may have been an expression of his sincere revolutionary ardour to fight openly all the "enemies of the proletariat". And it is well to remember that he was inwardly so unhappy at Trent and so anxious to leave that the danger of expulsion did not in the least disconcert him. On the contrary, it is probable that what he most desired, before returning to Italy, was a clamorous, dramatic departure which would please his vanity and add to his "laurels" as a persecuted revolutionist.

At the end of the first week in October 1909, we find Mussolini back at Forlì. Here he joined his father, who was eking out a bare existence as a tavern-keeper, and he enthusiastically participated in the world-wide agitation against the execution by the Spanish government of Francisco Ferrer, the noted Spanish anarchist, who had been accused of inciting the workers of Barcelona to rebellion. Ferrer was looked upon as a victim of vindictive clericalism and obscurantism and as a martyr of free thought. Several days before Mussolini's expulsion from Austria-Hungary and before the execution of Ferrer, the clerical *Trentino* tried to defame Ferrer and some of his publications by saying that his style was "Mussolinian". What the *Trentino* considered defamatory was doubtless considered complimentary by Mussolini. Was it not an honour for the young and obscure militant anti-clerical to have the famous Ferrer likened to him?

The execution of Ferrer was excoriated in a large number of mass meetings all over Europe. Forlì was the scene of an extraordinary demonstration. Among those who addressed a large crowd of Forlì socialists and republicans were Giuseppe Gaudenzi, the republican deputy from Forlì and the editor of the *Pensiero Romagnolo*, and "Professor" Mussolini. After the speeches, the crowd smashed the windows of the Bishop's home, set fire to the wooden fence which surrounded a tall column surmounted by a statue of a Madonna, and destroyed the slabs of marble at the base of the column. The onslaught on this religious monument, which was an example of the type of destructive revolutionary fury dear to Mussolini, was for many years remembered at Forlì as a symbol of anti-clerical and anti-religious feeling. After Mussolini's accession to power as the fascist Duce, the influence of the Catholic Church was immeasurably increased, and when the Forlì religious monument was repaired, the church officials of Forlì paid a lofty tribute to the man whom they had despised in 1909.

(*Isidore Giazzi*)

MUSSOLINI SHAKES HANDS WITH TODESCHINI.

CHAPTER VI

THE PROTAGONIST OF DIRECT ACTION

1. THE EDITOR OF *THE CLASS STRUGGLE*

HITHERTO Mussolini had led a nomadic and irregular existence. There had been nothing striking in his experiences as an emigrant adolescent in Switzerland, as a school teacher in various places, and as a journalist and propagandist. His place in the revolutionary ranks had been obscure, and while a goodly number of young anarchists, syndicalists, and socialists had come quite prominently before the public eye, he had been generally unnoticed. It is all the more remarkable, therefore, that in 1912 when he was twenty-nine years old, he became the editor-in-chief of the *Avanti!* and the virtual leader of the socialist party.

For about three years, from the autumn of 1909 to the winter of 1912, Mussolini lived in his home province of Forlì, among his own Romagnuoles, in an atmosphere "saturated with revolt". In the Romagna, he could fully express his revolutionary sentiments to people who understood him, while at Gualtieri, at various Swiss towns, at Tolmezzo, Oneglia, and Trent where most socialists were reformists, his extreme ideas were shared only by a small and insignificant minority.

Towards the end of 1909, about two months after his expulsion from Austria-Hungary, he was asked to head a reorganization of the federation of socialist clubs in the electoral college of Forlì and to edit a new socialist weekly.

Nothing could be more pleasing to this rebellious young man of twenty-six. Here was his first chance to lead a movement, albeit a provincial one, to edit a paper all by himself, albeit a four-page weekly, to have a real place of command, albeit on a small scale, to exercise his yearning and capacity for leadership, to become and act like a Duce of a movement that he could call his own. Signor Bonavita, the ex-reformist socialist and friend of Alessandro and Benito Mussolini, about whom he has written irresponsible books, claims credit for suggesting Benito as the editor of the Forlì socialist paper. While this is not certain, it is not improbable.

Mussolini becomes at Forlì what he was to be in the Italian socialist and fascist movements—the dominating leader, the Duce. His rather brief career as editor of the *Lotta di Classe* (*The Class Struggle*) and as secretary of the Forlì socialist federation shows the principal traits of his personality. His is the same character, temperament, manner of approaching problems, philosophy of action, style, and demeanour revealed later as the editor of the *Avanti!*, as the fascist editor of *Il Popolo d'Italia*, and as the leader of the fascist party and state. Change the shibboleth socialism to nationalism or fascism, shift the scene from provincial Forlì to Milan, the industrial capital of Italy where he spent ten years of his life from 1912 to 1922, and then to Rome, the political capital of Italy, and you will find the same personality.

The socialists of Forlì were in a grave minority as compared with the republicans who dominated the province to such an extent that it might well have been called a little republic. Although Mussolini had an up-hill fight, the violent and tempestuous struggles between the socialists and the republicans appealed to all the tenses and moods of his belligerent nature. Revealing is the title of the new paper of the Forlì socialists—*The Class Struggle*. This title was doubtless dictated by Mussolini, and it was intended as a warning to both the reformist socialists and the republicans that a temperate view of revolutionary action would not be countenanced. The first number of the paper appeared on January 9, 1910.

Mussolini's constant and minute supervision of *The Class Struggle* made him at once its editor, managing editor, chief reporter, and copy-reader. He did all the work but the printing. At every point, the paper bore the imprint of his fiery temperament. It was virtually his personal organ, for he had a completely free hand and would brook no interference from anyone. He wrote all the leading articles, and he edited all the news items covering the activity of his local comrades. *La Lotta di Classe* was not filled with reprints or clippings from other newspapers, as was and is the case with many provincial weeklies. "I write the paper", he exclaimed, "and I do it with my pen, not with my scissors." Given the small format of the paper, he said it was impossible to publish long articles that were being sent to him, articles which were "pretty indigestible stuff ***. I throw and I shall continue to throw in the waste-basket articles that are too long even if they should contain all the learning of Karl Marx."[1]

The collection of *The Class Struggle* abounds in valuable illustrations of Mussolini's extreme views on a wide range of subjects, including patriotism, militarism, reformist socialism, the United States of America, religion, Freemasonry, parliamentary government, and the virtues of political assassination and violence. It has been sought by enemies and friends alike—by the former, in order to expose his violent revolutionary past, and by the latter, in order to conceal it. One of the few complete collections of the paper was at the Forlì city library. In accordance with Italian law, all newspapers must be deposited at the public library of the place where they are published. Shortly after the fascist "March on Rome" in October 1922, the collection of the *Lotta* for the years when Mussolini was its editor was withdrawn from the Forlì

[1] I think that Mussolini had some editorial assistance from March 1912, when he returned to edit *The Class Struggle* after spending five months in prison, until December 1912, when he left his post to become editor-in-chief of the *Avanti!* at Milan. In April 1912, the format of *The Class Struggle* was considerably enlarged because it had been made the weekly organ of the socialist federations of the electoral colleges of Forlì, Cesena, San Arcangelo, and Rimini, all of which were located in the province of Forlì.

library and brought to Rome at the order, I think, of Mussolini himself, and it was deposited at the Ministry of Foreign Affairs. At that time, one of Mussolini's influential henchmen was Cesare Rossi, who was later seriously implicated in the murder of the socialist deputy Matteotti by fascists in June 1924. Rossi had somehow managed to appropriate and send the collection to Paris where it was kept by a lady friend. A few months after Rossi had made his way to Paris in 1926, four or five meagre fragments from this collection were published by anti-fascist exiles. These fragments made the rounds of the Italian anti-fascist press and have been incorporated in several anti-fascist books. It is most unfortunate that it did not occur to anyone who knew Rossi or could gain access to him, to buy or to photostat the entire collection or to republish its most important parts. To-day, Rossi is in an Italian prison, and I have not been able to learn whether the collection has been recovered by the fascists or whether it still remains in the possession of Rossi's rather elusive friend.[1] I am strongly inclined to believe that the fascists now have it. The story of this collection reveals the difficulty of access to much of the material relating to Mussolini's life before the "March on Rome".

In the course of my pursuit of the sources on Mussolini's life, I succeeded, despite great difficulties, in consulting a collection of the *Lotta di Classe* in Italy, first in 1926, then in 1927, and again in 1932 ; and now, it seems to me, it is possible for the first time to present a fairly complete picture of Mussolini's views and doings between 1910 and 1912, without having to rely on the untrustworthy and fragmentary accounts of his apologists, especially the novelist Beltramelli and the "official biographer" Signora Sarfatti, and on the few extracts from the paper used by anti-fascist writers.

Mussolini threw himself into his new work at Forlì with all his energy and enthusiasm. Preceded by the reputation of his father as one of the first internationalists in the Romagna and by a revolutionary record of his own to which he could point with pride, he soon fulfilled the most ardent hopes of his

[1] On Rossi, see below, p. 276.

Forlì comrades. He revealed the restlessness and fanaticism characteristic of many revolutionists who are always anxious to assume an extreme position on all questions lest they appear timid or cowardly. It was certain that on any issue, Mussolini would take, or appear to take, a "leftist" position. He had accustomed his followers to expect that.

Under his direction, the small four-page *Lotta di Classe* steadily increased its circulation and became one of the liveliest of the two hundred or more socialist weeklies in Italy. Besides writing editorials on important contemporary problems, he kept his readers informed of socialist activities in Italy and in other countries. The *Lotta* reflected his habit of reading periodical literature, and he frequently printed and commented upon extracts from foreign and Italian socialist, republican, and anarchist papers.

Another feature of the *Lotta* was the publication of a series of articles—"socialist medallions", sketches, and essays on—such thinkers or agitators as Thomas More, Babeuf, Fourier, Robert Owen, Blanqui, Leroux, Lassalle, Louise Michel, Malon, Bebel, Lafargue, and Kotoku (the Japanese anarchist who was executed by the Japanese Government in 1911). Some of these articles were reprinted from other papers; others were written by Mussolini. Incidentally, the "medallion" on Louise Michel was a translation by Mussolini of an article on the Communard and "Red Virgin", which had originally appeared in the German revolutionary paper of New York, the *Freiheit*.

These features formed a part of Mussolini's cultural programme for educating his comrades. Time and time again, he stressed the importance of the "human element" in the progress of socialism, for he maintained that the revolution could not be a mechanical event and a result of forces that were unaffected by the human will. A real revolution must solve not only economic problems but also moral problems. It must not only effect a better economic order but also develop a higher type of man. Hence the necessity of preparing the human element, of emphasizing moral and intellectual as well as material and physical improvements. In their political groups, he said, the socialists must prepare "the human element, the new men who strip themselves of mental and moral habits inherited from the old society that is on the decline. The socialist political groups must diffuse instruction through speeches, newspapers, books, and pamphlets; they must found schools of propaganda and libraries open to all. The brain of every man has sparks that sleep under the grey ashes of ignorance; it is a matter of kindling these divine sparks! The work of the school is deficient; it is necessary to complete it. In the most advanced nations, every socialist has his home library."

Mussolini was very active in encouraging the members of the various Forlì socialist clubs to build a socialist centre, to maintain a library and to invite speakers to address them on socialist questions. It was doubtless through his influence that Angelica Balabanoff and Costantino Lazzari, both of whom later helped him attain a leading post in the national socialist organization, went to Forlì to speak before socialist gatherings and contributed articles to the *Lotta*. Referring to the plan for a socialist library at Forlì, Mussolini declared that it should be the aim of socialist propaganda "to create 'the human element', the indispensable element for the realization of our ideas, the element whose importance did not escape any of the theoreticians, both old and modern, of socialism. The *Socialist Library* will contribute to form this element ***. We close this comment by noting to the comrades that resolutions must not remain on paper, but must be translated into facts, for only then are they efficacious."

In one of his early articles in the *Lotta*, Mussolini somewhat shocked and scandalized his comrades and the local bourgeoisie by his rude and sarcastic and, as he put it, "heretical" comments on the low state of culture at Forlì. He went around the town, visiting book-shops, news-stands, and political clubs to see what Forlì was reading, and he found that the town was doting. "The city library is rich and quite up-to-date, but it is frequented by professors and students." As for the political organizations, have they "institutions of culture like libraries, reading rooms, etc.? Nothing. I go into a republican club, and I see that under the picture of Mazzini—the mystic soul *par excellence*—*la morra* [an Italian game] is played. I go into a socialist club, and I find that under the picture of Marx, my dear comrades are often possessed of the devil over a badly played *briscola* [card game]. Intellectual pursuits at Forlì are left in the background. The mass of the people wastes its time and energy in taverns, dances, brothels and sports. The lower and upper bourgeoisie gather together in clubs to play a game of cards and to chatter often on subjects that would interest washerwomen. The residues of the nobility live miserably on in physical and moral inertia. This is the situation in broad outlines. That a false patriotic feeling may not put a bandage over our eyes!"

On another occasion, Mussolini wrote that "Forlì which was at one time a city of strong enthusiasms is doting on dancing, sports, the tonic reading of the *Amore Illustrato*, and the protection of socialistoid Freemasonry. I propose that the city's coat of arms be changed: in lieu of the eagle, let there be placed a large mirror and a well-groomed beardless youth who is looking at himself and strumming a guitar."

Mussolini made his comrades understand that socialism was no mere fad. He urged them to study, to attend meetings regularly, and to conform their daily activities to socialist principles. When a goodly number of socialists were absent from a local congress because of rain, he sarcastically jibed them for their fear of rain and their slight enthusiasm. "Sometimes they have the courage to walk kilometres through the snow on severe winter nights to say a few stupidities to a woman at a dance."

He set before his followers the example of the prominent Romagnuole agitator Andrea Costa. It will be remembered that Alessandro Mussolini was an ardent follower and admirer of Costa and probably knew him personally. One of the baptismal names that Alessandro gave to Benito was Andrea. In the course of his long political career, Costa became a believer in evolutionary, "parliamentary", reformist socialism, a type of socialism that was repellent to the youthful and volcanic Benito. Costa, in fact, was even a vice-president of the Italian Chamber of Deputies. When he died in January 1910, Mussolini passed over his later career and praised, instead, his earlier efforts in fanning the flames of insurrection.

"Andrea Costa does not belong to the well-fed socialists of the new era *** or to the young folks who take much care of their hair and little of their brains; he does not belong to the pseudo-intellectuals of academic positivism, who look upon all ideal efforts with a smile of incommensurable asininity; he does not belong to the company of cheap politicians, to the Rabagas of electoral and mercantile clienteles, who see the well-being of the workmen in the sterile formula of a law; he does not belong to the company of the sceptics, the discouraged, and the critics who scornfully retire to the Aventine as soon as they see that socialism does not assure fixed incomes; finally, he does not belong to the imbecile herd that is ignorant of the great crises of thought, simply because it has not the habit of thinking. Andrea Costa—the first to spread socialism in an epoch when socialists were considered criminals and were treated to all the rigours and snares of the bourgeois Penal Code, Andrea Costa who passed several years of his life in prisons and in exile, Andrea Costa who knew privation, poverty, hunger, and never sought flattering haloes of martyrdom—Andrea Costa belongs to the workers' mass which, in its economic and political organizations, is forging the weapons of its own emancipation and feels and fights for socialism. . . The life of Andrea Costa is an example. Do not sophisticate over the twilight [of this man], O petty censors who are condemned to impotence; look at the dawn and virility of this man. Understand him and bow your heads!"

The socialist clubs over which Mussolini presided had to be active centres of genuine revolutionary propaganda and culture. "We have an organization, numerous and disciplined, but poor in respect of intelligence, and superficial in respect of culture." He did not care about those chaotic, amorphous multitudes "that gather around a political orator, urged on by that same curiosity for which they would gather around a charlatan salesman of miraculous pills".

Instead, "what we want to initiate is socialist propaganda directed to socialists!*** Socialists have the duty of knowing how they must act in order to call themselves socialists and how they must fight for the triumph of our ideas. To *quantity* we prefer *quality* ***. I have already begun and I shall continue the propaganda tour of the entire [electoral] college. I shall speak to socialists and on socialist subjects. I ask the comrades for one thing only: attention. I shall try to substitute ideas for phrases. Even the old oratory based on rhetorical flights has done its time; brevity and precision are wanted. Your minds, like your stomachs, O proletarians, do not need to be stunned or deluded, but nourished. Begin to separate the chaff from the wheat."

Although the socialist forces at Forlì were meagre as compared to those of the republicans and although Mussolini did not expect them to constitute a majority in such a republican stronghold, he nevertheless carried on a vigorous campaign intended to make them independent of all other political parties and to make them fight their battles alone. For a decade or so before he took charge of the Forlì socialist federation, the Forlì socialist leaders had generally followed a policy of a "united front" with the republicans in opposition to the more conservative parties. This was true in local and parliamentary elections. Mussolini would have none of this. He insisted on putting an end to the socialist habit of forming coalitions with other advanced parties. Coalitions were deleterious because they did not accustom parties and men to rely exclusively on their own forces. Not union but independence would make for clarification of political issues. The practice of forming coalitions was a gospel only for weak and sluggish subversives. Mussolini's motto was: let each party go into the public arena with its own programme and seek support and votes from its own followers, not from the followers of other parties. He wanted the Forlì socialists to set a good example by fighting alone and by adhering to a policy of political intransigence. If in this way the socialists could not overcome the conservative and clerical control of local municipalities, then he had ready his favourite appeal to violence. The socialists could always resort to street demonstrations, to agitation in the public squares, and, as he expressed it, "force will have the last word".

Mussolini had a clear notion of what a revolutionary party should be. He was a firm believer in the efficacy of minorities, minorities conscious of the aims of a revolutionary programme, capable of heroism and sacrifice, and ready to serve as the vanguard of a mass movement and to use any means whatsover, however extreme and violent, to attain their object. The socialist party, therefore, should be composed of a revolutionary *élite*. He scorned the idea that socialism could be attained in an evolutionary manner through the gradual conquest of the bourgeois state by means of parliamentary methods. He had no faith in the idea that the transformation of the capitalist society into a socialist society could be achieved by peaceful means. He had no use for the majority principle and was sceptical of mass action. What he demanded was the organization of a class conscious party, however small it might be, that would constantly insist on the expropriation of the bourgeoisie. The tactics of the reformist socialists would be only an auxiliary means in the plan to overthrow the bourgeois order. Continuous and permanent revolutionary agitation was needed in order to keep the revolutionary *élite* in a state of exaltation and readiness for the historic revolutionary moment.

Mussolini's conviction that minorities are dynamic and active while majorities are static and passive constituted a basic part of his revolutionary philosophy, which he later turned to effective use when he became a fascist. He maintained that pre-war Italy as well as other countries was ruled by a bourgeois minority and that the majority merely submitted to its rule. This bourgeois minority, he believed, could be overthrown by a socialist and revolutionary minority. If the majority passively accepted or submitted to a regime of iniquity and injustice—the bourgeois order—why should it not accept a better regime—a socialist order? What was urgently needed was the creation, in the midst of the proletariat, of a minority sufficiently audacious and conscious of its revolutionary aims to be able to replace the bourgeois minority at the opportune moment. Of course, Mussolini was confident that the majority would follow the revolutionary minority.

Therefore, he envisaged the class struggle as a war between two minorities, the bourgeois minority and the revolutionary minority. His absorbing ambition was to be a leading protagonist, a Duce of the revolutionary minority or *élite*. In matters of revolutionary tactics and strategy, he was a thoroughgoing Blanquist, and he might well have been called a spiritual brother of Lenin. Like Lenin and the Bolsheviks, Mussolini was not as much concerned with the organization of a mass party of workers on a democratic basis as he was with forming a group of ardent, resolute revolutionists who would be prepared to execute a violent revolutionary uprising and to lead, if not to "drag along", the mass of workers to support such an act. Implicit in his tactical considerations is what we should now commonly call the "dictatorship of the proletariat" as a necessary step in the building of a socialist state.

At Forlì, Mussolini elaborated in his mind a system of revolutionary technique that was to serve him very effectively as the leader of the Italian socialist and fascist parties. "To *quantity*", he declared, "we prefer *quality*. To the obedient, resigned, stupid herd, which follows the shepherd and disperses at the first cry of wolves, we prefer the small, resolute, audacious nucleus which has given a rational basis to its own faith, knows what it wants, and marches directly towards its goal. We desire that the forty clubs in our federation be socialist clubs, not places for mere Sunday reunions."

Besides being the editor of the *Lotta*, Mussolini was the leading officer and the principal orator of the Forlì socialist federation: he had to be sure that members paid their dues; at times, he was called upon to act as arbiter in cases of disputes among party members and to intervene in quarrels between socialists and republicans; and he often delivered the oration at the funeral of a comrade. Some of these duties irked him, and he would show his exasperation whenever too much was expected of him. About every three months, he made a report to a congress of the socialist clubs in the federation. In one of these reports, he told about his having made speeches on such topics as Giordano Bruno, the Commune of Paris, socialism and socialists, the social question, anti-clericalism and socialism, why we are socialists, the principles of socialism, the duty of the socialists, and the contemporary political situation.

"In these speeches", he said, "I have sought to explain the principles of socialism, and I have preferred an audience of socialists to the usual audience of curiosity seekers. The work of proselytism is now accomplished or, at any rate, it has reached a good point in our region. It is now a question of giving a socialist conscience to those who are enrolled in our party. We must not only preoccupy ourselves about *quantity* but pay attention, and this seems to me the most important thing, to *quality* ***. I have sought at every meeting to disseminate socialist pamphlets and newspapers, and I have encouraged contributions for our newspaper."

Anticipating possible criticism from some of his comrades that he did not make enough speeches, Mussolini asserted in his defiant manner that he would not be a walking phonograph. He would give up his position if his comrades did not like his manner of doing things. "I do not think that on counting my speeches someone would say, 'they are few!'; should anyone say so, I must declare that I could not give a larger number. I cannot out of respect for my brains, become a peddler of propaganda, a walking phonograph. I must read an untold number of daily newspapers, many periodicals and books in order to keep myself in touch with the contemporary socialist and intellectual movement; and in order to read, a convenient margin of time is necessary. Besides, a few speeches compact with thought are better than a rosary of idle talk on the basis of verbal pyrotechnics, superficialities, and rhetorical bursts of anger. I shall continue my tour of the socialist clubs, and I shall not refuse my oral propaganda whenever it is necessary. But I ask for a reasonable attitude on the part of the comrades because if to-morrow my propaganda should take me completely away from intellectual work and should threaten me with 'progressive idiocy', I would find myself forced to place another dilemma before the party."[1]

After making these declarations, one of his comrades, Medri, although admitting that the secretary, Mussolini, had to keep himself posted, pointed out that he should not neglect the minute work of propaganda for all that concerned—in addition to the speeches—the activity of the clubs. According to Medri, it would be necessary for the secretary to do work of inspection, to see, for example, if the number of those who paid dues corresponded to those who were enrolled. At no time in his career has Mussolini ever liked the slightest unfavourable criticism of his work, and doubtless piqued by Medri's remarks, he got up to say: "I cannot be a doorkeeper. If the clubs want to be accomplices in a petty swindling of the federation, so much the worse for them! I lose nothing since I seek neither clients nor votes. I cannot be ready for all calls, especially when it is a question of useless personal quarrels that the clubs themselves should settle."

Mussolini's frankness endeared him to all, or almost all, his comrades. He had the reputation of being a hard worker and in dead earnest about promoting the revolutionary cause. No one ever thought of him as a "careerist" or as an "arriviste" who wanted to make a living by being a professional agitator. Although his salary was meagre, one hundred and twenty lire—twenty-four dollars—a month, he never protested or bickered about it. At a congress of the federation held in April 1910, a delegate from the socialist club of the town of Carpinello suggested that Mussolini's pay be increased from one hundred and twenty to two hundred lire a month. The Executive Council proposed one hundred and fifty lire. Mussolini rose to remark:

"I declare as I have already done at a meeting of the

---

[1] It seems that on at least three other occasions, Mussolini found himself in such disagreement with some of his comrades that he threatened or was ready to leave his post.

Executive Council that I refuse any increase whatsoever. I do not want to become a canon of the socialist organization nor am I thinking of opening an account at a savings-bank as a result of your compensation. Our federation is too young to take upon itself such a financial burden. I also declare that I prefer 120 lire that are sure, to 150 lire that are uncertain or to 200 that are impossible, and I add that if to-day I accept the compensation that comes to me from the small dues of all the [local] socialists, to-morrow I would refuse a salary that was picked up by knocking at the doors of well-to-do socialists. Do not consider the proposal of Carpinello, and table the increase to three months from now. If the fine enthusiasm continues, we shall discuss the matter."

As the *Lotta di Classe* wrote, "the Congress applauds the candid declarations of Mussolini, but almost all declare themselves in favour of an immediate increase. Zanchini recalls that the salary was to have been 150 lire from the beginning. Saviotti declares that such compensation is not even worthy of the party. Utili, Lanzoni, Medri, and Monti speak on the subject. Mussolini insists, and the Congress reluctantly decides to prorogue the proposed increase to three months from now."

Several months later, in January 1911, an increase in Mussolini's salary was again considered. "Antonio Zanchini proposes an increase of 20 lire to the present monthly salary of the editor-in-chief. Mussolini declares himself flatly against it and accounts for his refusal on considerations of an administrative character. Medri proposes tabling the matter, but the Assembly rejects this proposal and approves the increase."

It appears, therefore, that one year after Mussolini assumed his duties, he received an increase in salary from one hundred and twenty to one hundred and forty lire—from twenty-four to twenty-eight dollars—a month. No other data seem to be available on the salary matter, but it should be pointed out that Mussolini's attitude towards it brings out one of the finest traits that he revealed as a young man. He was not venal nor, so far as I have been able to see, did he ever show any signs of venality while he was associated with the socialist movement. He was ambitious, excessively so, but he was not venal. He yearned to be the leader, the Duce, among his socialist comrades, and he cared little for financial reward. Whatever else might be said of him, he was not, during his socialist career, a "socialist bureaucrat", a routine and well-fed propagandist, a man who would not agitate ideas unless he made a living by so doing. It has frequently been charged that when he resigned from the *Avanti!* in 1914 and founded *Il Popolo d'Italia* in order to advocate Italy's entrance into the Great War, he did so because he received considerable sums of money from the French government. Where, it has been asked, did he, a poor man, obtain the funds to launch a daily newspaper? Was not his "betrayal" of the socialist cause a result of venality? The subject is too complicated to be discussed at this point. Suffice it to say for the present that, after an extensive study of all the available evidence, it seems clear to me that venality was not the motivating force in causing Mussolini's abandonment of the socialist cause.

It is necessary to remark that when we say that Mussolini was not venal, we do not wish to imply that such is synonymous with the absence of that kind of vainglory, ambition, and intellectual and emotional instability which frequently causes rebels to become the most perfect types of renegades and which may reveal moral qualities that are baser than straight-forward venality. To betray a cause and a class to which all "proletarian" agitators and writers give their allegiance over a long period of years may be more reprehensible than venality. Mussolini's transfer of allegiance from socialism to fascism, the almost complete somersault in his views from the time he was a socialist to the time he became a full-fledged fascist as the dictator of Italy naturally give rise to a difficult problem of interpretation, important aspects of which will be taken up at various places in this volume.

At Forlì, in 1910, 1911, and 1912, Mussolini lived on a meagre income. He was in sore need of money in order to help pay the hospital expenses for his father, who was seriously ill during the year 1910, and to support Rachele Guidi, whom he had met while she was working in his father's tavern and with whom he had begun to live in a common-law union or *faux ménage*.[1]

An interesting document, hitherto unpublished, and of which I possess a photostatic copy, attests Mussolini's poverty while at Forlì. It is a postcard sent by him sometime in 1911 to Luigi Bertoni, the editor of the anarchist *Il Risveglio* of Geneva, who had asked him to translate from the French a considerable part of Kropotkin's *French Revolution*. In 1911, Bertoni and his *Risveglio* group published the Italian translation of this work in two volumes. Though Mussolini had neither requested nor received from Bertoni any compensation for translating the major part of Kropotkin's *Paroles d'un Révolté* in 1904, he received in instalments three hundred Swiss francs for his work on Kropotkin's *French Revolution*. Apparently being in great need, he wrote to Bertoni as follows:

"CARISSIMO,

"If you can send me the balance of 30 lire—always at Forlì—you will do me a distinct favour. I am in want. Awaiting your reply, I greet you and I thank you.

"Yours,

"MUSSOLINI".

[1] Mussolini has the average Italian's appetite for women—an appetite that men of other countries might consider excessive—but this has been wholly subordinate to his lust for political power. We need not go into detail regarding his two illegitimate children: one, a girl who died in her childhood and whose mother is dead; the other, a boy, now an energetic adolescent whose mother, when we last heard of her, was in an insane asylum. The public is aware of Mussolini's five children by Rachele Guidi, a fine and unobtrusive woman of simple tastes, with whom he began his common-law union in 1909 or 1910. The absence of a marriage ceremony is not surprising considering Mussolini's atheistic principles and Bohemian habits at that time. The first child of this *faux ménage* was Edda, wife of the present Italian Foreign Minister, Count Galeazzo Ciano. Some time during the Great War there was a civil marriage, but it was not until after Mussolini became Prime Minister in 1922 that there was a religious marriage.

2. SOCIALISTS VERSUS REPUBLICANS

Ever since the Risorgimento, when the Romagna had given many enthusiasts to the republican cause of Mazzini, that part of Italy was the chief stronghold of the republicans until Mussolini established the totalitarian fascist state and, among other things, swept aside all traces of open republican propaganda throughout the peninsula. After the annexation of Rome to the Kingdom of Italy in 1870, the disputes between the monarchists and the republicans rapidly receded in importance. The majority of Italians was so impressed by the patriotic rôle of the Savoy dynasty that the republican propaganda seemed to lack vitality for them. Accelerating the decline of the republican party was the rapid rise of the social revolutionary movement which found numerous and ardent recruits in the Romagna. The furious polemic between Mazzini and Bakunin and their respective followers marked the beginning of a long and bitter struggle between republicans and anarchistic or socialistic revolutionists. According to the latter, the republican doctrine was retrogressive, essentially bourgeois, and incapable of solving pressing economic and social problems. Up to the Great War, the existence of the monarchy was never seriously threatened; but in the years immediately following the war, the agitation for a republic in Italy gained formidable strength from two sources: the revolutionary socialist movement and Mussolini's fascist movement. Though at first the fascists demanded a republican form of government, they gradually became reconciled to the monarchy, and with its collaboration, they eventually seized power and set up a totalitarian state.

It should be observed that before the Great War, the republicans and the socialists often co-operated in times of stress, especially when constitutional liberties were threatened. After the reactionary events of 1898, the followers of Marx and of Mazzini in the Italian Parliament constituted the most important nucleus of the Extreme Left which on major issues acted as a single group. We have already seen how Alessandro Mussolini and his son Benito did not find collaboration with *Il Pensiero Romagnolo*, the Forlì republican paper, incompatible with their socialism.

The history of the alternate periods of co-operation and dissension between the Romagnuole socialists and republicans would entail a long digression. Suffice it to say that they frequently formed coalitions in municipal and parliamentary elections in order to check the power of the monarchical, the clerical, and the more conservative groups. When Mussolini became the editor of the *Lotta di Classe*, he demanded a radical change in the province of Forlì, which he regarded as the "republican Mecca of Italy", a "republican fief" and the "spiritual and temporal domain of the republican church", by insisting that there should be no coalitions with the republicans. He sought to destroy their influence because in his eyes the republicans were, at bottom, bourgeois patriots, capitalists, defenders of the conservative *mezzadri*—the share-tenants, and enemies of the property-less *braccianti*—the day-labourers.

The republicans, in turn, were ready to do battle. They were the heirs of a fine revolutionary tradition. Many of them were men of high purpose and intelligence. In order to maintain their dominant position in various parts of the Romagna, they embraced advanced economic doctrines although they never went as far as the socialists. Some of them tried to show that Marx and Mazzini could be reconciled, that the work of one complemented the work of the other. Their weekly *Il Pensiero Romagnolo*, which was founded at Forlì in 1894, was edited by Giuseppe Gaudenzi who, for many years, was a republican deputy in the Italian Parliament. In 1905, when Mussolini was twenty-one years old, the Milan syndicalist paper *L'Avanguardia Socialista* published his interview with Gaudenzi, whose acquaintance he had made in 1902. Gaudenzi is one of the few men who could do a real service to the literature on Mussolini if he would write about him and his parents, whom he once knew very well.

Under the leadership of Gaudenzi and Mussolini, the sectarian fight between the republicans and the socialists reveals the turbulent nature of Romagnuole politics and recalls the feuds between the Guelphs and the Ghibellines in the Middle Ages. At first the *Lotta* and the *Pensiero* tried to make it appear that they were journals fighting for a cause in a respectable manner, but Gaudenzi and Mussolini were too factious, too anxious to discredit each other and each other's cause to maintain such an appearance for very long. A few months after becoming editor of the *Lotta*, Mussolini wrote a short article listing the defamatory phrases that the *Pensiero* had directed against him and the Forlì socialists:

"We glean from the last number of the *Pensiero Romagnolo* the following very polite expressions which an anonymous writer addresses to us in an editorial: Our language is *vulgar, indecent, lurid, nauseating, insensate.* We are *rascals, tramps, pimps in the pay of Jewish societies, jesuitical minds, unscrupulous men, paranoiacs, hot-headed persons who madly abandon ourselves to the obscene brawl of provocative actions, probably we are also men who have been bought by police headquarters, sinister men, furious madmen, self-styled socialists, deceitful intriguers, unconscionable madmen, most cowardly delinquents and sowers of hatred, jugglers, scribblers hardly worthy of the contempt of gentlemen, maniacs, madmen of the type belonging to a criminals' insane asylum, stupid men, imbeciles, cretins,* and, dulcis in fundo, *most loathsome reptiles.* Amen."

When the *Pensiero* said he was "harebrained", Mussolini replied: "I am by this time used to this adjective. The little monarchists of Oneglia threw it to my face in 1908; the clericals of Trent did so in 1909; and the republicans do so in 1910. I should already be in an insane asylum. The monarchists *** succeeded in driving me out of Oneglia. The clericals of Trent had the great satisfaction of seeing me expelled [from Austria-Hungary]. Do *even the republicans* wish to 'drive me away'? *** It is clear that socialist heretics are not wanted in the spiritual and temporal domain of the republican church. When the heretics write, they are naturally 'harebrained'. Harebrained, even if they document what they affirm. Anyhow, all these acts of folly are shared by all my comrades. Might it be a matter of 'collective insanity'? Answer us, O subtle psychiatrists of the Forlì republic."

To the *Pensiero*, the *Lotta di Classe* was the *Lotta di Carta*, while to Mussolini, the writers for the *Pensiero* were "Jesuits of the Republic". When he was described as "the professor of syndicalism who edits the *Lotta di Classe* amid the compassionate hilarity of the public", he retorted: "They have a face that no longer knows the blush of shame." He resented the accusation that he was a syndicalist and termed it a lie. When the spelling of his name was altered so as to read Musolino, the name of the notorious Italian brigand, his answer was: "This is one of the arguments of the shepherds of the yellow herd: the alteration of a name. Not even the priests of Trent had gone as far as that." For the benefit of a republican writer who inaccurately quoted what he had said in a speech about Ferrer and the Spanish republicans, Mussolini wrote: "No, bilious vestryman of your bilious republic. Don't make lying your polemical weapon."

The "intellectual" debates between the *Pensiero* and the *Lotta* usually concerned the relative merits of Mazzini and Marx. Who was superior? Who was more ignorant of social doctrines, the socialists or the republicans? How much had socialism derived from Mazzini? Mussolini was not so ignorant or so narrow as to deny many eminent qualities to Mazzini, but he denied the claim that Mazzini could be considered an economist or a socialist: "Comparisons are always odious, but in this case, they are also absurd. If you speak to me about Mazzini as a philosopher and as a man of letters, I bow; if you present Mazzini to me as a national political agitator, I take off my hat; if you present Mazzini to me as a man of character, I say to you: he was great even when he exaggerated and went to extremes; but when you wish *** to eulogize Mazzini as an economist and as a socialist, I say to you: no. Socialism has not taken anything from Mazzini. While in the Mazzinian ideology, we find elective assemblies which will work for the good and for the interests of the people, in scientific communism, it is the proletariat that will work for its own interests, using its own, and not traditional or bourgeois institutions. The Mazzinian ideal culminates in the republic. Marx calls the republic the *'new ball dress for the old bourgeois society'*.*** Mazzini and Marx *** are two types that cannot be compared. Both are great, but in their respective fields. And they do not even complement each other because a harmonious whole cannot arise from discordant tones. Mazzini and Marx have only this in common, and it is, alas! a misfortune: both are remembered very much, but both are little or not at all read and understood."

Mazzini, declared Mussolini, had become for the republicans a "saint", an idol and a fetish to be adored, but not to be discussed. He gave currency to the fairly widespread rumour that Ernesto Nathan, the prominent Italian Jew, Freemason, and anti-clerical Mayor of Rome, was the illegitimate son of Mazzini—"Saint Joseph of Genoa".

The Forlì republicans and socialists also engaged in a debate over Carlo Pisacane (1818–1857), an important figure of the Risorgimento. Was Pisacane a socialist or a republican? Quoting passages from Pisacane's *Saggio della rivoluzione*, Mussolini tried to show that he was a socialist, indeed describing him as "the first exponent of socialism in Italy", but when the argument became protracted, he decided to cut it short by telling the republicans: "If Pisacane is yours, you may keep him! We are a party of living, not of dead people. This obscene merry-go-round among tombs disgusts us."

The asperity of the feud between the republicans and the socialists was caused chiefly by differences over economic issues. The *Lotta* is replete with attacks on the republicans who were accused of supporting the share-tenants against the day-labourers. Mussolini advocated the abolition of the share-tenant system so that the proletarians would be united in combating the landowners. "We think that the share-tenant should not fight against the day-labourer, but united with him, should attack the landlord." When the Rome republican daily *La Ragione* called the day-labourers "barbaric hordes, organized *canaille*, bands of criminals, blind instruments of oppression", etc., Mussolini replied: "Well then, long live the barbarians of Ravenna! Long live all the

exploited who rise with the destructive gesture of barbarians ***. Forward, most modern barbarians! Above and
against monarchies, republics, and all bourgeois exploitation!
Like all barbarians, you too are the precursors of a new
civilization."

The *Lotta di Classe* was certainly full of articles against the
republicans, but Mussolini resented the republican charge
that the paper was wholly taken up with fighting them. Incidentally, he took pride in and enjoyed flaunting the fact that
he had attacked all sorts of people and groups. In May 1911,
about a year and a half after the founding of the *Lotta*, he
wrote:

"Here is the collection before us. I have dealt with everything and everybody. I have denounced near and distant
adversaries without distinction. Here is an article on
Murrism and Christian democracy;[1] here are two or three
articles against the anarchists; then follow the syndicalists to
whom I have devoted several articles; then the revolutionists.
No newspaper has criticized the socialist party, its attitudes,
and its representative men as bitterly as this one. It is sufficient to read the issues that preceded and followed the
[national socialist] congress of Milan and even the most
recent issues. . . . While the socialist weeklies have neg-
lected the anti-militarist campaign, the *Lotta di Classe* has
frequently had its Anti-Militarist Section. We have also dealt
with the clerical danger, documenting the progress of the
Rural Banks in the Romagna . . . The polemics with the
local republican party were forced upon us by its equivocal
conduct in economic organizations and by its brazen administrative nepotism. I have been violent not only against the
republican party but also against other parties, not excluding
my own. In this great liberty of criticism lies my complete
justification, and if the pacification that has been invoked
must mean renunciation of this liberty, I renounce, for my
part, pacification and send the conciliators to hell. If someone
else with a more flexible backbone wants to tie the donkey

[1] Murrism, after Romolo Murri, a leader of a Christian democratic
movement and an excommunicated priest who is now a fascist.

where the boss, republican or even socialist, orders, let him go ahead if he wishes. But I do not lead donkeys and I do not tolerate bosses."

Mussolini never missed an opportunity to vilify the republican form of government and to point out examples of oppression and injustice in republics like Switzerland, France, Argentina, and the United States. With Switzerland he had had personal experience, and he reminded his Forlì republican adversaries of the large number of expulsions from the Canton of Geneva. "Keep clear of republican justice!" was the conclusion of an article in which he condemned the sentence in France of Hervé, the French propagandist against militarism and patriotism. Mussolini recalled that strikers were hanged in Chicago and were executed by a firing squad in France. He excoriated various reactionary measures of the Argentine Republic and invited his Forlì comrades to organize a demonstration against the Argentine Consulate at Forlì. The Argentine residence law, which he decried, was similar to laws which he himself instituted some years later as the Duce of fascist Italy.

"In the Argentine Republic, there exists and there is applied on a vast scale the infamous *residence law* by virtue of which every suspect individual may be suddenly driven away from the republican territory. On the morrow of the *attentat* against Falcon, the odious butcher of workmen,[1] fully 500 revolutionists were expelled or relegated far away, to islands with a deadly climate. The *residence law* that reaps victims in the Argentine Republic is also in force in France and Switzerland. In 1904, there were expelled from the Canton of Geneva, fully 1,450 persons through administrative means, that is, without a trial. It is a liberticide law that is exasperating; it is a law unworthy of any republic that does not wish deliberately to place itself on the level of Holy Russia. Two years ago, the regional Argentine Workers Federation began an energetic opposition against this law, opposition that was to culminate with a general strike to be held during the

[1] Ramon L. Falcon, the chief of police of Buenos Aires, had been assassinated in 1909.

centenary celebrations. Either a general strike or the abrogation of the law, such was the dilemma that the Argentine proletariat placed before the rulers. The republican rulers have replied with the proclamation of martial law. Martial law means the unchaining of brutal police instincts; it means liberty to all equivocal, parasitical and cowardly individuals to reap a nice vengeance for themselves." To the appeal of the Argentine workers, "we Forlì socialists must in some way answer. And our reply will be significant because the land in which we live is a republican fief. How shall we reply? At Forlì, there is in Via Morgagni the consulate of the Argentine Republic. We do not know who the consul is nor, for that matter, will our demonstration be directed against him personally. But we must go under the windows of the consulate; we must gather together under that coat of arms on which the Phrygian cap is mounted and hiss and cry out our indignation and protest. We shall be few because the republicanized workers' element will not join us. But this doesn't matter. Our gesture will serve, if for nothing else, to stir the still waters of our local political life. Our hisses will give him our opinion of the liberticide Republic which he represents; our cries will invite him to resign. The hour is propitious. Let us agitate."

Shortly after this article was written, Mussolini addressed a protest mass meeting of about one hundred and fifty persons, the majority of whom were socialists and anarchists, and joined the parade to the consulate and the hissing. The secret police record of his activities states that he was sentenced to pay a fine of ten lire "for having promoted at Forlì a demonstration against the Argentine Republic without due notice".

3. UNITED STATES OF AMERICA—THE DOLLAR REPUBLIC

In the course of his attacks on the republicans and the various republics throughout the world, Mussolini had frequent occasion to denounce the United States as another abode of oppression and injustice. Who dominated it but a bloodthirsty and unscrupulous bourgeoisie? What could the law avail in the presence of this rapacious, self-seeking, and truculent class? What was the republican form of government but a label when the police and other public authorities were the instruments of the Trusts? Was not American public life corroded with venality? Was not the true name of the Republic of the United States the Dollar Republic? Was not the United States, controlled by a millionaire bourgeoisie, like Spain under Prime Minister Maura who instigated the execution of Ferrer and like Italy under the reactionary Prime Minister Crispi?

Mussolini, the revolutionary socialist in the provincial town of Forlì, viewed the United States as it would now be viewed by many communists. Famous episodes in the history of the class struggle in America, particularly the Haymarket Affair at Chicago in the eighties, were familiar to Romagnuole socialists, including, of course, both Mussolini and his father.

The earliest recorded reference by Mussolini to the United States is to be found in his debate on religion with the evangelist minister Taglialatela at Lausanne in 1904. The twenty-year-old socialist criticized the minister's argument that the deeply religious Quakers were liberal and very progressive, by declaring that the Quakers were liberals not because of, but despite their religiosity. Their liberal attitude was dictated by certain economic conditions in their environment. In addition, Mussolini asserted: "But to-day, the descendants of those great liberals shoot down the striking miners of Pennsylvania."

When he was editor of the *Lotta di Classe* between 1910 and

1912, a noteworthy feature of the paper was brief reports on the progress of socialism in various countries. One of them, relating to the history and organization of socialism in the United States, was probably based on Mussolini's reading of *Il Proletario* of New York and of widely circulated pamphlets describing the spread of the socialist doctrine throughout the world. Perhaps he also gathered information about the United States from some of his Romagnuole comrades who had emigrated there and had helped the *Lotta* with their subscriptions and financial contributions.

Two striking incidents in the American labour struggle commanded Mussolini's attention: the McNamara case and the case of Ettor and Giovannitti. A sensation was caused in the spring of 1911 by the arrest of two labour leaders, John J. McNamara and his brother James, on the charge of having bombed the building of the Los Angeles *Times* in October 1910. Mussolini's contribution to the protest in labour and radical circles against this "frame-up" was a virulent editorial about the "sanguinary" American bourgeoisie. After recalling the acquittal, in 1907, of the labour leaders William D. ("Big Bill") Haywood, George A. Pettibone, and Charles Moyer who had been accused of planting the bomb that killed Governor Frank Steunenberg of Idaho, he wrote on May 27, 1911:

"The freebooters of the piratical and sanguinary bourgeoisie of the West are preparing a fresh murder. To retrieve the defeat undergone four years ago when Moyer, Haywood and Pettibone were snatched away from the homicidal noose of the law by the huge, spirited and tremendous protest that the entire working class of the land roared out, they have prepared another colossal blow to break the back of the proletarian organization.*** The rapacious and powerful American bourgeoisie knows no limits, and it does not have the scruples, the fears, and the cowardice of our bourgeoisie. It is violent, despotic, criminal. If necessary, it stains its hands with proletarian blood. It is inhuman. It wants only to exploit and exploit!... For it, there exists no law; there are no sentiments and no rights. The dollar guides it, obsesses it, pushes it on to crime and murder, and strains the law to satisfy it, to satiate it and to approve it. The arrest of [John J.] McNamara was followed by his extradition to California. He was not allowed to defend himself, to get a lawyer, a defender, and thus he was denied that which the law allows even to a madman who cuts his mother's throat. The American proletariat was left surprised and stunned when the newspapers announced to it the first blows of the odious and infernal plot of the industrialists against McNamara. The leaders of the workers' organizations have, however, already cried out aloud that they will never permit the law of their masters to entrap those who were arrested. Just as Moyer, Haywood and Pettibone were snatched away from the gibbet, so will the handcuffed ones of to-day be snatched away. Behind them are the crowd, the huge army of organized workers, and the country. It is time that the country should wake up and cry out *basta!* to the brutal and criminal insolence of the bourgeoisie of the dollar!'"

When James was sentenced to life imprisonment and John to fifteen years' imprisonment in December 1911, Mussolini made no comment because he was then in prison for opposing the Turco-Italian War. During most of the year 1912, labour and radical agitation in the United States centred around the case of two labour leaders, Joseph Ettor, an American of Italian descent and a prominent I.W.W. organizer, and Arturo Giovannitti, an Italian of uncommon literary talents and the editor of *Il Proletario*. Both were charged with having incited to the murder of a girl striker and with having engaged in "unlawful conspiracy" during the famous textile strike at Lawrence, Massachusetts. Their trial was delayed for several months, and it was feared that they would be condemned to death. In August 1912, Mussolini had this to say about them in the *Lotta di Classe*:

"The international agitation of the proletariat, aimed at saving the lives of Giovannitti and Ettor who are threatened with death in the electric chair, is every day being more intensified. The masses, now enlightened by the terrible precedents of Chicago and of Barcelona, know that every delay, every hesitation can be fatal.[1] The American bourgeoisie has no humanitarian scruples. It is violent and brutal. Powerfully supported and defended by the republican government, the millionaire bourgeoisie of North America treats workmen like cattle that can, when it is desired, be massacred with impunity. The class struggle in America has not the idyllic, temperate forms with which it is fought in Italy. But instead, it is an incident of war, a furious, and almost always bloody hand-to-hand fight between the oppressed and the oppressors. The democratic, indeed the republican, form of government must not delude anyone. It is a matter of a label and nothing more. The government puts the formidable clubs of its policemen and the guns of its soldiers at the complete disposal of the slave-dealers of the Trusts. For some time, that very civilized and very free republic of the stars has descended to the level of Maura's Spain and Crispi's Italy.*** The danger that Giovannitti and Ettor will end in the electric chair is not illusory, as certain people are suggesting. It is real. In the United States, given the idea of venality and of speculation that regulates the entire social organization, it is relatively easy to obtain provisional liberty through bail. Well, this provisional liberty, which at times has not been denied to very dangerous criminals, has been refused to Giovannitti and Ettor. There is more. Several co-defendants for the occurrences in the Lawrence strike have already appeared before the Court to answer for the alleged crime of conspiracy, and they have been sentenced to seven years of imprisonment. Symptomatic and disquieting is the fact that the judicial authorities of Massachusetts, with the evident aim of wearing down the agitation and of catching the masses by surprise with an accomplished fact, have ordered another postponement of the trial to the early part of September. There is still time to make our cry of protest resound aloud and solemnly, to unite ourselves to the millions of proletarians who, from one con-

[1] Mussolini has reference to the "Chicago Massacre" and to Ferrer's execution in Spain on a charge of having incited to rebellion at Barcelona.

tinent to another, renew and consolidate the inviolable pact of class solidarity in the name of Ettor and Giovannitti. The moral pressure of the European proletariat joined to the material and moral pressure of the American proletariat, which is bent on resorting to extreme measures, will not be in vain, as some sceptics think. Whether or not the freedom of Ettor and Giovannitti be obtained, whether or not the tragic epilogue be averted, we socialists must do our duty. The comrades of overseas throw out to us a desperate appeal. Socialists of the Romagna, who have never been second to anyone in supporting the causes of humanity and justice, take it up and agitate!"

In November 1912, when the fate of Ettor, Giovannitti, and Caruso (a co-defendant) hung in the balance, Mussolini wrote the following stirring editorial in the *Avanti!*, the daily paper of the Italian socialist party:

"The drama of Salem, which for two months has kept the soul of the entire international proletariat in suspense, in anguish and in a state of perennial oscillation between dark fears and trembling hopes, is fast approaching its end. In a few hours, the telegraph will bring us the last word, the word of life or death. It seems as though we were dreaming, as though we were living in another world, as though we were evidently projected not towards the future, as in one of the Wellsian phantasmagoric anticipations, but towards the past, towards a dark past that we thought had disappeared forever. Have we been deluded? No: We believed that the persecution of thought, the violence perpetrated against ideas, the coercion of minds by means of the gibbet were an exclusive heritage of monarchies, but Attwill[1], the fierce prosecutor who, impassive, without a quaver in his voice, has demanded the sentence of death for Ettor, Giovannitti and Caruso, is the spiritual brother of Maura, the assassin of Ferrer, and the republic of the starry flag descends to the

[1] Mussolini says "Quinn" who was the judge, not "Attwill" who was the prosecutor in this case, but since it is quite clear that he means the prosecutor, I have substituted "Attwill" for "Quinn" in two places in this editorial.

level of the nations governed in an absolutist manner by emperors and kings. Shades of Franklin and of Washington, where are you? Nostalgic evocation. The republic has become a word without meaning, a mask, a mockery. The ideas of justice, liberty and unselfishness have remained on the one hand with impotent Quakerism and on the other they have been taken over, vivified and perpetuated by the red proletariat that ascends toward, but is still far away from its goal. The ruling class, the American bourgeoisie, the brutal people of the dollar—for whom the saying of Heine is true that gold is the god of our epoch and for whom Rothschild is the true supreme prophet—is no longer fettered by the old and romantic democratic caprices that inflamed the minds before the war of secession. The patriarchal period of the republic has for a long time been buried. To-day, bureaucracy and plutocracy, Rockefeller and Morgan dominate, and the voracious capitalism that fights its great battles at the Stock Exchange entrusts to the clubs of policemen and to the administrators of mercenary justice the task of repressing, of subduing and of driving back the working class when it abandons the gigantic industrial prisons and cries out its imprescriptible and sacred right to a more human life. In this tragic hour, the sky of our hopes is darkening. We remember another episode of the bourgeois vendetta. The memory of those who were hanged at Chicago, innocent like those on trial at Salem, and their innocence was later—too late!—officially recognized and proclaimed, the memory of the Chicago martyrs drives from our souls any exaggerated illusion and places before us the fatal omen of to-day and the eventual and terrible reality of to-morrow.

"O workers of Italy, workers of all faiths who for months and months, have agitated in order to snatch away the lives of our heroic comrades from the legal snares of North American capitalism, will you now allow the horrible crime to be perpetrated? Will you permit Attwill and the twelve jurors to send to the electric chair three men innocent of any blame and crime and guilty only of having fought for the cause of the oppressed? Ah, no. You will make the supreme effort. You will fold your arms. You will desert the booming factories and you will rush from the countryside to the cities. The fires in the locomotives will be extinguished; all the complex, enormous activity of the nation will be suspended, delayed and stopped. And to the indifferent, the ignorant and the enemies who will ask about the reason for the general strike, you will answer: it is a question of saving three lives in danger; it is a question of reaffirming, by every means, the raging solidarity of the proletarian class, united in a granitic block against the bourgeois class; it is a question of impelling the Italian Government—which is always slow except when the clerical interests of the Banco di Roma are involved—to an act, in duty bound, of protection and defence of three of its nationals.

"The accused of Salem are already in the purest realm of the knights of the ideal. The jurors will tremble in declaring a death sentence. The accused will not reel on hearing it: they are strong; they are resolved; they have the calm conscience of martyrs. Not a word has ever come from their lips, either during the preliminary questioning or during the trial, that has impaired their dignity or the cause for which they fought, for which they suffered and for which they are now ready to go to their death as to the arms of a smiling bride.

"Ah, the sceptics who for some time have been saying sardonically that the indomitable characters, the very noble souls who do not belie themselves, the heroes, in short, capable of fighting and of sacrificing themselves for an idea, were carried away and submerged by the surge of pedestrian and philistine utilitarianism, these sceptics to-day, with the trial of Salem before them, will remain pensive and uncertain. Ettor, Giovannitti and Caruso are the new heroes of the new generation. They are the precursors, the predestined, the soldiers who die that others may live, the workers who sow that others may reap. They are not the first; they will not be the last. The classes that push on towards the conquest of the world have, each of them, their bloody martyrology. It is inevitable. But we cannot accept this inevitability. We do not submit to destiny. We want to break it, to transcend it with our will. Ettor, Giovannitti and Caruso must not fall into the ambush of bourgeois legality.

"As we write, we have before us a letter of Arturo Giovannitti, written to his family from the Lawrence prison in September. It is a memorable document. The warm sense of tenderness that pervades it reminds you of the testamentary letter of Ciro Menotti, and the calm confidence in the triumph of his own innocence reminds you of the defence of Socrates. If your heart is not made of stone, you will feel moved to the point of tears. A class that gives birth to men of this moral elevation cannot fail in its historic task. And these men must live! And to snatch them away from the executioner, let us, on the eve of the verdict, issue a desperate call to arms.

"Socialists, workers of Italy, take up our appeal; prepare yourselves to perform your full duty; support the work of the American proletariat which is resolved to resort to any means whatsoever in order to save our intrepid comrades, and you will win and we will win. In any case our conscience will be free of regrets. If the North American bourgeoisie should dare provoke the rage of the entire proletariat by convicting the three innocent men, it will lose the right to invoke the mercy of the rebels who, on the day of victory—mindful of the past—will apply, without hesitation, the inexorable law of the desert."

Ettor, Giovannitti, and Caruso were acquitted. Among those who were active in their defence was Nicola Sacco, then an obscure Italian worker in the United States. Had Mussolini been there at that time, he surely would have allied himself with the defence forces. In describing and encouraging the widespread agitation on behalf of Ettor and Giovannitti and against the "horrible reprisal that the bourgeoisie is trying to inflict on two innocent persons", he said: "Although forced to witness it from a distance, we offer to our brother workers and socialists of North America all our moral and material solidarity."

Fifteen years after he wrote these articles on the Lawrence case, Sacco and Vanzetti were executed in Massachusetts. In

1912, he demanded that the Italian government protect and defend its nationals. In 1927, he was the all-powerful Duce of fascist Italy, indeed the Italian government itself, and the question of saving two Italian nationals from the electric chair was involved. But his doctrines and beliefs were profoundly different from those he held in 1912, and his government made no representation on behalf of Sacco and Vanzetti.

4. THE ANTI-CHRIST

The Romagna was fertile ground for Mussolini's savage and blasphemous attacks on Jesus Christ, Christianity, and religion in general. Agnosticism and atheism were widespread among the Romagnuoles who spoke out their anti-clerical and anti-religious views with the same zeal and fervour with which they had fought papal rule and had embraced the Mazzinian or socialist gospel. Among Mussolini's favourite formulae in his anti-religious propaganda were Blanqui's "Neither God nor Master" and Marx's "Religion is the opium of the people".

In December 1910, Mussolini paid his respects to the Christmas holiday in the following language: "December 25: the price list at the Bourse of moral values has a stock that is going up—compassion; but it has a stock that is going down—Christianity. Our century is not Christian, not even in compassion. It feels it at fixed intervals. Is it perhaps anti-Christian? No. It pretends to be Christian, as Carducci says. The last great Christian [Tolstoy] died yesterday in a small railway station in Russia. The bankruptcy of Christianity is documented. It wanted to realize brotherhood among men, but men continue to hate and to kill each other. It was to be a purification of souls, but human wickedness is still widespread. The Christians have disappeared everywhere. There are baptized people and there are followers perhaps of the letter, but such people are far away from the spirit of the Gospel. The Catholic Christmas is a mystification. Christ is dead, and his teaching is moribund. But there is a living Christ: the slave who for centuries has carried and still carries the cross of poverty. This slave cannot celebrate the Christian Christmas. He lives in preparation, in expectation. He awaits the Anti-Christ; he prepares the Revolution. The Human Christmas will come."

Mussolini went farther than most socialist propagandists by demanding that followers of Marx should not countenance any form of religious worship for themselves and for members of their families. He insisted that the Forlì socialists should carry out their anti-religious views in their daily lives. At a congress of the Forlì socialists held in 1910, Mussolini laid down the law on the religious issue when he said: "The question is delicate, but it behooves us to face it. It is necessary to distinguish between 'individual belief' and 'religious practice'. The first cannot be controlled, and to it can be applied the formula of the German socialists, 'religion is a private affair'; but 'religious practice' resolves itself into a direct and indirect, a mediate and immediate support of the Church which to-day is, indeed, not a community of believing souls, but a hierarchy of an economic and political character. The Church is an obstacle to the advent of socialism. The socialists who support the Church retard the march of socialism. This is clear. And from these premises, it is easy to deduce the conduct of the socialists. If they wish to destroy the Church, they must begin, with themselves and with their families, to do without it."

Mussolini concluded by presenting the following resolution which was carried by a large majority: "The Collegial Congress maintains that the practice of the Catholic or any other faith is incompatible with socialist consistency, and it resolves upon the expulsion from the party of those members who follow religious practices or tolerate them in their children. Therefore it imposes upon the socialists the strict obligation to avoid religious marriage, baptism of children and all other religious ceremonies."[1]

The broad character of the *Lotta's* propaganda against the "gangrenous and shameful sore of superstition" is noted in Mussolini's review of the paper's activity in the year 1910: "We affirmed that traditional anti-clericalism had to be completed by anti-religionism, and our ideas found full confirmation in a congress of our federation that forbade socialists to take part in religious practices and to tolerate them in their children."

Under his old pseudonym *Vero Eretico*, he commemorated the anniversary of the birth of the Spanish anarchist and free-

[1] On Mussolini's relations with women, see above, p. 192.

thinker Francisco Ferrer, "the last one—in order of time—sacrificed by the Church of Rome. The 'old ravenous Vatican she-wolf', against which Carducci imprecated, still has thirst for blood.*** If the holocaust of Ferrer, plotted at Rome and carried out at Montjuich, has filled our being with horror and indignation, the present work of the clerical sect, designed to defame the dead man, has proved to us that calumny is still the sovereign weapon of the priests." In his conclusion, Mussolini attacked Cardinal Della Chiesa, the future Pope Benedict XIV. "Cardinal Della Chiesa, the present archbishop of prosperous and clerical Bologna, on being interviewed by an editor of the *Vita*, dared to say that '*the anti-clerical agitation in Italy might lead to the execution of another Ferrer*'. Ah! no, reverend cardinal of the criminal Church. Your prophecy will not come to pass. The proletariat, which no longer wants to be driven back again to the times of theocratic barbarism, will overturn you parasites who enjoy this earth while mortgaging heaven for the imbeciles; you and your churches, made the seats of your material rapine; you and your idols—without name and without life—already for a long time mute for free men."

To a series entitled *Martyrs of Free Thought*, issued by the small Roman publishing house of Podrecca and Galantara, Mussolini contributed a small volume entitled *Giovanni Huss, il veridico* (*John Huss, The Man of Truth*). Although this volume was not published until 1913, when Mussolini was editor of the *Avanti!*, he probably began writing it during the years 1910 and 1911. An announcement in the *Lotta*, September 23, 1911, said that the book was about to be published. On October 14 of that year, Mussolini was arrested for his propaganda against the Turco-Italian War, and it is quite likely that he continued to put together parts of the biography during his five months' term in prison. The book is now rare and very difficult to obtain, owing in part to the fact that a large edition was not issued and owing in part to the anxiety of the fascists to suppress it in order to conceal Mussolini's anti-Catholic opinions. Signora Sarfatti mentions the book, remarking that "not a copy of it is now procurable, so little importance has its author attached to it!" This is hard to believe, all the more so since Mussolini was her collaborator. The important thing is that she says nothing of its contents. The author of the present volume has possessed a copy since 1926, and he knows of another in an American library. An English translation of the book was published in 1929.

The virulence of Mussolini's anti-religious opinions is illustrated in his denunciation of a rather formal and conventional anti-clerical demonstration at Rome on the anniversary of Bruno's death, February 17, 1910. The celebration committee was made up of too many diverse groups and a host of "unclassifiable" anti-clericals who were such only for a day. In an article entitled "Minestrone"—the name of the well-known Italian vegetable soup—he declared that among the unclassifiable anti-clericals of February 17 were those who on February 18 would go to confession "in expiation and lead even their wives to the confession booth. Yes, wives too must co-operate in the salvation of husbands. And that it is possible to attain the glory of the heavens even through the womb of a woman, Christ has demonstrated by making love to Mary Magdalene and to the wife of the good Pontius Pilate."

5. DOWN WITH FREEMASONRY!

Mussolini seems always to have had a special hatred for Freemasonry. Almost everything about it was repugnant to him. Masonry represented a democratic, humanitarian, and bourgeois attitude of mind which he had repeatedly lampooned. Its anti-clericalism was conventional and formal. It was just another organization of petty politicians and "careerists". Its "bourgeois" and insincere internationalism repelled the propagandist for whom the only true international was that of the exploited workers. As an enemy of "secret" factions and as a lover of fighting in the open, he held in contempt the Masons' rigmarole of secrecy. At heart a sectarian himself, he vilified the Masonic sect not because it was a sect, but because it was a sect other than his own. The factious socialist would prohibit his comrades from worshipping in the "great sect"—the Church of Rome—and from joining the "lay congregation"—the Masonic Order.

Masonry in Italy, as in other Latin countries, has been primarily a political organization with no single party label, but anxious to dominate as many parties as it could, whereas in Anglo-Saxon countries, this order has been primarily a social organization. A halo of dignity surrounded Italian Masonry ever since it took an active part in favour of Italian unification. After 1870, many of its "brothers" were prominent leaders in various Italian political parties. As Italian socialism became more reformist and democratic, many Masons joined it, reconciling in their own way their allegiance both to socialism and Freemasonry. Mussolini, the anti-reformist and anti-democratic revolutionary socialist, attacked such dual allegiance as a mark of that "political and moral hybridism" which he despised. His formula was: no man can be at once a socialist and a Mason.

After the revolutionary elements had gained control of the socialist party in 1912, Mussolini, their Duce, demanded at the Congress of Ancona in 1914, that all Masons within the party choose either socialism or Freemasonry. The result was an exodus of several prominent members who were Masons. In 1923, Mussolini, the Duce of fascism, declared that no one could be at once a fascist and a Mason, and he demanded that the fascists in the Masonic Order either give up their Masonic membership or leave the fascist party. After 1925, Mussolini became a sectarian *par excellence* when he established the so-called totalitarian state, suppressing the Masonic Order entirely and, along with it, all political parties except the fascist party, which eventually was made identical with the Italian state and the Italian nation. The fascist sect is now the state in Italy. Consequently, anyone opposed to the fascist party is not only anti-fascist but anti-national and anti-Italian as well.

As the obscure editor of the *Class Struggle*, Mussolini sought to extirpate all Masonic influence from the socialist party so as to make it less bourgeois and more proletarian. "The politics of the Italian subversives will always be a ludicrous comedy until the republicans and also the socialists have the courage to free themselves of Masonic tutelage and of the longing for immediate success." In 1910, he had no hesitancy in taking a clear stand on a referendum about to be called by the Executive Committee of the Italian socialist party on the "vexatious Masonic question", and it was doubtless because of his intransigent attitude that the delegates at a congress of the Forlì socialist federation unanimously voted the incompatibility between the two positions of socialist and Mason. "Recent events have again shown what dangerous Masonic gangrene is hidden in the bosom of our party ***. To the question—can a socialist become a member of the Masonic Order?—we will answer: No. Must a socialist who is in the Masonic Order be expelled from the party? We will answer: Yes. We have several hundred leaders who work for the interests of the lodge to which they belong instead of working for the interests of the proletariat. It is necessary to sweep them away, to purify the air infected by the old sinister lay congregation.[1] Then we shall breathe better."

[1] I think the Masonic Order was first called a lay congregation by the historian and independent socialist Ettore Ciccotti, whom Mussolini admired.

In 1911, Mussolini wrote: "We are happy not to have any point of contact with this ridiculous [Masonic] association, which if it had reasons for existing in other times, is to-day—in the century of enlightenment—an anachronistic and ruinous relic like the Church of Rome."

Mussolini's anti-Masonic bias was stimulated by his hatred of the republicans, many of whom were prominent Masons. While some Masons reconciled the triangle with Marx, others reconciled it with Mazzini. When certain Forlì republicans shouted "Down with Masonry!", the editor of the *Lotta di Classe* questioned their sincerity: "No paper—not even the local republican paper [*Il Pensiero*] which always has known how to be prudently silent on the Masonic question—has attacked with such consistency and violence the old anachronistic institution as ours has done. We have fought and we shall fight the Masonic infiltration in socialism. The first Forlivese to refuse our paper were the Masons. Everyone knows that between us and the Masons there do not exist relations of any kind, either political or personal. We can cry out 'Down with Masonry!' without anyone's taking us by the ears and admonishing silence. But the republicans!! Their party is the servant of Masonry. Their tradition is Masonic."

It is clear that during his career as a socialist up to 1914 and during his career as a fascist since 1923, Mussolini hated and fought the Freemasons. One qualification must be made: from the time he began advocating Italian intervention in the Great War in 1914 up to a month or so after the fascist "March on Rome" in October 1922, he closed his eyes to his anti-Masonic scruples and often co-operated with the Freemasons, not to join them, to be sure, or even to strengthen them, but rather to exploit their powerful aid for his own political purposes. The Masons were aware of this, but they thought they could exploit Mussolini and his followers for their own objects. Of course, the Masons and Mussolini actually distrusted one another. When Mussolini became Italian Prime Minister, he received a warm telegram of congratulations from the Grand Master of the Italian Grand

Orient, Domizio Torrigiani. As friction rapidly developed between the Masons and the fascists, Mussolini first had all Masons expelled from the fascist party and then destroyed the entire Masonic Order. Torrigiani was sent to the penal islands as an enemy of the state, that is, of the fascists, that is, of Mussolini.

While we are on the subject of Freemasonry, it is amusing to note that a considerable number of people, orally and in writing, have frequently called Mussolini a Mason—meaning membership in the fraternity of Freemasons—and a mason— meaning his alleged occupation as a stone-mason. It is sometimes hard to know which is meant, but in any case Mussolini was never a "mason" in either sense of the word.

6. "AN EYE FOR AN EYE"

As editor of the *Lotta di Classe*, Mussolini continued to extol the virtues of violence and showed none of the horror for it that was characteristic of most socialists. He had what he called a "barbaric" conception of socialism. "I conceive of it as the greatest act of negation and of destruction that history records."

Towards the end of June 1910, the Colon Theatre in Buenos Aires was bombed. A few days later, in the course of a debate with a republican at Voltre, a small town near Forlì, Mussolini was reported by the *Lotta* to have "had words of approval for the unknown thrower of the bomb". The report was complemented by an article in which Mussolini justified the bombing: "The other night, while all the upper nobility and bourgeoisie of Buenos Aires were at the immense and splendid Colon Theatre for a gala performance, an audacious man threw a bomb in the orchestra. Result: one dead and several injured. The perpetrator of this *attentat* has not yet been found although the police have promised an award of 20,000 lire to whoever finds him. The bomb is evidently the first reply of the revolutionists to martial law. Since meetings are prohibited, newspapers are burned and the militants are put in prison, they could not help resorting to extreme measures. Against violence, violence."

This extreme position caused a certain stir among Forlì socialists who, though far from being moderates, were neither terrorists nor apologists for terrorism. But Mussolini did not waver. He heaped scorn on the "sensibilities" of some socialists, and in a manner characteristic of him when he must have his way, he told the Forlì socialists that if they did not like his views, he would not hesitate to leave them. In an article entitled "Sensibilities", Mussolini, who had been editor of the *Class Struggle* about six months, wrote:

"What I said at Voltre and what I wrote in this paper regarding the *attentat* in Buenos Aires have aroused a certain sensation among some comrades and have made the very delicate chords of their sensibilities vibrate. It would certainly not be worth while to bring out the matter if it did not furnish the occasion for some considerations of a general character.

"I admit without argument that bombs cannot constitute, in normal times, a means of socialist action. But when a government—republican or monarchical, imperial or Bourbon—gags you and throws you outside of the law and humanity, oh! then, you must not curse against violence which answers violence, even if it results in some innocent victims. I find that many socialists are too frequently moved by the misfortunes of the bourgeoisie and remain impassive to those of the proletariat. So much is this true that we have grown accustomed to proletarian massacres. At one time, there were protests; to-day, there are no protests. It is found natural that the skin of the proletariat should serve as the target of the Centannis and associates.[1] But when it is a question of some bourgeois son of a bitch who all of a sudden goes to the devil, when it is a question of the tender and perfumed skin of young and pretty aristocratic ladies, many socialists unloose their reserve of lachrymal liquid. They become merciful in the face of a bourgeois tragedy, while the bourgeois have not been and they will never be merciful in the face of a proletarian tragedy . . . The parts of a machine matter more to the capitalist than the limbs of a worker. The speculator gambles on the misfortunes of human society, and he does not care if his acts fill the streets with victims. The law does not have pity for the unfortunate one who has fallen into the abyss of poverty, but it deprives him of his last rags and auctions them off. Thiers had no pity for the Communards; [General] Bava-Beccaris emptied the streets of Milan with grape-shot [in 1898]; Alphonso [XIII] of Spain was not moved on Ferrer's account . . . But instead, some socialists are moved on account of the victim at the Colon Theatre in Buenos Aires . . . Oh, do not fear! . . . The workers of the Pampas certainly were not present on that gala evening. The dead per-

[1] Enrico Centanni was an Italian police officer who was notorious for his brutality in the "proletarian massacre" at Candela in 1902.

son is not a proletarian. These unilateral sensibilities of many socialists are produced by residues of Christianity that are still alive in their souls. It is Christianity which has given us this morbid mercy that is characteristic of hysterical women. Socialism instead is a rude, fierce thing, made up of contrasts and of violent elements. Socialism is war. And in a war, woe to the merciful! They will be vanquished."

A certain "G. M.", doubtless a socialist of the Forlì group, wrote a letter to the *Lotta* expressing his unfavourable opinion of Mussolini's views, calling the bomb-thrower "a cowardly person" and emphasizing the fact that socialism had been revised and corrected and that the true strength of the new socialism lay in organization.[1] But the fiery Mussolini would brook no criticism. The bomb-thrower, he insisted, was not a coward. And those who committed violent acts were not madmen. Angiolillo—the assassin of the Spanish Minister, Canovas del Castillo—Bresci—the assassin of King Humbert of Italy—and Sophia Perovskaia—the Russian nihilist who was implicated in the assassination of Czar Alexander II— were not insane. Part of Mussolini's reply to "G. M." follows:

"I admit that the socialism of to-day is very different from the one I long for, provided that socialism as an idea is distinguished from the socialist party. I know that socialism has been revised and corrected. Too much so! Too much so! So much revised, so much corrected that it no longer frightens anyone, and the bourgeoisie jokes and hums a lullaby to the old lion that no longer has any teeth, no longer has any claws and no longer roars but bleats. The devil with revised and corrected socialism! If it is corrected still a little more, it will no longer be distinguished from the humanitarianism of the intelligent bourgeois who are represented to-day by that Luzzatti before whom the very much revised and correct socialists of the Italian parliament prostrate themselves ***.

"All those at the Colon Theatre on that famous gala evening were representatives of the governmental reaction.

[1] I think "G. M." was Giovanni Medri, one of the more moderate Forlì socialists and a member of the Executive Committee of the Forlì socialist federation, who disagreed with Mussolini on a few occasions.

Is the thrower of the bomb a cowardly person simply because he lost himself in the crowd? But did not even Felice Orsini try to hide himself?[1] And do not the Russian terrorists try to avoid arrest, after striking a blow? Are those who commit an individual act heroes and madmen at the same time? Nearly always they are heroes, but almost never are they insane. Insane, an Angiolillo? Insane, a Bresci? Insane, a Sophia Perovskaia? Ah, no. Their behaviour has wrung lines of admiration from bourgeois journalists of great intelligence, like Rastignac.[2] In judging these men and their acts, let us not place ourselves on the same level of the bourgeois and police mentality. We socialists must not throw stones at each other. Let us recognize, instead, that individual acts also have their value and, at times, mark the beginning of profound social transformations. I notice that I have been a bit lengthy, but the subject is worthy of being amply treated. To conclude, let us hope that the revisions and corrections of socialism will cease. Socialism must remain a terrible, grave, sublime thing. Only at this price will it be able to realize the hopes of the proletariat. Revised and corrected socialism is the haven of graft for the politicians and the weak."

In a postscript to this article, Mussolini added:

"It is needless to say that if the majority of the socialists grouped around this newspaper should declare itself favourable to revised and corrected socialism of the G. M. type, I would go immediately among those who practice a socialism that is unrevised and uncorrected, indeed very incorrect. At any rate, this will be seen at the coming collegial meeting."

Nothing happened at this local socialist congress; Mussolini remained at his post and kept on glorifying violence and recalling with pride the violent deeds of various revolution-

[1] Orsini (1819–1858) was an Italian patriot and conspirator who was executed for attempting to assassinate Napoleon III. He was born at Meldola, a Romagnuole town near Forlì.

[2] The pseudonym of Vincenzo Morello (1860–1933), a well-known Italian conservative journalist who later became a fascist and was made a member of the Italian Senate by Mussolini in 1923; see above, p. 149.

ists. Though he had reservations about the utility of assassinating the King of Italy on the ground that such an act would not necessarily lead to a revolution or to substantial changes in the Italian political system, he had no hesitancy in applauding political assassination in a country like Russia where the government was so personalistic. According to him, the Russia of the proletarians was waiting to smash the bones of the Czar, the "Little Father", whose hands were red with blood. Another of his Russian heroes, besides Sophia Perovskaia, was Sazonoff who was implicated in the murder of the Czarist minister Plehve in 1904:

"He is dead. The Reuter Agency laconically announces his death. Sazonoff, you will ask, who was he? Subversives, your memory is in truth slippery. Remember Plehve, the sanguinary minister of Russia, the man who had filled up the Schlüsselburg [Russian prison for political offenders], who had populated Siberia and had authorized and encouraged the 'pogroms' of Kishineff? Well, one day Plehve paid with his life for all his crimes. He died, torn to pieces by a bomb. Sazonoff, one of the bomb-throwers or one of the accomplices, was arrested. They did not want to hang him. They preferred to relegate him to Siberia for the rest of his life. There, after several years of suffering, he committed suicide. We remember him with reverence."

When the Russian Prime Minister, Peter Stolypin, was murdered in September 1911, Mussolini hailed his assassin: "Nemesis has struck him dead. He had it coming to him. Stolypin, oblique, sinister, bloodthirsty, deserved his fate. The Russia of the proletarians is celebrating and waits for the dynamite that will smash the bones of the Little Father whose hands are red with blood. Is the tragic end of the minister of Nicholas II probably the beginning of a new period of revolutionary action? We hope so. Meanwhile, glory to the man who has accomplished the sacred act of the Avenger!"

It is obvious that in his apologia for violence, Mussolini resembled the terrorists rather than the socialists. In January 1911, there occurred the famous Battle of Sidney Street in

London, which the *Annual Register* called "one of the most amazing scenes of disorder and bloodshed in English history". Two well-armed Russians, allegedly members of a gang of burglars, had for some time evaded the police and had finally found refuge in a house on Sidney Street. A formidable barrage of bullets was exchanged between them and an unusually large police force, and the "battle" did not end until the house was burned down and the bodies of the two men were found in the ruins. Were these men criminals or anarchists? Mussolini hastened to their defence and exalted their resistance to authority in an article he wrote for the syndicalist paper *Pagine Libere:*

"No. The tragedy of London cannot be measured by the yardstick of current morality. Were the men who were burned in the house on Sidney Street perhaps criminals? No. They cannot be jumbled together in the same cage of the Assizes along with the brute who in a moment of alcoholic delirium, plants a knife in the stomach of his drinking companion. Were they thieves? Not at all. Would you perhaps want to put them in the company of a trolley-pickpocket? They did not rob in order to enjoy themselves, to have something to squander, to indulge in debauchery. They were filthily dressed; they slept in an attic in the most miserable section of the metropolis.

"Anarchists, then? Yes, anarchists. But in the classic sense of the word. Haters of work because physical work—and let us have the courage to proclaim it once and for all!—brutalizes and does not ennoble man; haters of property which seals the differences between one individual and another; haters of life; but, above all, haters, deniers, destroyers of society. The social apocalypse! Do you recall Sandor Petöfi in his *Dream of a Madman?* The madman, with immortal hatred, drills the bowels of the old earth. Getting to the centre, he fills up the hole with dynamite and sets it on fire . . . Our planet and its inhabitants are dispersed in pieces through sidereal space . . .

"This palingenetic anarchism explains the tragedy of London. And only Russians could have been its protagonists. Only in Russia are there still Christians and anarchists.

Among us, the one and the other have disappeared. Anarchism that is adapted to the masses loses all its grandiose, heroic quality because the mass, be it a crowd or an army, is cowardly. Only these sublime, violent people who live beyond good and evil can call themselves anarchists. The battle of London, the new event amid the grey English happenings, this Shakespearian drama is full of very eloquent warnings. It is well that the upper stratum of society, made up of men and women who have attained the *quid medium* of material happiness, should realize from time to time that underground volcanic explosions are being prepared. It is a salutary nervous shock; it is an appeal cried out by the voice of dynamite.

"Are these volunteers of destruction—so distant from us in life and in death—the last violent men of the old world or the first violent men of the new world?"

On March 14, 1912, Antonio D'Alba, an Italian stonemason, attempted to assassinate King Victor Emmanuel of Italy. The congratulations to the King on his escape sickened and repelled the editor of the *Lotta di Classe*, who had just been released from prison for his violent opposition to the Turco-Italian War. He quoted with approval passages from a brilliant book by Arturo Labriola, in which was portrayed the "indescribable spectacle" of Italians of the Right and of the Left, including many socialists, after the assassination of King Humbert in 1900. Labriola stated that the people who were supposed to be citizens were instead "serfs freed by chance" and that they recognized their servile condition by prostrating themselves without any sense of dignity at the foot of the throne.[1] Twelve years had passed, and Mussolini saw in the popular reaction to D'Alba's act a justification for writing: "After the attempt of March 14, we can declare with a calm conscience that the people of serfs freed by chance are more slavish and servile than ever." He was so disgusted with the reformist socialist deputies, like Bissolati, Cabrini and Bonomi, who had gone to the Quirinal to express their congratulations to the King that he demanded their expulsion from the party. It was one thing for socialists like himself

[1] *Storia di dieci anni, 1899–1909*, Milan, 1910, especially p. 77.

to reject political assassination as a tactic in Italy, and quite another for socialists to go out of their way to use the attempt on the King's life as a pretext for visiting or sending telegrams to the monarch, thus performing "a political act of subjection to a system". Mussolini also had this to say:

"The reprobation of violence does not in any way carry with it homage to the Head of the State. This homage must be left to the monarchists.*** It may be that the King is the head of the state, but we socialists are not subjects of this state except by force; it may be that the King is the symbol of the nation, but we socialists are not citizens of this nation except by force. The personal qualities of the King are out of discussion. For us, the King is a man subject, like all other men, to the comic and tragic extravaganzas of destiny. There is no reason why the socialists should be any more moved for him than for any one else. Quite the contrary! If we introduce into our subjective evaluation an objective element, that is, the value of the individual as a producer, then between the accident that strikes a King and that which strikes a worker, the first can leave us indifferent while the other wrings tears from us.

"The King is a citizen who is 'useless' by definition. Many peoples, ancient and modern, have dismissed their kings, when they did not wish to safeguard themselves better by sending them to the guillotine, and those peoples find themselves in the vanguard of civil progress.*** Those socialists who avail themselves of every occasion to show themselves devoted to the King are ready for government jobs. *** The King is a man, and an attempt on his life does not transcend the limits of a news item. Now, he who helps to exploit the sordid monarchical speculation, he who follows Giolitti to the Quirinal must be eliminated from our ranks. It is necessary to have the courage to disqualify publicly and solemnly a handful of men who are prostituting the party. Or must we then fall headlong into the ridiculous? Alas, everything is possible in the country where the orange, the socialist-monarchical idyll, and the compromising and unprincipled politics of 'serfs freed by chance' flourish."

Mussolini's disapproval of political assassination, not on grounds of principle but on grounds of expediency—rejecting it as a matter of policy if it could not help the revolutionary cause as in Italy and commending it if it could help the revolutionary cause as in Russia—is amplified in his comment on an article by Francesco Ciccotti, who had been in charge of the *Lotta* when Mussolini was in prison. Ciccotti also assailed the socialist visitors to the Quirinal, but, unlike Mussolini, he maintained that human life is inviolable. "We socialists", he asserted, "have been and remain alone in proclaiming the inviolability *without exception* of human life." Mussolini criticized this premise as follows: "As the readers see, the premise from which Ciccotti sets out in his article is different from mine, but the conclusion is the same. For Ciccotti, human life is 'always' and for everyone sacred; that is, it has in itself an absolute, immanent value. Instead, I consider life a relative good, a means, not an end. In any case, whether the political *attentat* be disowned because— as I maintain—it is useless to the ends of the socialist revolution or whether it be reproved in the name of the idea that human life is sacred, one fact is certain: that nothing in socialist thought and tradition justifies the courtier-like act of Bissolati and his comrades."

At the national socialist congress held at Reggio Emilia in July 1912, Mussolini had the satisfaction of delivering a philippic against Bonomi, Cabrini, and Bissolati and of presenting the resolution which resulted in their expulsion from the party.

In another important comment about D'Alba in June 1912, Mussolini censured the inquisitorial methods of the Italian police and judges who were trying to force D'Alba to implicate others in his attempted crime. The reader should bear in mind that the "third-degree" methods which were condemned by Mussolini and which were rather unusual in pre-fascist Italy from 1900 to 1922, have become a regular feature of Italian police and judicial procedure under Mussolini's fascist rule. "The old methods still prevail. The Italian investigating judge is always an 'inquisitor' judge. The Italian judiciary does not believe in Beccaria; instead, it follows Torquemada. Antonio D'Alba has been tortured. 'They made him say it.' Take a man, be he the strongest in the world, imprison him, subject him to daily interrogatories, crush him under the exasperating barrage of questions, promises, insinuations and threats, and this man, to save himself, to withdraw and to flee in some way from the diabolical, atrocious persecution of the judge, will talk, will invent, will lie."

The fundamental law of Mussolini's life is "an eye for an eye, a tooth for a tooth". There is nothing he could better understand than an attempt to assassinate him. His primitive love of violence is so deeply ingrained in his nature that it would seem idle to discuss at length his "teachers" on the subject of violence; and yet, so much confusion has arisen on this matter that it is worth while to consider his relationship to one of his alleged teachers, Georges Sorel, the French "apostle of violence".

7. GEORGES SOREL

Although a host of writers, ranging from scribblers to "social scientists", have talked about the profound influence of Sorel (1847–1922) on the intellectual formation of Mussolini, not one of them, it appears, presents a single bit of documentary and reliable evidence to show that Mussolini had ever read Sorel or had ever been acquainted with his ideas. The Sorelians, in their enthusiasm for their *maître*, say that Lenin as well as Mussolini owed a great deal to Sorel, while Mussolini's hero-worshippers have been anxious to show that their Duce has had great mentors like Sorel and Nietzsche. Assuming *a priori* that mentors there must be, they display in their writings absolute disregard for texts, documents, chronology and other difficulties attending the writing of intellectual history. All this has led to confusion. We do not wish to minimize in the least the importance of intellectual currents in history. We are inclined, in fact, to attach the greatest significance to them. What we protest against is the careless use and clever invention of sources, the guess-work, false assumptions and speculation that characterize so much intellectual history.

In discussing Mussolini's early and obscure connection with Sorel on the basis of the sources, we shall see how he was familiar with Sorel's ideas, cited him often, reviewed his famous work *Reflections on Violence*, admired him for a time and eventually became one of his most violent defamers. Our main concern is Sorel's relationship to Mussolini as an individual rather than his relationship to fascism as a movement.

Before the Great War, Sorel had achieved considerable prominence as a social philosopher and as one of the most intelligent and profound students of Marx. Unfortunately, the importance of his works on Marxism and revolutionary philosophy has been obscured by the popularity of his *Reflections on Violence*, a sort of bible for revolutionary syndicalists. As a theoretician of syndicalism during the first decade of this century, he was better known in Italy than in his native country. Some of his best writings—books and articles—appeared for the first time in Italian. This Latin interpreter of Marx and his "glosses" on the author of *Das Kapital* appealed more to the Italian revolutionist of the extreme left than did the more staid, *terre à terre*, mechanistic, and "prosaic" interpretation of Marx by most German socialists. There was not a socialist in Italy with a modicum of culture who had not heard of him. The average Italian syndicalist or syndicalist sympathizer regarded him as his *maître*, and it was fashionable to cite and quote him or talk about him.

Mussolini learned about Sorel as a result of his intimate contact with the revolutionary milieu in which he had moved since he was a boy. Even as a youthful immigrant in Switzerland between 1902 and 1904, he was aware of Sorel's growing reputation, and in an article written in 1904, he referred to Sorel's well-known attacks on intellectuals, the *professionels de la pensée*. He early became one of a large category of socialist agitators and journalists who could easily cite a Sorelian phrase or allude to a Sorelian idea. Anyone who carefully watches revolutionary movements will soon observe that almost all those who take an active part in them are in some way familiar with the ideas and phrases of the "intellectuals" of these movements, such as Marx and Sorel who, besides being provocative thinkers, were brilliant phrase-makers. The revolutionary press, including daily newspapers, periodicals, pamphlets, and books, and revolutionary oral propaganda have greatly aided in the diffusion of "socialist culture" among the masses. As an omnivorous reader of the revolutionary press and as an active socialist of the left, it was easy for Mussolini to know about Sorel.

The name of Sorel was constantly brought to the fore in the factional disputes between various elements in the Italian socialist movement. What was first called the revolutionary and later the syndicalist element in the party popularized Sorel in its propaganda. In 1902, Arturo Labriola and Walter Mocchi, two of the earliest Italian exponents of syndicalism, founded *L'Avanguardia Socialista* (*The Socialist Vanguard*). In his contributions to this weekly, Mussolini clearly showed his syndicalist leanings. These are further illustrated by his writings in *L'Avvenire del Lavoratore* between 1902 and 1904 and by his exalted praise of the general strike of 1904 and the Parma strike of 1908. Sorelian ideas were also disseminated by *Pagine Libere*, a syndicalist monthly founded by Arturo Labriola and A. O. Olivetti in 1906, which Mussolini read and to which he contributed a few articles. It must always be borne in mind that at no time was Mussolini a reformist socialist and that his sympathies with the syndicalists quite naturally brought Sorel's name frequently before him.

Another syndicalist monthly which popularized Sorel was *Il Divenire Sociale* (*The Social Future*), founded by Enrico Leone and Paolo Mantica in 1905. It is important to observe that this Italian review began to publish the essays of Sorel, which later constituted his *Reflections*. Thus, Mussolini had easy access to them. The essays on violence that Sorel had written for the *Divenire* in 1905, 1906, and 1907 were collected in a brochure published in 1907 under the title *Lo sciopero generale e la violenza* (*The General Strike and Violence*) with a preface by Leone. Consequently, the ideas in the *Reflections* had gained currency in Italy before they were printed in volume form in France. For the sake of completeness, it should be added that during the first half of 1906, the *Mouvement Socialiste*, the French syndicalist review edited by Hubert Lagardelle, also published Sorel's essays on the subject of violence. This periodical was widely circulated in Italian extreme left circles, and it is highly probable that Mussolini read it and thus became further acquainted with Sorel.

In May 1908, Sorel's views on violence, expressed in the *Divenire Sociale* and the *Mouvement Socialiste*, were published in volume form under the title *Réflections sur la Violence*. On May 18, the day when the first edition appeared, the *Matin* of Paris published Sorel's article entitled "Apology for Violence", which was added as an appendix to the later editions of the *Reflections*.

One of the first Italian translations of this article appeared on May 29, 1908, in a socialist weekly of Turin, *La Guerra Sociale* (*The Social War*). Several days later, Mussolini republished this translation in *La Lima* of Oneglia. In his small way, he too was helping to circulate Sorel's ideas. Mussolini prefaced this translation with a brief statement to the effect that his own ideas on violence had found "a sufficiently authoritative confirmation" in Sorel's article. However immodest this remark may appear, it seems to be accurate, for I think that on the subject of violence, Mussolini sincerely felt that he had little or nothing to learn from Sorel. Sorel merely confirmed Mussolini's faith in violence, on which he had been nurtured by his native, "red" Romagna. Because Mussolini was a believer in the efficacy of violence as an agency of social transformation and because Sorel was a philosophical exponent of such an idea, it does not at all follow that Mussolini derived his views on violence from Sorel. Social "scientists" who like to talk about Sorel's influence on Mussolini and on other political contemporaries are prone to isolate the Sorel phenomenon. They easily forget that men like Mussolini were reared in a tradition of revolutionary socialism and from their early youth, were exposed to ideas on violence expressed by anarchists and by Marx and many of his interpreters, not to speak of the Mazzinian "theory of the dagger", the deeds of political assassins, the example of the French Revolution and the Paris Commune, the voluminous literature of revolt, and practical exponents of violence since time immemorial. Numerous historians and writers on the "social sciences" have been so deeply imbued with pacifist, humanitarian, and democratic sentiments that they find it difficult to attain a sympathetic understanding of the restless, passionate anxiety on the part of social revolutionists to overthrow the established order by violent, extra-legal means. A more intimate knowledge of the literature of revolt in the nineteenth century would help enormously in properly estimating the influence of Sorel's writings on revolutionary movements.

Unless such factors as these are kept in mind, the discussion of Sorel's influence on Mussolini and others is likely to become ridiculous. In Mussolini's case, let us remember, above all, his temperament and his Romagnuole background. Of him it would almost suffice to say that he was a typical Romagnuole revolutionist, a revolutionary child of that Romagna which abounded in rebels who almost instinctively understood the need for violence. Preceding pages of this book are so full of allusions to Mussolini's exaltation of violence and of the "voice of dynamite" that we need not recapitulate them here.

Philosophers of force or violence like Sorel made brilliant contributions to methodology in interpreting historical events and may also have helped "critics" originating from the democratic, pacifist, and humanitarian bourgeoisie to appreciate the significance of violence. But to acknowledge this is not to see in every twentieth-century political exponent of violence a student of Sorel. The revolutionary socialists and syndicalists who appealed to the authority of Sorel during the first decade of the present century were pleased to have this "intellectual" of "bourgeois origin" as a new ally in their exaltation of violence. Moreover, since Sorel himself professed deep faith in the creation of a new society by the proletarian class, they regarded him as a militant in their own ranks.

The appreciation of Sorel's intellectual merits by Benedetto Croce, the great philosopher, spread the Frenchman's fame in Italy. In 1907, Croce wrote a celebrated article on Sorel, which appeared in modified form as the introduction to the Italian translation of Sorel's *Réflections sur la Violence* in 1909. Sorel became a fad in Italy not only in syndicalist and revolutionary circles but also in what might be called "bourgeois" and "intellectual" centres. At Italian cafés and intellectual salons, he was a favourite topic. The serious agricultural conflicts in 1908 in the Parma district, a stronghold of Italian syndicalism, deepened the interest in syndicalism and in Sorel who loomed large as its leading exponent. At the height of Sorel's reputation in Italy in 1908 and 1909, numerous articles appeared on him in the Italian press. The *Corriere della Sera*, the great conservative-liberal daily of Milan, published an extensive article on "the apostle of violence"; other non-socialist newspapers and periodicals, as well as the small, provincial socialist weeklies, carried articles on him and popularized his phraseology. Few were the professional Italian publicists who did not have something to say about the French writer.

With this background in mind, it is not surprising to find Mussolini among the many socialist journalists who spoke of Sorel in 1909. For example, he summed up and reviewed at some length the Italian translation of the *Reflections* and showed an intelligent understanding and grasp of many of Sorel's favourite ideas and sentiments: the theory of myths, especially in its relation to the myth of the proletarian general strike; the antipathy to democracy in general and to the democratic, parliamentary, and humanitarian brand of socialism in particular; the contempt for an "intellectualized" socialism; the exhortation to proletarian violence as an essential characteristic and manifestation of the class war; the high moral values of proletarian violence as an heroic and sublime expression of the spirit of the revolting masses; the great promise of a new and vigorous ethics of producers; the importance of arousing the "terrible", bellicose instincts of the proletarians in their struggle against the bourgeoisie; and the insistence on a constant state of war between the proletariat and the bourgeoisie. Incidentally, Mussolini linked together both Sorel and Croce as thinkers who avoided "learned verbal manipulations" and as men who manifested a "desire for clarity, sincerity and probity in research. Both are opposed to superficial positivism as well as metaphysical cloudiness; both teach men that life is struggle, sacrifice, conquest, a continuous 'surpassing of one's self'."[1]

That Mussolini was well acquainted with Sorel can therefore admit of no doubt. The most important thing to emphasize here is that he responded with considerable enthusiasm

[1] It is well known that Croce, probably the greatest living philosopher, is an opponent of Mussolini's fascist, "totalitarian" state. The fascist Duce has encouraged his press and his intellectual sycophants to indulge in vulgar defamation of Croce.

to Sorel (and for that matter to all other writers whom he has cited with favour) because he found in the French writer a brilliant rationalization of his own political impulses and sentiments, particularly his passionate hatred of reformist, parliamentary socialism and his passionate love of violent political struggle.

But Mussolini's enthusiasm for Sorel was short-lived indeed, for it disappeared by the end of 1910 when he began calumniating the French writer. The history of the estrangement between Sorel and certain extreme revolutionary groups is instructive and will help to explain Mussolini's contemptuous opinion of Sorel. In 1908, Sorel ceased to contribute to the *Mouvement Socialiste*, and in the following three years, he further dissociated himself from the syndicalist movement, partly because he was tired of the ambitions and polemics among its various factions and partly because he thought that its revolutionary ardour was somewhat spent. In a series of articles written for the *Divenire Sociale* in 1910 and published in pamphlet form in the same year under the title *Confessions (How I became a syndicalist)*, Sorel discussed the reasons for his diminishing interest in syndicalism. About this time, French and Italian syndicalism was experiencing a "crisis", intellectual as well as practical. Even revolutionary syndicalism was becoming reformistic, too wholly engrossed in economic problems. Lagardelle forgot about his anti-parliamentary propaganda and announced his candidacy to the Chamber of Deputies.

Sorel turned his attention to the writings and doings of the French royalists, neo-monarchists, and clericals, many of whom had as their organ the *Action Française*. Men of action they were, at least in words. Like the Sorelian syndicalists, they were anti-democratic, anti-bourgeois, and anti-humanitarian, with no scruples about the use of violence for their own purposes. Sorel had strong words of censure and disdain for the general strike against the execution of the Spanish anarchist Ferrer, while he had words of indulgence and praise for General Gallifet, who is best known to history for his pitiless repression and persecution of the Paris Communards. He became a contributor to the conservative and, from the revolutionary point of view, the reactionary and clerical newspaper of Bologna, *Il Resto del Carlino*. In 1911, an announcement was made that Sorel would edit, with the collaboration of two writers on the *Action Française*, a new review entitled *La Cité Française*, but although this review never appeared, the announcement further associated Sorel with the royalists. On various occasions, he made it clear that he would have nothing to do with the syndicalist and socialist movements. Perhaps the fundamental reason for Sorel's flirtation with the royalists was that he was pre-eminently an intellectual who was interested more in the play of ideas than in a practical political movement. He gave his acute mind, but not his sentiment, to the study of Marx and revolutionary problems. After the Great War, he wrote an apologia for Lenin and dedicated a book to two of his "chers camarades", written, he said, "par un vieillard qui s'obstine a demeurer comme l'avait fait Proudhon, un serviteur désintéressé du prolétariat". Apparently, it was his personal wish to go down to posterity as a friend of the proletariat.

And yet, his flirtation with the royalists was symbolical of new and important intellectual alignments. In Italy, syndicalists like Paolo Orano and Olivetti corresponded to Sorel, and nationalists like Enrico Corradini corresponded to Charles Maurras.[1] Particularly between 1909 and 1912, the Italian syndicalists and nationalists whom we have mentioned flirted with one another. In this flirtation lay the seeds of the marriage between revolutionary syndicalism and reactionary nationalism. The child of the marriage was "totalitarian fascism", born in 1925.

We see the curious phenomenon of the extremes of reactionary nationalism and revolutionary syndicalism meeting in the persons of their respective theorists, Maurras and Sorel in France, Corradini, Orano, and Olivetti in Italy. Although

---

[1] On this page and the pages immediately following, we are not referring to all the Italian syndicalists. We cannot in this book present a detailed account of all the complicated currents in the Italian syndicalist movement.

seemingly at opposite poles, these syndicalists and nationalists were drawn together by powerful affinities. They despised
democracy, liberalism, pacifism, humanitarianism. They saw
nothing but mediocrity in the bourgeoisie. The nationalists
heaped abuse on the democratic bourgeoisie, while the syndicalists heaped abuse on the democratic socialist party. For
different reasons, the syndicalists and the nationalists found
parliamentary and liberal institutions insufferable. They
could not think or live in terms of orderly, democratic
methods. They placed their faith in small minorities, in *élites*.
The *élite* of the nationalists would represent the elect of the
nation; the *élite* of the syndicalists would represent the elect
of the producers. The nationalists' talk of "proletarian
nations" and the syndicalists' talk of a workers' *élite* with a
nationalist ideology foreshadowed the basis of the so-called
fascist corporative state. Both the syndicalists and the nationalists developed a cult of activism, of the "heroic", and of the
volitive instincts in men, for to them, real men, the race
of *homines novi*, must be hard, "realistic", unsentimental,
energetic, combative. It was not long before the syndicalists
lost themselves in their intellectual orgy of heroics and forgot
their revolutionary goal.

What bound together the syndicalists and the nationalists
was a *forma mentis*, a state of mind. The special forms of
syndicalism and nationalism that blossomed in Italy were
manifestations of the same psychology. Since the syndicalists,
a peculiar brand of so-called "individualist anarchists" like
Massimo Rocca (the pseudonym of Libero Tancredi),
raucous futurists like Marinetti who affected a yearning for
the complete freedom of the individual, legions of men who
were morally, emotionally, and intellectually unstable, and
revolutionary socialists like Mussolini had never understood
or sympathized with democracy and liberalism, they found
it easy to trample upon these principles, to regard them as
corpses and to embrace an extreme nationalist ideology.
Hence the presence of many ex-syndicalists and ex-revolutionists in the fascist ranks.

The first crisis that exposed their fragile moral and intellectual fibre was the Turco-Italian War which some of them favoured for "revolutionary" reasons. In another crisis, the Great War, when Italy was undecided as to whether she should remain neutral or enter the war, others among them became interventionists, also for "revolutionary" reasons. And in the post-war crisis, many of them rushed to the fascist camp, also for "revolutionary" reasons. Always they spoke of "revolution" while they steadily furnished new and unexpected recruits to the forces of reaction.

The propaganda of the syndicalists and the nationalists served further to discredit democracy and to lay the intellectual foundations for that anti-democratic movement *par excellence*, fascism. The censure of democracy that Sorel and the Italian syndicalists had expressed in their early writings with the avowed intention of helping the proletariat, fed the reactionary, traditionalist, and monarchical movements which demanded the destruction of every vestige of democracy. Is this not a revolting form of betrayal, this intellectual sport so cynically practised by men who speak in the name of the proletariat and concentrate so much of their contempt and bile on democracy and liberalism that they end up in becoming the allies of the most reactionary elements in society? We leave this question to the consideration of the reader.

After the fascist "March on Rome", Mussolini did everything in fact that he had excoriated Sorel for doing in word during the years 1909–1912. As editor of the *Lotta di Classe*, he bitterly assailed Sorel's "somersaults" and by way of stressing his abjuration of whatever admiration he had had for the "*maître*", he went so far as to say that he had never believed in the "revolutionism" of the French writer. It was generally known that Sorel, after many years of service as a government engineer, had been pensioned and had been made a member of the Legion of Honour, a form of recognition customarily paid by the French government to all its ex-employees of a relatively high rank. Mussolini took heed to remind his readers of the pension and the decoration. In November 1910, under the title "The Last Somersault", he wrote the following savage attack on Sorel in the *Lotta di Classe*:

"Here is great news. Georges Sorel, the recognized and venerated *maestro* of Franco-Neapolitan[1] syndicalism, has passed definitely into the ranks of the French monarchists who long for a 'restoration'. Already for some time, Georges Sorel has been saying 'my realistic friends'; already for some time, the theoretician of syndicalism has been flirting with the representatives of the most reactionary forces of the past. It is sufficient to read his articles in the *Resto del Carlino*. It is sufficient to recall his latest manifestations.

"Right after the assassination of Ferrer, alongside of the obscene voices of the Jesuits who could not yet forgive and did not wish to abandon the cadaver and on it continued their defamatory speculations, here comes Georges Sorel, the comfortable bourgeois-minded *pensionné*, decorated with the Legion of Honour, who censures the general strike and describes Ferrer as 'one of the last vagabonds of the Renaissance'. Luigi Fabbri [the distinguished anarchist] could not restrain himself from crying out to him: 'Canaille!', and according to us, with reason. A few months later, we read a writing of Sorel, in which is justified the Catholic patriotism of the recently beatified Joan of Arc. Then there follow the articles in the newspaper of the Bolognese priests [*Il Resto del Carlino*], articles in which an apologia for the death penalty is made, the abolition of whipping and scourging is bewailed, and the ideas of the fatherland and religion are exalted. His *Confessions* appear. In its few pages, there is a paragraph which reveals the inner stuff of this theoretician of the revolutionary general strike. A perfect and perfected Jesuit. He writes: 'According to a widely circulated legend, Gallifet was one of the most brutal butchers of the Communards' . . . Do you see? The historically documented massacres perpetrated by the hyenas of Versailles become widely circulated 'legends' in which one may well cease to believe.

"To-day, Sorel performs the most clownish of his somersaults. His intellectual activity in these recent times

[1] Since leading Italian syndicalists such as Arturo Labriola, Mocchi, Leone, Mantica, and others came from southern Italy, they were commonly called Neapolitans.

has been nothing but a continual and violent attack against democracy, the republic and socialism. This man has a nostalgia for the *ancien régime*. And he returns to it together with the *camelots du roi* [King's henchmen]. For us, no surprise. We have known Georges Sorel for some time. We have never believed in the revolutionism of this pensioned bookworm. His syndicalism was nothing but a movement of reaction. It was a mask. To-day it has fallen. Sincerity is the gainer."

In addition to this article, which, by the way, is a perfect picture of the eventual conversion of many Italian syndicalists to his own brand of fascism, Mussolini enlivened some of his other writings in the *Lotta di Classe* with attacks on Sorel and syndicalism. For example, in December 1910, when Sorel told Italian syndicalists who were about to meet in a congress at Bologna that he was no longer interested in syndicalism, Mussolini greeted with a sarcastic *bon voyage* the "creator of syndicalism", the *maestro* who had "passed definitely over to the service of the *ancien régime* and of the gibbet". Again, in July 1911, speaking of the degeneration of Italian syndicalism, Mussolini declared that the "parabola of Georges Sorel is highly significant. This man has passed, almost with impunity, from the theory of the *syndicat* to that of the . . . *camelots du roi* . . ." He took a fling at the "intellectual politicians of Italian syndicalism, oscillating between Sorel and . . . Corradini", and at those "ex-socialists who after a parenthesis of professorial syndicalism, cherish the 'nation' and harbour a nationalism, literary to-day and jingoistic to-morrow."

In July 1912, shortly after the national socialist congress of Reggio Emilia, where Mussolini made his great debut as a leader of the extreme left group, he wrote another trenchant attack on Sorel in the *Avanti!* This was his first important article in the daily organ of the Italian socialist party. The occasion for it was an interview which Sorel had given to a Paris correspondent of *L'Italia*, a Milan Catholic daily. The French writer was quoted as saying, among other things, that "the struggle being carried on by the various groups of

Italian socialism is more difficult to understand than the history of the Renaissance. I still ask myself if a Guicciardini would not find himself perplexed." The Italian socialist party, continued Sorel, did not have the aptitude to be revolutionary. After trying to point out the contradictions and "the concatenation of inaccuracies and banalities" in Sorel's interview, Mussolini dwelt upon his mania for giving interviews. Interviewmania he called it, admitting that he was coining a horrible word. His lively account of Sorel's interviewmania is a fine description of his own interviewmania as Duce of the fascist state. In reading this fragment from Mussolini in 1912, the reader should remember that in an interview he gave in 1926, he spoke of his great debt to Sorel:

"I am coining a horrible word. I am very sorry for the purists, but at this moment, I haven't the time to consult the Petrocchi dictionary and find a better word. Let me come to the point. Whoever reads the newspapers frequently encounters the name of Georges Sorel. At one time, he was an assiduous collaborator of the reactionary landowners' *Resto del Carlino*; now he accords interviews with an astonishing facility. There isn't an Italian journalist passing through Paris who does not go to interview Sorel. And the good old *ex-ingénieur des ponts et chausées*, already completely liquidated in French syndicalist circles, still enjoys, thanks to the flood of interviews, a certain popularity in Italy. I am beginning to believe that the accusation that was being made against him to the effect that he was vain and a *poseur* (for example, he cares much about the *Legion d'honneur* decoration) was not exaggerated or unfounded. A man who has a great sense of dignity for his thought does not lend himself to interviews with the condescending manner of theatrical actors and professional politicians. The interview is a bad journalistic habit. It is something highly immoral. It is always a form of exhibitionism. As a means of transmitting ideas, it is not free of dangers."

Since 1914, Mussolini has gone through the same parabola for which he had criticized Sorel. He not only flirted with, but also joined the most anti-democratic and reactionary forces in Italian society, the monarchical, nationalistic movement of Corradini and the futuristic movement of Marinetti. At one time or another, many Italian ex-syndicalists associated themselves with his fascist movement, among them being Michele Bianchi, Alceste and Amilcare De Ambris, Dinale, Dini, Forges Davanzati, Arturo Labriola, Lanzillo, Masotti, Mocchi, Monicelli, Olivetti, Orano, Panunzio, and Rossoni (the present fascist Minister of Corporations who spat on the Italian flag when he was a syndicalist agitator in the United States). Some of these men became prominent fascist "hierarchs". Especially since the "March on Rome", the various currents of syndicalist nationalism, reactionary nationalism, and bombastic futurism have entered the large stream of fascism. Those who gave fascism the larger part of its ideology were the same nationalists whom Mussolini had once called bluffers, litterateurs, dandies, and pimps. From many points of view, his fascism is the synthesis of two Italian movements which he once severely condemned as importations from France, reactionary nationalism and certain forms of revolutionary syndicalism. Not to be overlooked is the type of liberal, represented by Giovanni Gentile, who performs the intellectual acrobatic feat of declaring that liberalism and fascism are two aspects of the same thing and hence compatible with each other. Over these many currents, Mussolini has presided with extraordinary agility and equanimity, allowing each a certain freedom in expressing its ideological tendency, but always being certain that they were all subordinated to the theory of the totalitarian, anti-democratic fascist state; that is, the Mussolinian state or the personal state of Mussolini. Given his philosophy of life, he certainly cannot be blamed for encouraging the many intellectual sycophants, who surround him and whom he inwardly despises, to talk glibly about a theory of the fascist state, thus confounding the Italian people and numerous social scientists outside of Italy.

Has not Mussolini as head of the fascist government turned the "somersault" for which he savagely attacked

Sorel? In his ranks are the nationalists who longed for and realized the "restoration", the *ancien régime*. He has praised the Catholic virtues. What were once the "obscene voices of the Jesuits" are now among the most authoritative voices in the fascist state. Was Sorel's verbal apologia for the death penalty comparable to the law whereby Mussolini established the death penalty for certain crimes in Beccaria's very fatherland which had as one of its greatest glories the fact that the death penalty had been abolished? Even when King Humbert of Italy was assassinated in 1900, his assassin, the anarchist Bresci, was sentenced not to be executed, but to serve a long term of imprisonment; while to-day, in fascist Italy, the anarchist Schirru who, at most, was guilty only of an intent to kill Mussolini, was executed by a firing squad. Mussolini castigated Sorel for bewailing the abolition of whipping and scourging. In fascist Italy, the Italians who oppose or do not agree with Mussolini and his party soon learn what whipping and scourging and many refined forms of torture mean in practice. Is Gallifet comparable to some of the fascist "hyenas" who gloat over the use of violence? Mussolini excoriated Sorel for exalting the ideas of the fatherland and religion; and yet, no ruler in the history of the modern world has exalted the idea of the fatherland more than he. Religion, for the Duce, is one of the pillars of the fascist state. The Lateran Accord illustrates his conception of the relations between State and Church. Indeed, judging by the almost wholesale passage of Italian ex-syndicalists and ex-Sorelians to fascism, Sorel's syndicalism was nothing but a movement of reaction. In 1911, Mussolini clearly saw how certain deformations of syndicalism would cause it to end up in a "theistic, patrioteering, nationalistic, anti-socialist caricature". This is an acute description of what was to be known as fascism. As for interviewmania and passion for publicity, Sorel was like so many intellectuals who cannot restrain their vain desire to be talked about, to be discussed, and to be publicized. But in this field, Mussolini is unsurpassed by any individual in history.

Sorel's reputation grew at a formidable pace after his

death in August 1922. In obituaries, books, and pamphlets appearing after his death is to be found high praise of his work by men of the Right and of the Left. Fascists endearingly spoke of his great influence, while in Soviet Petrograd a Georges Sorel Club was formed in order to pay tribute to the man who had written an apologia for Lenin and the Bolshevik Revolution. Some writers appealed to the authority of Sorel to buttress the general bourgeois and anti-democratic offensive that they yearned for. Obviously, the author of the *Reflections on Violence* could easily be invoked and acclaimed by reactionaries as well as revolutionists.

Especially since the fascist "March on Rome" in October 1922, numerous reports, written and oral, have been circulated about the relations between Sorel and Mussolini. Most of them are apocryphal; all of them are questionable; and however interesting they may be from the viewpoint of the history of legends, we cannot afford a long digression to deal with all of them. One of these legends—that Mussolini and Sorel knew each other personally before the Great War—is a myth.

Once Mussolini was in power as the Duce of the fascist state, all sorts of people went on an hysterical hunt for his intellectual mentors, displaying fallacious, almost infantile thinking, false perspective, and ignorance of Mussolini's early life and of the social and intellectual history of contemporary Europe. To believe some of them, Mussolini was a special student of some of the "greatest" minds in recent times. Who had had the most decisive influence on his intellectual formation—Nietzsche, Pareto, or Sorel? Of course, for the Sorelians it was Sorel, for the Paretans it was Pareto, for the Nietzscheans it was Nietzsche. These are merely the chief candidates. Other candidates were nominated for the honour of having shared in the instruction of Mussolini—Machiavelli, Schopenhauer, Strindberg, Alfredo Oriani, etc. I think no political leader in modern times has evoked as much nonsensical speculation and discussion about his intellectual background as Mussolini.

As the Duce of fascism, he knew that students were ignorant of his attacks on Sorel, which have been revealed for the first time in this volume, and he was aware of Sorel's posthumous fame. From a political point of view, he found it easy to capitalize on this fame. Why should he not set agog the many "intellectuals" whose ignorance and vanity he sensed? Why should he not appear as a man who had been in close communion with "great" thinkers? He understands too well that the fabrication of a mythology on his intellectual origins would be politically useful to him. He has enjoyed playing tricks on credulous and vain intellectuals and professors who have taken his pronouncements seriously.

Mussolini's interviewmania, to use a word he himself coined, has frequently brought him to discuss his philosophical masters. In an interview he gave in 1926, he said that among those who had had an influence in shaping his character, including Nietzsche, William James, and Sorel (he temporarily forgot about Pareto), it was to Sorel that he owed the most. Considering his former judgments of Sorel, this opinion is quite entertaining. In another interview, given in 1924, Mussolini talked glibly of Nietzsche's profound influence on him, thus satisfying all the members of a Nietzschean cult, with Nietzsche's sister, Frau Elizabeth Foerster-Nietzsche as the high-priestess. With his flair for sententious statement, he has made glowing references to Machiavelli, Goethe, Balzac, Renan, James, Pareto, and many others. If approached properly, he will talk about his familiarity with or his debt to almost any man regarded as a great thinker. The monument to his interviewmania, to his exhibitionism at its best is his published *Colloqui* (*Talks*) with Emil Ludwig.

Mussolini has contributed to the growth of legends not only about his intellectual masters, but also about his entire life, in that shameless literary fraud which passes as his "Autobiography" (1928), published in English, but not in Italian. Although he said, "There is no other autobiography by me", the real author of the book was Mr. Child, an American journalist and the American Ambassador to Italy during the Harding Administration. Mussolini exploited the possibilities of impressing the English-speaking public with the story of his life after he had apparently been persuaded that this public was gullible. That he was not the author of the "Autobiography" clearly appears from his statement in his memoir on his deceased brother Arnaldo (*Vita di Arnaldo*, 1932), that he had entrusted the writing of it to Mr. Child.

8. THE NATIONAL FLAG—A RAG

Just as Mussolini went beyond mere anti-clericalism and preached opposition to all forms of religion, so he went beyond mere anti-militarism and preached anti-patriotism. The *Lotta di Classe* became a forum for violent anti-militarist and anti-patriotic propaganda which did not subside with the outbreak of the Turco-Italian War in September 1911. For his opposition to this "adventure", Mussolini served a prison term of five months. The reader will easily appreciate the similarities between this colonial venture and the Mussolinian or fascist war against Ethiopia.

Mussolini's anti-militarism and anti-patriotism were reinforced by his disgust with the vacillating attitude of most reformist socialists towards these issues. In a truculent speech which he delivered at the national socialist congress of Milan in October 1910—his first speech before a national socialist assembly—he declared that "the matter of the fatherland, this old *cliché* of the fatherland in danger, is the ideological *cliché* of all the bourgeois democracies, with which *cliché* the blood has been pumped from the poverty-stricken proletariat for the past 30 years". Although the congress tabled a discussion of the anti-militarist issue, he was determined to deal with it in the columns of the *Lotta di Classe*:

"We shall continue tenaciously and violently our anti-militarist and anti-patriotic propaganda. Anti-patriotic propaganda, we have said, because as long as one recognizes a political fatherland which has or can have interests that are antagonistic to other fatherlands, one must also allow for an army and a military budget. We have recently put ourselves in contact with anti-militarist newspapers and groups of the Yonne (France), and we shall intensify in the Romagna the propaganda designed not to win over the army, but to destroy it. We know well that this propaganda is dangerous, and legal action already instituted against us shows this, but we are ready to pay with our own person.[1] Meanwhile, every

---

[1] Mussolini, as editor of the *Lotta*, and the manager of the paper were indicted for publishing an anti-militarist article in the *Lotta*, but I have found no record of the trial.

number of our paper will have an *Anti-Militarist Section*. This propaganda will serve further to distinguish us from the official socialists who are beginning to admit the concept of a fatherland and from the other ex-socialists who after a parenthesis of professorial syndicalism, cherish the 'nation' and harbour a nationalism, literary to-day and jingoistic to-morrow. Proletarians, socialist day-labourers, cry out aloud: We do not have a fatherland. We will not defend the fatherland because in the fatherland, we have nothing of our own to defend!"

While reviewing the *Lotta's* work for the year 1910, Mussolini pointed out that "the prudent anti-militarism of many subversives concealed an equivocation that had to be undermined by preaching anti-patriotism. We have made a breach in the idea of the fatherland, and we have unmasked the patrioteering prejudice."

The tone and content of many of his articles bear a striking resemblance to the type of anti-militarist and anti-patriotic propaganda known as *Hervéisme* which derived its name from the French revolutionary socialist Gustave Hervé. Although Mussolini had arrived at his anti-militarist and anti-patriotic convictions quite independently of Hervé, his convictions and those of Hervé were so nearly alike that it is useful to describe him as an *Hervéiste* and to associate him with the widespread current of *Hervéisme* in Latin countries. To all revolutionists of the extreme left, Hervé was a hero because he had frequently been sentenced to prison for his violent attacks on militarism and patriotism. His ideas were widely circulated in the Italian revolutionary press, including the *Lotta* which published several articles extolling him. When Mussolini stated that he had got in touch with anti-militarist newspapers and groups in the Yonne, he had reference to that section of France where Hervé had begun his propaganda about 1901. Rightly or wrongly, Hervé came to be identified as *"l'homme du drapeau sur le fumier"*, the "man of the flag on the dunghill" fame, for having written, under special circumstances, that the flag should be "planted" on a dunghill. He had also spoken of the sacred emblem of a country as a "rag". Mussolini almost

literally copied Hervé when he declared in 1910 that the
"national flag is a rag to be planted on a dunghill". It is
significant that both Hervé and Mussolini, hot-headed anti-
militarists before the Great War, became hot-headed militarists during the Great War, the latter eventually glorifying
war and starting one against Ethiopia, which was almost
entirely of his own making.

With regard to the severe sentences imposed at Vienna on
certain Austrian anti-militarists, Mussolini remarked in
March 1910: "The bourgeoisie does not tolerate attacks
against the army. For this reason, we must intensify our anti-
militarist propaganda." He applauded a congress of French
and German workers in the summer of 1911 as a sign of
international and proletarian solidarity: "If the fatherland—
a lying artifice that has already done its time—should ask for
new sacrifices of money and blood, the proletariat that
follows the socialist policies will answer with the general
strike." Having been a *réfractaire* himself, the report that there
were more than 17,000 *réfractaires* in France in 1909 heartened
him: "Not less is the number of Italian, Austrian and German *réfractaires*. Let the patriotic press shed its warm tears if
it wishes . . . but *ça ira*. That is, the *réfractaires* and the
deserters will increase in spite of all the devices of Boeotian
nationalism founded on student battalions and irredentist
mirages. The proletariat is beginning to tire of serving the
fatherland . . . of their masters. A good sign, for us." The
huge cost of a new battleship built by the Italian government
despite the need for many improvements in the country,
called forth the following statement: "For us, who are completely free of all the scoriae of jingoistic nationalism and
patriotism, the launching of a battleship is a fact that lends
itself to melancholy reflections."

When an article in the *Lotta* on military discipline was
censored and a search was made of its offices, Mussolini
asserted: "In any case, we are happy about the censorship. It
proves to us that the only propaganda that is disturbing to
the Constituted Authorities is precisely the anti-militarist and
anti-patriotic propaganda. We shall continue in spite of the

socialist deputies who vote for Luzzatti and for the 61 millions for new military expenditures, in spite of some of our ex-socialistoids who call our anti-militarist propaganda 'anarchical'. To demolish in the minds of socialists respect for the economic, military, political and religious bureaucratic authorities: that is our purpose! To ruin the Bastille of bourgeois authority: that is our goal!"

Soon after the outbreak of the Turco-Italian War in September 1911, Mussolini observed that aligned with the nationalists, whom he despised, were the clericals and the Vatican whose "patriotic" attitude was based on economic and financial interest: "In truth, the most excited Italian nationalists to-day are the priests. Irony of history? Economic determinism, Marx answers us. The patriotic exercises of clerico-nationalistic journalism and literature are nothing but the irridescent and deceiving disguise of a different and more prosaic reality. Under the poetry, there is the prose; behind the phrases, there are the figures, that is, the dividends of the Banco di Roma. Economic interest: here is the determining factor of the spiritual and political attitudes of the clericals. The doctrines of economic determinism again find their confirmation in the facts. Self-respect, national pride, the sentiment of the fatherland are commonplaces and rhetorical motifs to inebriate the public, but if we tear away the rosy veil of ideologies, we find that it is a matter of protecting economic interests with the brutal force of arms. The contemporary patriotism of the priests is explained by Marxist economic determinism. It is probably the first time that the Vatican finds itself with Italy against a foreign country, for in the past centuries it was always with the foreigner against Italy. The Banco di Roma, however, explains this exception to the rule.[1] Business is business. Let the clerical newspapers continue, if they wish, to extol self-respect with the ready-made phrases of nationalistic literature.

---

[1] The Banco di Roma was generally reputed to be controlled by clericals and closely associated with the Vatican. There is good ground for believing that the Vatican supported the recent fascist war against Ethiopia.

They will never succeed in deluding us about the purity and honesty of their sentiments, the evident insincerity of which we shall proceed to document in the future."

Mussolini was a pitiless critic of the incipient nationalist movement led by Corradini, Federzoni, and others who were destined to hold important positions in the fascist regime. If any movement before the Great War can be said to be the spiritual precursor of fascism, it is certainly that of the Italian nationalists who set forth their programme and formed a party at a congress held in Florence in 1910. Anyone reading their aims would easily observe how their ideology was taken over almost bodily by the fascists. Shortly after the congress, Mussolini ridiculed this movement in characteristic fashion:

"O my proletarian brothers, it is fitting to speak to you to-day about a novelty which made its appearance a few months ago in the fertile soil of Italy. For some days, indeed weeks, there has been everywhere talk of nationalism.*** In the name of nationalism, two hundred litterateurs who write in the newspapers have convened at Florence. Nationalism! Do not pay any attention to endings, my friends. To-day, how many words end in ism, like socialism. When all these words will have a right of citizenship in dictionaries, the bulk of these odious sacred words will become larger and thus more academic.

"Here they are, the newspapers of Florence, spread out before us like slightly soiled tablecloths. We have read carefully. We have with difficulty sought between the lines, beyond the report [of the congress], which is almost always a false caricature of the text, an idea that was not old, an act that was not an everyday occurrence (imagine! there was even a duel!), a backbone that did not remind us of the backbones of seminarists, a complexion that was not that of blasé frequenters of drawing-rooms perfumed by iris . . . Well, we have consumed the oil of our lamp in vain.

"Monarchy, the army, war! Here are the three spiritual-ideological beacons to which the butterflies of Italian nationalism have come rather late. Three words, three institutions, three absurdities. A monarchical nationalism is a gouty nationalism, paralysed even before moving. The Italian monarchy cannot be nationalistic, but it must be anti-national because of its alliances and traditions. The army? It is undermined by the clerical tabes. Moreover, an Italian army has never won. A sad affirmation, already made by Niccolò Machiavelli. War? With an army that cannot win? Are there perhaps in Italy the warlike traditions that France and Germany have? War against Austria? Perhaps to repeat Lissa and Custoza?[1] No. When these nationalists speak of war, we seem to see them blowing cracked tin trumpets; we seem to see them seriously taking aim with a wooden rifle.

"We would have understood and perhaps regarded with sympathy a nationalism from within, a democratic, cultural movement for the betterment, enrichment and renovation of the Italian people. We would have wished that these national-ists who dream about carrying Italian arms across Europe had not so lightly abandoned themselves to illusions of nationalism imported from beyond the Alps. They should have reflected that before conquering Trent and Trieste or Tripoli, Italy remains to be conquered: bringing water to the Puglia districts, draining the Agro Romano, introducing justice to the South [of Italy] and literacy everywhere! But if they had thought this, if they had directed their energies to do this, these litterateurs of doubtful reputation would have belied themselves. Nationalism? An exotic flower, budding in Italian hot-houses. Brought to the sun, exposed to the winds, it will lose its foliage and its fragrance. The inevitable cannot be checked. The world goes towards the socialist international, towards the federation of fatherlands, no longer enemies but sisters. These nationalisms are nothing but efforts and makeshifts of the bourgeoisie to retard for a year, for a day, the great event which will mark the end of the pre-history of mankind."

Mussolini's judgment of pre-war nationalistic movements is precisely in accord with the view of communists to-day

[1] Where Italy was defeated by Austria in the war of 1866.

towards fascist movements when they describe them as the last efforts of a crumbling bourgeois and capitalist society. What was Italian nationalism, he asked, but a movement of dandies, pimps, and bluffers? Was it not a caricature of the French nationalism of Maurras and others? He answered these questions while ridiculing a government measure providing for the opening of enlistments for volunteers: "Whoever desires to die for his country—*decorum pro patria mori*—according to what is being taught in modern schools, which, it seems, are pursuing a sole objective, that is, blighting the free development of plant-man by a heap of conventional lies, whoever aspires—we were saying—to die for his country in the manner of the ancients should give thanks to the provident Giolittian act and rush to enlist. The minimum age is 18. Of the maximum age, nothing is said.*** Why doesn't Italian nationalism which has given wings to the fatherland, also give an army of volunteers? Why haven't the nationalistic newspapers given special attention to the decree which opens the enlistments? Where have the thirty thousand volunteers who postulated the Ministry of War gone to? Why don't they go from idle chatter to deeds? Ingenuous questions. The nationalism of poets, story-tellers, dandies, pimps and bluffers cannot elevate itself to the dignity of real drama. It arose in Italy as a caricature of French nationalism. Its field is the farce, indeed the *pochade*. Here it must live; here it must die and will die."

What was the fatherland to Mussolini but the patriotic Moloch? What was the "national flag" but "a rag to be planted on a dunghill"? On July 2, 1910, the *Lotta* reported the following from the oral rebuttal of its editor-in-chief to a speech by a local republican: "The fatherland? While the republicans wish to defend it and so they declared in their last national congress, we transcend it and deny it. The worker does not have fatherlands, and not even has the bourgeois. In case of war, instead of rushing to the frontiers, we will stir up an insurrection within the country. The republicans want a national pact. We want an international pact. The proletariat must no longer shed its precious blood in sacrifice to the patriotic Moloch. For us, the national flag is a rag to be planted on a dunghill. There are only two fatherlands in the world: that of the exploited and that of the exploiters."

That Mussolini was ready to urge a general strike and an insurrection in case of war is illustrated by his uncompromising opposition to the Turco-Italian War, which broke out on September 29, 1911. On September 23, he asserted in the *Lotta* that "millions of workers *** are *instinctively* opposed to the African colonial undertakings. The slaughter of Abba-Garima [Adowa] is still very much alive in the memory of the people. The adventure of Tripoli was to be for many a '*red-herring*' that would distract the country from posing to itself and solving its complex and very grave internal problems. For the moment, [Italy] will not go to Tripoli; but in the mediate or immediate eventuality of an occupation, the Italian proletariat must *keep itself ready to effectuate the general strike.*"

Events moved rapidly during the last week of September. After the Italian government had sent an ultimatum to the Turkish government, Mussolini penned a short article, entitled "War?", in which he said: "To-day, Italy begins a new period of her history, a period that is uncertain and pregnant with many terrible unknown elements. Confidently we await events. War is almost always a prelude to Revolution."

The Italian socialist party and the General Confederation of Labour called a general strike in protest against the expedition to Tripoli. On the whole, it was a platonic demonstration, but among the few places in Italy where it assumed violent form was Forlì. With his usual contempt for the pusillanimity of the official socialists, Mussolini termed the national general strike a "fiasco" and attacked the Socialist Parliamentary Group and the Confederation of Labour for being insincere in their resolutions for a strike. "Either there is a desire simply and platonically to protest, in which case the Sunday or evening meetings with the usual resolutions are enough, or there is a desire to overthrow a political regime, in which case the duration of a political strike cannot be fixed. It is necessary to continue until the aim is reached. Thus, the general strike means insurrection, and an insurrection can triumph in a day or in a month according to the resistance that it encounters."[1]

At Forlì, the republicans and the socialists were intent on tumultuous opposition to war. The *Lotta* tells us the following about the Forlì strike: street-car service between Forlì and a nearby town was sabotaged; a car was overturned, spikes were broken and rails were covered with stones; there was a violent demonstration near the railway station, designed to prevent the departure of men called to arms; and there was sabotage of the wires along the railway line. The *Corriere della Sera*, the great Milan daily which had the best news service in Italy, reported that "between Forlimpopoli and Forlì, a telegraph pole was cut down and placed across the rails; besides this, telegraph wires were cut". All this, the *Corriere* went on to say, was done because it was thought that the train was carrying men called to arms.

The agitation at Forlì lasted from September 24 through September 27. Mussolini spoke three times during these days. Only the speech he delivered at the Forlì socialist Chamber of Labour is reported in the *Lotta*. In the absence of any other contemporary record of it, it is desirable to present its important parts because it furnished the essential basis for criminal charges against him and because it will help us clarify certain later misapprehensions about his anti-war stand. We are told that in a "lucid and documented" speech to his comrades, which lasted more than an hour and which was greeted with great applause, he gave the reasons militating against the adventure in Africa. He cited the investigations made in Tripolitania by the English, by the Zionists, and by the Italians; he referred to the danger of an Austrian march on Saloniki, facilitated by the distraction of Italian military forces in Tripolitania; he recalled the judgment of Salvemini, Ricchieri, Ghisleri, and many other very competent scholars; he proved on the basis of figures that the Tripolitan undertaking might afford occasion for nationalistic

[1] In *Lotta*, September 30.

and jingoistic bragging, but that it constitutes great waste of wealth and energies which could much better be utilized to colonize the many Tripolis of contemporary Italy; then he examined the question from the socialist point of view and concluded by calling upon those present to intensify the agitation in order to avert the mad adventure.

In addition to this speech, Mussolini published an editorial in the *Lotta* of September 30, in which he praised the unity of the proletariat in the Forlì strike and made an apologia for sabotage: "Proletarian Forlì has given a magnificent example. The general strike was fully successful.*** This general strike has revealed a new revolutionary mentality which is exposing and smashing to pieces reformist and calculating pacifism. We have been the first to familiarize the workers with the weapon of sabotage. And sabotage has been put into practice. Attempts, we know, but significant attempts. By their sabotage and complete abstention from work, the workers have demonstrated that they thoroughly understand the revolutionary importance of the general strike.*** The socialist workers now turn from pacifism with disgust. A few more years of good propaganda and this mass will be capable of great acts of heroism and of fruitful sacrifices.*** For two days and two nights, the anonymous people, exploited and despised, was the sovereign master of the streets and squares of the city.*** The days of September 26 and 27 will remain etched in letters of fire in the history of the Forlì proletariat."

The Turco-Italian War began on September 29, 1911. About two weeks later, on October 14, Mussolini was arrested along with Pietro Nenni, the twenty-year-old secretary of the Forlì republican Chamber of Labour, and Aurelio Lolli, another republican who took care of the premises of this organization. Interesting is this encounter between Mussolini and Nenni. The latter eventually became a socialist, and after the Great War, he was made editor-in-chief of the *Avanti!*, the post previously held by Mussolini from 1912 to 1914. For the past several years, he has been carrying on active anti-fascist propaganda in Paris.

While Mussolini was in prison awaiting trial, the *Lotta* had this to say: "It is our conviction that the arrests would not have been made nor would a trial have been hatched if the pot of reaction had not been stirred by a handful of national-ists who *** had vomited all their gall of hatred because Forlì had been unanimously opposed to the war." After the trial, it was rumoured by some local socialists that the trial and the sentence of Mussolini had been desired by those in high places, who had had an interest in showing that Crosara, the prefect of the province of Forlì, had not done his duty during the two days of the Forlì strike.

Mussolini was arrested while sipping his coffee at the Garibaldi Café of Forlì in the company of the labour organizer Umberto Bianchi. At police headquarters, he, Nenni, and Lolli were searched. It was announced that a small revolver had been found in Nenni's pocket, while in Mussolini's pockets, "much glorious poverty and nothing more!" Apparently, Mussolini had been warned of his arrest. When someone said to him, "Take care, the police are looking for you", he replied with a shrug. When a friend told him that the danger was certain and imminent and urged him to give himself up, he answered: "If they are looking for me, they will find me. I have no crimes on my conscience and I won't run away!" And when he was arrested, he exclaimed: "I understand! I understand! They want me to finish my work on John Huss in prison! They don't know that they are doing me a favour!"

The numerous charges against Mussolini for inciting to crime and to class hatred, for complicity in causing damage, and for resistance to the police led the *Lotta* to remark that for its chief, "there was half the Penal Code and two or three centuries of imprisonment" and to wonder whether the authorities had not mistaken Mussolini for Musolino, the notorious Italian bandit.

The trial of Mussolini, Nenni, and Lolli took place at Forlì towards the end of November 1911. Mussolini's long answer to the indictment merits careful exposition and analysis, for besides containing some striking phrases and demonstrating his capacity to impress an audience, even of judges, it reveals him also as an artful man, with consummate agility in introducing elements in his defence calculated to minimize his part in the Forlì movement against the Turco-Italian War and to show that his opposition to the war was inspired by patriotic motives. If his defence at the trial were read by itself, without reference to his propaganda in the *Lotta* and the events leading to his arrest, one might easily be convinced that Mussolini agitated against the war because he thought it was against the best interests of Italy. This is the approach of Mussolini's numerous apologists. Thus the anti-militaristic and anti-patriotic Mussolini is transformed into a patriot!

In presenting in full, and for the first time, the fundamental report of Mussolini's oral defence at the trial, published in the *Lotta* on November 25, 1911, we shall accompany many of his remarks with comments intended to clarify the relationship between what he said at the trial and what he did as editor of the *Lotta* and as an agitator in the anti-war strike. A word about his appearance when he made his long address to the court. "This morning", we are told, "Mussolini is cleanly shaven. His eyes are more alive and scintillating than usual. He is smartly dressed, almost dapper. He speaks with his habitual precision, incisively."

After the reading of the indictment, Mussolini began to address the court as follows:

I am sorry that I cannot be brief because I must complete the deposition which I made when I was not familiar with the indictment. I immediately deny that the general strike broke out at Forlì because I had proposed it. This deduction is amazing! The general strike is the merit of the Forlì proletariat, not mine. The indictment would exaggerate the importance of my personality among the proletariat of the city of Forlì, the great majority of whom not only would not obey me, but would do the opposite of what I say. The epoch of instigators, Mr. President [of the Court], is over, just as the epoch of apostles is over! The mass has already acquired a conscience and will of its own; it does not allow itself any longer to be towed by its so-called leaders, but it tows them. At times, it disavows them and even gets rid of them. And it almost always does well.

All this sounds flattering to the Forlì socialists, but Mussolini is too modest in underestimating his leadership. From a very legalistic and literal point of view, the responsibility for the strike may not have been entirely his, but the effect of his statements in court is in sharp contradiction to the provocative tone of his articles and speeches before the outbreak of war. Time and time again, he preached a general strike, not platonic but insurrectionary in character, in case of war. What is amazing is Mussolini's deduction that he, the acknowledged leader of the Forlì socialists, had so little to do with the calling of the strike. In fact, he had contributed as much as he could and certainly more than any other Forlì socialist to stir up enthusiasm for a strike. Had he not written on September 23, six days before the beginning of the war, that in the eventuality of a war, the Italian proletariat was to keep itself ready to effectuate a general strike?[1] Had he not, in a speech that lasted more than an hour, urged his listeners to intensify their agitation in order to prevent the "mad adventure"?[2]

The *Lotta* continues to give the text of Mussolini's defence at the trial, sometimes quoting him directly and sometimes quoting him indirectly.

And let us come to my . . . incendiary article.[3] On the eve of the expedition, I did not know it would take place. Not only, but I did not even foresee it (and in proof of this he reads an article of his published in the *Lotta* when the expedition was imminent). Only on the night of the 24th [of September] did we learn that the landing at Tripoli was imminent. And a mass meeting, which turned out poorly, was called for the 25th.[4] At

---

[1] See above, p. 253.   [2] See above, pp. 254–255.

[3] Mussolini seems to be referring to his article in the *Lotta*, September 23: see above, p. 253.

[4] Mussolini says the meeting turned out poorly apparently because there was a drizzling rain on the day it was held and the weather threatened to become worse.

this meeting, he made a speech illustrating historical and geographical aspects [of the Tripolitan situation], as is confirmed
even by the police witnesses. In that speech, I said that between
us socialists and the nationalists, there is this diversity: they want
a vast Italy, and I want a cultured, rich and free Italy. I should
rather be a citizen of Denmark than a subject of the Chinese
Empire. Thus I took my stand on love of country. And I was
. . . somewhat incoherent; and for this, I was even reproved as
showing a weakness towards nationalism.[1] Well, I have been
redeemed of this charge in a bizarre manner, by this trial!

Mussolini's reference to the patriotic element finds no
substantiation in the *Lotta's* report of his speech. Since he
wrote almost every line of the *Lotta* himself and carefully
edited what he did not write, it is scarcely possible that anything of importance which he said and which he wanted to
have reported could have been omitted. His speech contained only the following allusion to conditions in Italy: "He
[Mussolini] proved on the basis of figures that the Tripolitan
undertaking might afford occasion for nationalistic and jingoistic bragging, but that it constitutes great waste of wealth
and energies which could much better be utilized to colonize
the many Tripolis of contemporary Italy; then he examined
the question from the socialist point of view and concluded by
calling upon those present to intensify the agitation in order
to avert the mad adventure." While the report explicitly
states that Mussolini considered the war from a socialist point
of view, it says nothing about his considering it from a
patriotic point of view. The report does not tell us that Mussolini made any distinction between the socialists and the
nationalists. Moreover, at the trial itself, the making of such
a distinction was not alluded to by a single witness for the
prosecution or for the defence. If such a distinction had been
made and if there had been a patriotic element in Mussolini's
speech, at least the witnesses for the defence would have
brought it out in their testimony.

Mussolini's reference to the many Tripolis in Italy is not
at all out of harmony with his revolutionary and anti-

[1] I have found no evidence that he was ever "reproved", etc.

patriotic outlook. In any case, it is too tenuous to warrant the conclusion that patriotic impulses motivated his opposition to the Turco-Italian War. It must be remembered that a revolutionary socialist like Mussolini fought "bourgeois", "capitalist" patriotism. His particular type of allegiance to extreme forms of revolutionary doctrine did not preclude love of the country where he was born and preoccupation with seeing it free itself of moral and economic impoverishment. These elements in Mussolini did not belie, but rather accompanied his revolutionary socialism. When a revolutionist like him speaks of redeeming his own country from its economic and moral blights, he is no less a revolutionist and certainly he is not necessarily a patriot. The spiritual and economic redemption of a given country can very well form part of the programme of a revolutionist who lives in that country. Of course, what would be evoked is the development of that country in accordance with socialist ideals. The advance of the country in the direction of socialism would be regarded as a step forward in the international diffusion of socialism. Confusion takes place when the viewpoint of a revolutionist like Mussolini is ascribed to national and patriotic, not to revolutionary, motives. Mussolini could and did remain a revolutionary socialist while demanding that the rulers of the particular country in which he lived should devote their energies not to colonial adventures but to the improvement of conditions within their country. Even granting for the moment that in his speech before the Chamber of Labour, he made a distinction between socialists and nationalists and expressed a desire for a cultured, rich, and free Italy, it does not at all follow that he was uttering patriotic sentiments. It means that he hoped for a new Italy developed and organized along socialist lines. Let us always bear in mind that Mussolini belonged to the most rabid anti-patriotic and anti-reformist, not to the reformist and rather patriotic, element in the socialist movement.

The absence of any report of the speech contemporaneous with its delivery showing that Mussolini was guided by patriotic motives leads us to conclude that the intrusion of the patriotic note at the trial was an after-thought on the part of Mussolini and of his lawyers, calculated to minimize the revolutionary and anti-patriotic motif in Mussolini's propaganda. In his address to the court, one of Mussolini's lawyers, Gino Giommi, said: "Mussolini performed a work of clear-sighted patriotism by opposing war and arousing against it the intense hostility of public opinion. And he was right in saying that he was incoherent because if he had wanted to be coherent with his standing as a revolutionary socialist, he would have kept silent in the expectation of seeing official Italy fall into the abyss of the mad undertaking in order to attack her and give her a mortal blow!" At this point of Giommi's speech, Mussolini interrupted: "Good, that is the truth!" Another lawyer for Mussolini, Francesco Bonavita, had this to say on behalf of his client: "Where is the *pravity* of the end which the protestants against the Tripolitan expedition obeyed? But they wish to protect the Nation from an undertaking that they judge to be injurious . . . Mussolini rendered a noble patriotic service in speaking and writing against the expedition because he saw in it a draining of the money and blood of his own fatherland."

The identity between Mussolini's testimony about his patriotic stand and the defence speeches of his lawyers is striking. The lawyers apparently took their cue from Mussolini. Since there seems to be no evidence showing that either Giommi or Bonavita was present when Mussolini delivered his anti-war speech, they probably knew nothing about its contents except what Mussolini had told them. To return to Mussolini's defence at the trial, he went on to say:

The mass meeting did not proclaim the general strike because it was incompetent to do so; at the meeting, we confined ourselves to *calling upon* the Chamber of Labour to bring it about. Mussolini denies that at the mass meeting, he uttered provocative phrases against the public authorities [the police] who had put their foot in it.

And he declares: *I did not formulate the resolution for the strike; in my function as president of the mass meeting, I read it.* The general strike broke out at Forlì, in part in obedience to the orders of the Confederation of Labour and to the invitation of the Socialist Parliamentary Group,[1] which had convened at Bologna, and it was called on the night of the 25th at the Old Chamber of Labour[2] by a very imposing assembly, in which he did not want to speak. And why? Neither on account of fear nor on account of prudence, but out of political fairness because—he says—*I was not a workman, but a journalist, and I did not intend to exercise any influence on the proletariat with my political criteria.*

How did the demonstration break out? Through my instigation? If I had done this, I would now take responsibility for it here. But the truth is that when 15,000 workmen gather together at Forlì, the demonstration breaks out spontaneous, unrestrained.[3] I did not take part in any of the incidents that occurred in the two days [of the strike].

Like most defendants in any trial, Mussolini was prepared to disclaim all connection with anything that might incriminate him. His categorical statement that he took no part in the incidents during the Forlì strike is very questionable. I have learned from more than one eyewitness that he was one of the most active leaders of the strike. After a careful scrutiny of the facts, I find that the two principal leaders of the strike were Nenni and Mussolini. One eyewitness whose testimony I regard as trustworthy and disinterested told me that he saw Mussolini in the centre of a crowd trying with his own hands to tear up some railroad tracks. Of course, Mussolini's statements were made at a trial, and obviously he saw no reason for telling the truth to a "bourgeois" court of law. But it should also be observed that his defence at the trial, made up of so many denials and so many feeble arguments, was anything but heroic.

Mussolini then took up his newspaper articles:

The indictment would discover in my articles, published in the

---

[1] For Mussolini's criticism of these two bodies, see above, pp. 253–254.

[2] The Old Chamber of Labour was a socialist organization of workers and was so named in order to distinguish it from the New Chamber of Labour, a republican organization of workers.

[3] Included in Mussolini's rather large estimate are not only socialist but also republican workers.

Lotta immediately after the strike, the confession of my . . . crimes. That is grotesque! I did not confess anything because I did not have any offences to confess. Those articles contained only theoretical criticisms and doctrinal comments on the events that had occurred, and they amounted to a presentation of the *myth* of the general strike and of the *religiosity* of this new form of action which takes the place of that of past religions. My articles, in substance, tried to tell those gentlemen of the Confederation of Labour: do you want a general strike in earnest or for fun? Because, take care, if you want it in earnest, you must engage in a mortal duel with the government which has already decided upon the expedition.[1] I do not reject any of the responsibilities originating from my articles although I could have hidden myself behind the manager [of the paper]. But for these, my purely theoretical affirmations of revolutionary thought, I invoke the co-responsibility of thinkers of great dignity, whose . . . subversive writings circulate everywhere with impunity.

As Mussolini continued his defence with an explanation of his views on sabotage, he was interrupted by the President of the Court, Pietro Carboni, and by the Prosecutor, Pietro Bagnoli.[2]

I have been accused of having incited to sabotage. Well, I am favourable to sabotage, but my sabotage is not that of vandals and hooligans. For me, that is immoral. My sabotage is that which makes effective the protest, respecting, as in every war, even in the social war, the right of neutrals, that is, the safety of citizens.

The PRESIDENT: But in any event, the damage is immoral.

MUSSOLINI: Mr. President, your interruption places in relief the difference between my morality . . . and that of others. I think that the highly civic *end* of sabotage, the sabotage that I accept, justifies and moralizes the *means*.

The PRESIDENT: Then, you are for the theory that the end justifies the means!

[1] He refers to his articles in *Lotta*, September 30: see above, pp. 253–254, 255.

[2] Carboni heard the case together with two other judges, Manaresi and Dini. There was no jury in this case. By the way, Carboni had also been the President and Dini one of the judges of the Forlì Court which had tried Mussolini in 1908: see above, p. 135.

MUSSOLINI: Mr. President, the well-known Machiavellian theory has been rehabilitated by Giovanni Bovio . . . and it is, above all, rehabilitated by the finest realities in the realm of experience and thought.[1] But let that pass. I deny and reject the charges of complicity in the acts of vandalism perpetrated by the crowd simply because, as a matter of fact, I remained entirely extraneous to these incidents.

PROSECUTOR: When Professor Mussolini wrote the well-known article on sabotage in the *Lotta*, did he already know about the acts of vandalism that had been perpetrated?

MUSSOLINI: Yes, I was not ignorant of them.

PROSECUTOR: And still he made an apologia for them in his articles.

MUSSOLINI: Apologia for acts of vandalism? Absolutely not, in no case. I have already explained the profound diversity, morally and factually, between the sabotage I approve of and which is the logical continuation of the general strike and the acts of vandalism for which I reject any responsibility and any complicity.

Some of these assertions by Mussolini are ingenious, perhaps even theatrical. Fine and subtle and perhaps not very meaningful distinctions about the sabotage that suited him. Nevertheless, Mussolini, in his article on sabotage, had written with pride after the strike that "we have been the first to familiarize the workers with the weapon of sabotage. And sabotage has been put into practice." Surely, he did not mean temperate sabotage, for was he not anxious to smash to pieces the reformist and calculating spirit of pacifism? And why should he have singled out the vandal-like acts of the

---

[1] Giovanni Bovio (1847–1906) was a well-known Italian philosopher. Although a republican, he was, because of his liberal views, also dear to socialists who freely quoted his aphorisms. Mussolini probably had in mind Bovio's contention that acts cannot be judged as good or bad independently of the end in view. If one kills for robbery, one is an assassin; if one kills in self-defence, one is innocent; if one kills to liberate his country, one is a hero. Three killings, Bovio concluded, not three culprits. For this argument of Bovio, see his *Saggio critico del diritto penale*, Part I, chap. x. Bovio was arguing against those who followed the scholastics in judging the acts of men in themselves, irrespective of the end in view. Mussolini's end was, of course, the social revolution.

"crowd", he who had always sneered at the unfair use of the words "crowd", "mob", "hooliganism", and "*teppa*" by those seeking to discredit revolutionary movements? Moreover, his article on the success of the strike applauded the "magnificent example" given by proletarian Forlì. Therefore, his remarks at the trial, while they may have sounded impressive in the court room, were at variance with his philosophy of revolutionary action and his practice of it.

The end of Mussolini's defence is dramatic and eloquent:

And now I conclude. I conclude like that philosopher who had written on the door of his house: He who enters here gives me pleasure; he who does not enter does me an honour! Well then, I say to you, gentlemen of the Tribunal, that if you acquit me, you will please me because you will restore me to my work and to society. But if you condemn me, you will do me an honour because you find yourselves in the presence not of a malefactor, not of a common delinquent, but of an asserter of ideas, of an agitator of consciences, of a soldier of a faith that commands your respect because it bears within itself the presentiments of the future and the great strength of truth.

The *Lotta* remarked that the "close of this vigorous, lucid, and noble deposition of our comrade Mussolini, which produced a great impression, visible even in the judges themselves, aroused on the part of the public, applause and approval which were immediately quelled by the President's act in adjourning the trial to the afternoon".

Mussolini's speech was delivered before the court on November 19. In the few remaining days of the trial, the witnesses for the prosecution and for the defence contradicted each other on all disputed matters. By his interruptions of the testimony of various witnesses, Mussolini showed his remarkable ability to be theatrical and to adhere to the version of the facts which he had presented to the court. On the question—did Mussolini write the resolution calling for a general strike at Forlì?—Umberto Bianchi, the secretary of the Forlì socialist Chamber of Labour, testified that he, not Mussolini, had written and presented the resolution, adding that Mussolini, in his capacity as President of the meeting, had confined himself to reading it. Bianchi went even farther, declaring that he, not Mussolini, had spoken in animated fashion about the general strike. At this point, Mussolini interrupted: "For a month, the accusation against me has been denied, and yet, we are drifting towards the grotesque and the ridiculous. Here is the newspaper proving that the incriminating resolution is not mine. For a month, Bianchi has shouted to you that it is his. He is not believed, but there is a desire to believe at any cost your officers who lie. (Mussolini throws the newspaper[1] to the Clerk of the Court and cries out contemptuously): I shall speak no more; it disgusts me."

After this outburst, Pisani, a police officer whose testimony contradicted that of Mussolini and Bianchi on extremely important points, "whispers that evidently there is a desire to save Mussolini", and despite Mussolini's protestations, we think his suspicion was well-founded; it was apparently quite easy for Bianchi, who was not indicted, to assume responsibility for some of the acts charged to Mussolini.

There are other elements in the trial worthy of note. In the course of his summation, prosecutor Bagnoli, a man much despised then by revolutionists and who, curiously enough, became *Chef de Cabinet* of a Minister of Justice in one of Mussolini's ministries, had this to say about Mussolini: "He [Bagnoli] pays tribute to his intelligence, his culture and his character but, he adds, he has also the gift of speaking in a very convincing manner which renders him . . . dangerous!" Regarding this, one of Mussolini's lawyers, Giommi, remarked that for the prosecution, "Mussolini is an intellectually superior man, but the prosecutor renders this tribute to him only in order to infer from it that he is extremely dangerous. But this means establishing, before the law, the degradation of intellectual power!"

Before sentence was pronounced by the court, the accused were allowed to make declarations. Mussolini said the following: "After the excellent pleas of my lawyers, I have nothing to add. But I wish only to remind you, your honours,

---

[1] This is doubtless the *Lotta* for September 30, 1911.

that if I had been a man of that coherence that bends but does not break, of that coherence that does not allow compromise, I would have acted like the Christian during the decadence of the Roman Empire. He said: 'What does it matter to me if the Empire goes to ruin, so long as the cross of Christ rises in its place.' I too could and should have said: 'Let official Italy wear itself out in Africa, and let the tears of the mothers who have lost their sons render more prolific the sowing of my revolutionary thought.'"

However eloquent this statement by Mussolini might be, it is strange that he should have tried to make it appear that he was not coherent in his revolutionary views, he who had always had scathing words of condemnation for those who were in the slightest manner incoherent in their pursuance of revolutionary socialist ideals. But, as our analysis demonstrates, his concluding remarks as well as most of his other assertions at the trial were prompted by the desire to impress the court with his innocence, to minimize the revolutionary import of his anti-war propaganda and agitation, and to emphasize his patriotic attitude. Mussolini's stand at the trial does not reveal to us his patriotism, but rather his facile capacity for wheedling. In the light of his socialist writings and activities before and after the trial, which make it clear that he wished to be regarded as anti-patriotic, the inescapable conclusion is that he was deliberately insincere in the court-room. The greater part of his defence at the trial is a concatenation of feeble understatements and ingenious fabrications. He tried to hide himself behind all sorts of alibis. Although he had been outspoken in asserting his leadership of the Forlì proletariat, he exaggerated the "volitive" will of the proletariat which, he said, had acted quite independently of him. Some of his interruptions during the trial seemed to be the spontaneous outbursts of one whose sense of truth had been outraged, but, in reality, they were studied attempts to make himself appear innocent of any crime. Although his oral and written propaganda had been calculated to stir violent insurrection and violent sabotage, he affected the attitude of a man who had been merely pronouncing theories. In order to confound the court, he resorted to casuistic distinctions about his view of sabotage and played on the various meanings that could be attached to the word "patriotism". Although he had professed contempt for legalistic arguments, he used them freely when it was a question of avoiding a long prison term; for example, he said he had read, but had not formulated the resolution for a general strike. Throughout his stay at Forlì, he had arrogantly tried to dominate all local socialist activity to such an extent that, in certain cases, he threatened to resign his leadership unless he had his way; and yet, he declared in court that because he was not a workman, he did not want to intrude his political criteria as an influence on the proletariat's decision for a general strike. He also denied flatly that he had taken any part in the "incidents" of the Forlì general strike. Sometimes, in a single sentence, he attempted at once to display courage and to exculpate himself from any criminal responsibility by stating that the Forlì strike did not break out because of his instigation and then adding that if that had been the case, he would have assumed responsibility for it before the law. It sounded courageous to say that he would assume responsibility, and it served his ulterior purpose to deny that he had been an instigator although, in fact, he had been one of the leading instigators and organizers of the Forlì strike.

Mussolini's predominant preoccupation was to be acquitted, and he did not care to invite martyrdom by an open avowal of his agitation against war on revolutionary grounds. His lawyers and his local socialist comrades were anxious to spare him a prison term. The only hope for his acquittal lay in a series of denials of all the crimes imputed to him and in the intrusion of a mild socialist point of view, motivated by lofty and noble patriotic feeling. The "patriotic" alibi was the cue for Mussolini and his lawyers. Since socialists regarded courts of law as "bourgeois" and therefore "iniquitous" institutions, why should they tell them the truth? I think these factors explain in part Mussolini's shifty position at the trial.

His speech failed to convince the court, and although the

prosecutor demanded a sentence of eighteen months' imprisonment, the court sentenced him on November 23, 1911, to a prison term of one year for "inciting to crime" and rejected his plea for provisional liberty pending an appeal. Nenni was condemned to one year and fifteen days, and Lolli to six months of imprisonment.

The statements we have quoted from Mussolini are taken from his articles in the *Lotta* and from his testimony at the trial as reported in the *Lotta* of November 25, 1911. After his accession to power under a nationalist-fascist programme, his apologists minimized, misrepresented, or entirely overlooked his revolutionary and anti-patriotic propaganda and tried to bring into prominence the patriotic motives in his view of the Turco-Italian War. Had he been the leader of a communist revolution, his apologists would have shifted their emphasis. Writing after the fascist "March on Rome" in 1922, Beltramelli, the novelist, Bonavita, Mussolini's lawyer, and Signora Sarfatti, his official biographer, studiously omit any discussion of Mussolini's anti-militarist and anti-patriotic propaganda and any analysis of his opinions on the eve of the war; and in their fragmentary discussions of the trial and its outcome, they project in relief the patriotic motif, thus building up another legend.

In his biography of Mussolini, entitled *L'uomo nuovo* (1923), Beltramelli romanticizes to the effect that the editor of the *Class Struggle* maintained a position towards the war, which was "anything but socialist". In two and a half pages of his book, he purports to give the *Lotta's* report of Mussolini's speech at the trial, but he fails to reproduce the report in its entirety and to indicate the important omissions he has made. Even what he does set forth is not accurately transcribed.

Bonavita, in his book *Mussolini svelato* (*Mussolini Revealed*, 1924), also purports to give an account of his former client's attitude. Like Beltramelli, he writes loosely and is careless in the use and citation of sources. In one case, for example, he presents, about fifty pages apart from each other, two different versions of an alleged remark by Mussolini at the trial.

Signora Sarfatti, whose biography of Mussolini appeared first in English in 1925 and then in Italian in 1926, pretended to quote Mussolini's speech at the trial. Her version is utterly false in its conception and presentation and illustrates how sources of historical information can be distorted. Instead of giving us genuine textual quotations from Mussolini's speech, as she slyly implies, she invents a text which embodies, for the most part, a curious synthesis of extracts taken from Beltramelli and Bonavita, whom she fails to mention as sources for her information. Most of her quotations from Mussolini's speech are cleverly joined together in a running statement, part of which is taken from Bonavita, part of which is taken from Beltramelli, and part of which is not at all attributable to Mussolini. She begins her quotations from Mussolini's testimony concerning his responsibility for the strike and his views about sabotage with statements that are taken from Bonavita's version, not from the *Lotta's*. Then she attributes the following remarks to Mussolini: "At the station I exerted myself to prevent the crowd from forcing its way into the telegraph office. I fell and was injured by a blow from a sabre. The violence offered by the crowd was caused by the aggressive attitude of the police force." These remarks were never made by Mussolini and they were never ascribed to him except by Signora Sarfatti and those copying her. They originally appeared in the book by Bonavita who attributed them to Nenni, not to Mussolini. Signora Sarfatti, however, takes them bodily from Bonavita's book and incorporates them in her version of Mussolini's address to the court. Further quotations by the official biographer of the Duce are taken successively from Beltramelli, Bonavita, and again Beltramelli. The same criticism of Beltramelli's inaccurate transcription of parts of the *Lotta's* report is applicable to Signora Sarfatti who thus perpetuates Beltramelli's careless use of sources. She confuses the documents by not placing whatever can be credited to Mussolini in the order in which he said it. What she presents is a combination of the versions of her two predecessors plus certain variations of her own, obviously to suit her strong pro-Mussolini bias. In her treatment of the trial, Signora Sarfatti never indicates the variety of her sources.

Of course, the unconscionable use of documents by such fascist writers as Beltramelli, Bonavita, and Signora Sarfatti[1] was calculated to show that Mussolini had a "patriotic", not an "unpatriotic" or "anti-patriotic" past. The same is true of numerous other books written by apologists who took their cue from Signora Sarfatti, principally because her book, appearing as an official biography, was more widely circulated than Beltramelli's or Bonavita's. Unfortunately, some of the detractors of Mussolini and fascism have uncritically taken at its face value the Sarfatti version of Mussolini's speech at the trial, and thus they have unwittingly contributed to the legend about Mussolini's early "patriotic" attitude.

It is tempting to trace in great detail the history of the "patriotic" legend and other misconceptions concerning Mussolini's attitude towards the Turco-Italian War, from the time of the trial to the present; but this would take us too far afield, and we need not linger over it at this point. Instead, we prefer to pursue further Mussolini's personal point of view on the war and on militarism and patriotism.

Our contention that his opposition to the Turco-Italian War was inspired by revolutionary socialist, not by patriotic motives is amply substantiated by unequivocal declarations which he made after his release from prison in March 1912 and while the war was going on. In June 1912, on the eve of the national socialist congress of Reggio Emilia where the reformist and revolutionary elements of the party engaged in a momentous conflict resulting in the victory of the latter, Mussolini's paper carried on a debate with *L'Azione Socialista*, the weekly organ of the extreme right wing of the party, whose leading members were Bissolati and Bonomi. When *L'Azione* criticized Mussolini for identifying socialism with anti-patriotism, he replied: "*L'Azione Socialista* also finds that our socialism is aberrant because it is *anti-patriotic*. Let us

[1] By the way, both Bonavita and Signora Sarfatti are ex-reformist socialists.

confirm our heresy. We cannot conceive of a patriotic social-ism. In fact, socialism has a character of humanity and universality. Since our first years of adolescence when there passed through our hands the large and small manuals of the socialist doctrine, we learned that there are only two father-lands in the world: that of the exploited and that of the exploiters. For you, of the Right, the fatherland is a sort of fetish which can be worshipped by everyone; for us, it is a fetish which, like all other fetishes, does not deserve any pity. The fatherland is a fiction, a mystification and a conventional lie. This was recognized by the Humanists of the *Ubi bene, ibi patria*, by the Stoics who proclaimed *Man a citizen of the world*, and by Christ, the anti-patriot *par excellence*. We are not Italians; we feel ourselves to be at least Europeans. There are no longer any patriotic frontiers for science, philosophy, art, economics, styles and sports, and should there be for socialism? To-day, the fatherland has become identical with militarism. They are inseparable. Whoever says fatherland says militarism. We transcend the concept of the fatherland with another concept: that of class. And we are typical socialists. When Marx throws out his cry 'Workers of the world, unite!', he is a destroyer of the old patriotic ideology."

After noting various manifestations of militarism in Tripoli and elsewhere, Mussolini exclaimed in June 1912: "International militarism continues to celebrate its orgies of destruction and death. Every day that passes, the huge pyramid of lives that have been sacrificed rears its bloody summit upon which Mars stands waiting with his unsated and contorted mouth in an infernal grin. Sandor Petöfi, the Hungarian bard ***, asked in one of his verses: 'What have you eaten, O earth, that you are so thirsty and continually drink new tears and new blood?' It is not the earth that is thirsty for tears and blood, but an Idea: the idea of the Fatherland. So long as there are Fatherlands, there will be Militarism. The Fatherland is a spook ***, a spook like God, and like God, it is vindictive, cruel and tyrannical. The anti-militarism . . . of a patriotic kind . . . is a miserable absur-

(*Central Press' Photos*)

MUSSOLINI ARRESTED BY THE ITALIAN POLICE IN THE SPRING OF 1915.

dity. It resembles the anti-clericalism of the so-called free-thinkers. The evil must be struck at its roots. To demolish religions, it is necessary to efface every God from men's minds; to overthrow militarism, it is necessary to depreciate the idea of the Fatherland. Let us show that the Fatherland does *not* exist, just as God does not exist; that one and the other are two great fictions, two formidable, conventional lies. This propaganda must be carried on with tenacity and assiduity—methodically—among the proletarians who are condemned to be sacrificed to the patriotic Moloch."

In September 1912, while the Turco-Italian War was still going on, Mussolini declared: "As long as the war continues, I shall not desist from my anti-war campaign. I want to create an anti-war conscience that is lacking to-day."

These statements contradict the legend of Mussolini's patriotism, and they are in perfect harmony with his views on patriotism expressed on various earlier occasions. If he had really cherished any patriotic feelings, he never revealed them in a single article after his trial and imprisonment and while Italy was at war with Turkey. The collection of the *Avanti!*, which he edited from 1912 to 1914, abounds in tirades against the war. Accustomed as he was to outspoken expression of his own ideas, it is strange that, except for his speech at the trial, the editor of the *Class Struggle* did not utter a single word before the Turco-Italian War, or after he was sentenced to prison for trying to sabotage it, that would lend any support to the theory that he was opposed to the war for patriotic reasons.

9. PRISON AND FAME

Mussolini was sentenced in November 1911 to one year of imprisonment, but he was in prison only five months in accordance with the reduction of his term ordered by the Court of Appeals of Bologna. After the November verdict, Forlì republicans and socialists temporarily forgot their differences and joined in mass meetings protesting against the imprisonment of Mussolini, Nenni, and Lolli. The *Lotta* censured the refusal to grant Mussolini provisional liberty pending his appeal; provisional liberty that "we have seen granted even to recognized robbers and that recently has been accorded to a murderer is denied to him who has a right to it".

A writer for the *Lotta*, probably Francesco Ciccotti, reporting his visit to Mussolini in prison, said that he was in good health, passing his days "absorbed in his studies". Perhaps he was finishing his volume on John Huss.

After some delay, the appeal of Mussolini and the others was heard on February 19, 1912. The *Lotta* expressed the hope that freedom would be given to its "courageous comrade who, unjustly sentenced, finds himself in prison for more than three months." The Court of Appeals of Bologna reduced Mussolini's term to five months, Nenni's to seven months and a half, and Lolli's to four months and a half. Thus, the *Lotta* declared, the Court of Appeals recognized the injustice of the "Cossack sentence" of the Forlì court; if it had set aside the judgment of the lower court, "a very harsh lesson would have been inflicted on those who condemned him. And so . . . the punishment was reduced in order not to confess the injustice that had been perpetrated." Although the original sentence had been considerably modified, the *Avanti!* regarded the result of the appeal as "very severe". On February 20, Mussolini gave an interview to one of its reporters, in which he sent his greetings to the paper and to the comrades who "feel solidarity with him in this hour of judicial reaction which strikes those culpable of opposition to the war undertaking".

The day following his release from prison on March 12, 1912, a banquet was tendered to him by his Forlì comrades. Besides Mussolini, the speakers were Bonavita, Ciccotti, Umberto Bianchi, and the socialist deputy Bentini. Various tributes paid to him after his release show the high regard in which he was held. His opposition to the Turco-Italian War had spread his name in the Romagna and had made him better known to party leaders at Rome and Milan and to the revolutionary group in the party which issued *"La Soffitta"* (*"The Attic"*) at Rome.

On the eve of his release, the *Avanti!* referred to "our very dear comrade Benito Mussolini, a very noble type of idealist ***. Liberty will be doubly dear to him because he will learn that while he was in prison, all the socialists—having recovered the passion of a former time—have unflinchingly done their duty, defying unpopularity, violence and calumny. Thus, after five months, jingoistic vanity can now be said to be in liquidation." On March 12, a correspondent of this paper wrote: "Comrade Mussolini left the prison this morning more socialist than ever. We saw him in his humble home with his small family, which he adores, and we stayed a short while with him. He has not suffered at all physically because of his imprisonment. Numerous telegrams of congratulations and praise from every part of Italy have reached him."

The *Lotta* said this of its leader, now ready to resume his editorial duties: "Our comrade, who regained his liberty after five months [of imprisonment], is always the same: proud and indomitable for the socialist ideal.*** Mussolini did not like one thing: the banquet that the socialists had prepared in his honour. He did not want it, but even so, he had to resign himself to the will of his comrades." Incidentally, this dislike of banquets and all sorts of social affairs has characterized Mussolini throughout his socialist and fascist career.

Among those who sent congratulatory messages to him and to the banquet committee were his old acquaintance Angelica Balabanoff and his more recent acquaintances Battisti and Piscel. Messages were also received from two men who were

to become important figures—Cesare Rossi and Nicola
Bombacci. The former was then a syndicalist agitator at
Parma, the stronghold of Italian syndicalism. On behalf of
the syndicalist paper *L'Internazionale* and of the syndicalist
Chamber of Labour of Parma, Rossi sent a telegram in which
he referred to the "likeable and noble Mussolini". This is the
first written record I have found concerning the relations
between these two men, and it seems to imply either that they
had already met each other personally or that they had been
familiar with each other's work. When Mussolini resigned
from the *Avanti!* in 1914 and founded *Il Popolo d'Italia* in order
to advocate Italy's participation in the Great War, Rossi
became one of his intimate henchmen. After the "March on
Rome", Rossi enjoyed a powerful position among fascist
"hierarchs", for besides being head of the fascist Press
Bureau, he was said to be the chief of the fascist *Cheka*. He
became so deeply involved in the brutal murder of the
socialist deputy Giacomo Matteotti in June 1924 that he
was taken into custody. Feeling that he had been made the
"scapegoat" for this crime, he wrote, for self-protection,
several famous memoranda containing serious charges
against Mussolini and the fascist government.[1] In 1925, he
was released by an amnesty and in 1926, made his way to
Paris where he carried on violent anti-fascist propaganda
until 1929 when he was "captured" by fascist officials as he
was motoring near the Italian–Swiss border.

On behalf of the socialists of Modena, Bombacci signed a
message to "his friend Benito, courageous and cultured
apostle of the socialist ideal". Before going to Modena, and
while Mussolini was in charge of the *Lotta di Classe* in 1910
and 1911, Bombacci edited *Il Cuneo* (*The Wedge*), a socialist
weekly published at Cesena, a town near Forlì. The editors
of these two socialist weeklies met quite frequently and
resumed an acquaintance which began, I think, when both
were in their teens. They shared the same platform on September 7, 1910, when Mussolini delivered a speech at Cesena

[1] For a masterly analysis of Rossi's memoranda, see Gaetano Salvemini, *The Fascist Dictatorship in Italy*, London, 1928.

on the Romagnuole socialist martyr Pio Battistini, the eloquence of which won a glowing tribute from *The Wedge*. Bombacci remained an obscure figure in the Italian socialist party until the Great War was well under way, and then he became somewhat prominent as a spokesman for the party's intransigent anti-war position. After the war, this demagogue *par excellence* was elected to the Chamber of Deputies and became one of the principal leaders of the left or communist wing of the party, haranguing the masses, holding up Bolshevik Russia as a model for his country and demanding the establishment of a Soviet system. At the same time, his former comrade Mussolini was editing the *Popolo d'Italia* and clamouring for a "revolution" along nationalist or fascist lines. Bombacci seemed powerful because the Italian social- ists were so strong politically until the spring of 1921, but never perhaps in the history of socialism in any country has a man, seemingly so important, been so pusillanimous, vacil- lating, and, one might even say, empty-headed. Lacking in almost every important element of leadership, the irresolute Bombacci, this Bombastes Furioso, by talking continuously about the social revolution and never organizing genuine revolutionary steps to bring it about, did as much as any other single man effectually to "sabotage" the post-war Italian revolutionary movement. One is tempted to wonder if the Italian socialists would not have got closer to their avowed aim, had they had as their chiefs men with Mussolini's undoubted political capacity for revolutionary leadership.

For several years, Bombacci has been living undisturbed in fascist Italy, undisturbed because of the indulgence of its "master", Mussolini, who has uncannily completed the process of discrediting Bombacci. While Mussolini's motive is publicly to degrade "revolutionists" like Bombacci, it should be said that by accepting his "protection", such "revolu- tionists" reveal the stuff of which they are made. The apostasy of this shameless mountebank was fully revealed in April 1936, when he began publishing at Rome a fascist review entitled *La Verità* (*The Truth*).

Probably the most signal tribute paid to Mussolini in connection with his release from prison was contained in an article published on March 4, 1912, in *"La Soffitta"* (*"The Attic"*), the weekly organ of the revolutionary wing of the socialist party which was seeking to overthrow the dominance of the reformist elements. We have not been able to identify the author of the article, who signed himself "V." Mussolini was described as the "duce" of the Forlì socialists. He was destined to be the "duce" of the Italian socialist party, the "duce" of the revolutionary *Fasci* favouring Italy's entrance into the Great War, then the "duce" of the post-war *Fasci di Combattimento* and finally the "duce" of the fascist state. In a few days, "V." wrote, Mussolini "will be restored to us ***. Thus, Benito Mussolini will return, with his old serenity and with renewed fervour, to the political battles of his red Romagna, which he does so much to animate with the impetuosity of his socialist passion that does not know opportunisms and adaptations. Professor Benito Mussolini is, without doubt, one of the most likeable and outstanding personalities of our [revolutionary] group, to which he brings the contribution not only of his tenacious and fruitful work but also of his uncommon culture which he does not flaunt for vain advertisement, but which is profound and sure, as the quality of his character is proved. And at [the forthcoming national socialist congress at] Reggio Emilia, men of the Left and of the Right will realize that this time the Forlivese will count also in the statistical calculations of the congress and will count so much the more inasmuch as they have as duce, beloved and esteemed, a man of the character and incorruptibility of Benito Mussolini."

A few days later, *"The Attic,"* in an unsigned article, greeted the release of Mussolini, that "strong type of fighter" who could now "embrace his family again" and resume his work at Forlì.

The twenty-eight year old idol of the numerically small but well-organized Forlì socialists, their "Duce", now become a celebrity somewhat known beyond the confines of his province and familiar to the revolutionary leaders in the socialist party, was on his way to a great triumph—the editorship of the *Avanti!*, the most important post in the party. Fired with zeal for the socialist cause, Mussolini—on resuming his work as editor-in-chief of the *Lotta* towards the end of March 1912—said of himself that the return of brutal and stupid reaction as a policy of the Italian government had not broken or bent his backbone.

Mussolini has always hated parliaments and has always heaped vituperation and ridicule on these instruments of democratic rule. With reference to this subject, he has remained quite consistent throughout his socialist and fascist career. He had almost entirely made up his mind about parliamentary rule during his stay in Switzerland from 1902 until 1904. As editor of the *Lotta di Classe* at Forlì, where he had the advantage of being in Italy, directly on the scene, so to speak, he was ever ready and thoroughly prepared to denounce the Italian parliament and the faith of reformist socialists in parliamentary methods.

It is true that as a powerful leader of the Italian socialist party between 1912 and 1914, and as fascist leader after the Great War, he urged his followers to participate in elections, but this attitude was motivated purely by tactical considerations. Basically, he has always despised electoral methods, parliaments, and all kinds of deliberative assemblies. One of the most important reasons for this is that deliberation, discussion, and argument, all of which are implicit in the parliamentary system, are repugnant to his authoritarian and imperious temperament. His will must be supreme. A salient aspect of his style, in speech and in writing, is its declamatory character; hence his hatred for the dialectic method of socialist reformists like Filippo Turati and Treves and of his democratic and liberal anti-fascist opponents. Mussolini would rather settle a controversy by a duel or by ordering his followers to strike an enemy down by physical force than by a debate with an enemy in an open forum. Despite his great power as the fascist Duce, he is intolerant of any criticism within his own party. He has removed from office and power and has even sent to prison fascists who have tried to assert themselves in a manner not in conformity with his dictates. Instances are the expulsion from the fascist party of its former secretary Augusto Turati, and the relegation to the penal islands of the once-powerful fascist leader and Under-

Secretary of the Interior Leandro Arpinati. His demotion of Roberto Farinacci, Dino Grandi, and Italo Balbo, together with his constant replacement of men in ministerial posts, also shows that he will not brook the advance to power of any fascist who begins to develop a considerable following of his own. Mussolini is bored by the discussions that take place in his fascist Senate and Chamber of Deputies, and he hears speeches by his party members only because they constitute hosannas to his will and to his policies. Of such hosannas he never tires, although it is with considerable disdain that he listens to those fascists who think they express a will of their own when they rise to speak about a fascist policy.

Lest we digress too much on his later career, let us focus our attention on Mussolini as editor of the *Lotta di Classe* from 1910 until 1912. This paper contains an extraordinary collection of vigorous and virulent fragments of his contempt for parliamentary institutions, and they are well worth presenting because they reiterate in forceful language a fundamental aspect of his political outlook. For Mussolini, the Italian Chamber of Deputies was a "parliament of the underworld ***, a parliament of malefactors ***, the most illiterate, the most slothful and the most corrupt parliament in the world ***. In Italy, parliamentarism is exactly that great conventional lie denounced by Max Nordau."

Mussolini held up to the scorn of his followers the falsehood and the lie that underlay the belief in popular sovereignty. He told the proletarians that the parliamentary regime was an instrument of corruption, and that the school teachers and university professors who had praised popular democratic institutions had lied and had betrayed the good faith of their students:

"Chamber of Deputies, vain chimera, great circle of the corrupt and the bribers, sovereign without a sceptre, Circe of honest navigators, easy and ready bargainer with the pirates of national happiness and honour, away with you; we despise you. Chamber, you who are the false mirror of the Country, you who decree war laughing about death,[1] you

[1] Mussolini refers to the Turco-Italian War.

who extol the Fatherland forgetting its most jealous interests, you who slowly gnaw the conscience and emasculate the fibre of the upright men that the people send to you, false Chamber, you who dabble with the republic and belong to the king, you who fondle socialism and allow to capital the most bloody pageantry, you, sorceress of *trasformismo* [coalitionism] and juggler of character, you, hybrid, insincere and inglorious institution, away with you."

By the year 1910, the reformists had gained unquestioned dominance of the Italian socialist party. In 1892 they·had dissociated themselves from the anarchists, and by 1908, from the syndicalists. Among the reformists, however, there were two important factions: one, represented by Leonida Bissolati and Ivanoe Bonomi, displayed definite ministerial tendencies and a readiness to advocate the participation of socialists in a "bourgeois" ministry; the other, more numerous and powerful, led by Turati and Treves, although believing in parliamentary methods and in supporting by its votes various bourgeois ministries which proposed liberal social reforms, refused to encourage the participation of socialists in any bourgeois cabinet. Fighting both these factions was a small but vigorous minority, which called itself the revolutionary socialist group, led by Costantino Lazzari, Giovanni Lerda, Angelica Balabanoff, and others. Its biweekly organ, founded at Rome in 1911, was ironically entitled "*La Soffitta*" ("*The Attic*") by way of retort to the Giolittians and the socialist ministerialists after Giolitti's remark that the socialist parliamentary group had forgotten all about Marx and had tucked him away in an attic. Mussolini was a staunch adherent of this group, and the *Lotta di Classe* was one of the few socialist weeklies that championed its programme. In 1912, this group succeeded in expelling from the party the leaders of the extreme right wing, such as Bissolati and Bonomi, and took over the control of the party. Mussolini became its outstanding spokesman and Duce for almost two years, from 1912 until 1914.

For Mussolini, none of the bourgeois political leaders was worthy of any support by the socialist party. He assailed

Giovanni Giolitti, Sidney Sonnino, and Luigi Luzzatti, all of whom held the office of Prime Minister while he was editor of the *Lotta*. After Cavour, the dominant figures in Italian politics were Agostino Depretis, Francesco Crispi, and Giolitti. From the beginning of this century to the outbreak of the Great War, Giolitti, a gifted politician, expert parliamentarian, and clever manipulator of elections, managed to control the Italian parliament, and through his liberal social policy, he was able to "domesticate" the Italian socialist party. It was said, and with considerable truth, that he could make or break a ministry at will. Therefore, when he resigned as Prime Minister in December 1909, after holding this office since May 1906, and was succeeded by the more conservative Sonnino, the general opinion in Italy was that the Sonnino Ministry would be short-lived. Mussolini became editor of the *Lotta* when Sonnino was in power.

Although Sonnino enjoyed the reputation of being honest and incorruptible in contrast with Giolitti who was regarded by his many critics as unscrupulous, Mussolini saw no difference between them. Giolitti, he said, was the "guardian of the present ministry ***. A return of Giolitti to power is therefore not an absurd hypothesis. Everything is possible in Italy, and the English are not wrong when they call us 'the carnival nation'.*** Sonnino is on his feet because of the votes of the Giolittians. Therefore Sonnino rules fictitiously, while Giolitti governs in fact.*** The last elections prove to us that Sonnino follows the electoral methods of Giolitti: Buy and corrupt. The delusion must be bitter for the ingenuous people who swore on the political and moral honesty of Sonnino who, at bottom, is worthy of his predecessors."

Mussolini condemned the socialist deputies for being frequently absent from Montecitorio, the seat of the Italian Chamber, instead of giving regular battle to the Sonnino Ministry. Where was the combative spirit that they had shown in their policy of parliamentary obstructionism towards the reactionary Pelloux Ministry in 1899? The editor of

the *Class Struggle* bitterly attacked the Extreme Left, a parliamentary coalition group of the popular parties, including the
socialist, radical, and republican deputies. On one occasion,
when a good many members of the Extreme Left were absent
from a session in which Sonnino delivered an "empty" speech,
Mussolini excoriated them for not fighting Sonnino. His
special target was the group of socialist deputies. "Our very
glorious [socialist parliamentary] group is always equal to
its great mission. Among all the paralytics that encumber the
halls of Montecitorio, the socialist deputies suffer from the
most grave forms of paralysis. Where are they? What do they
do? Of 45 deputies, hardly 20 are present at the sessions. And
where are the other leaders idling? What Capua takes the
fight out of them? And where are the young members ***
who came out triumphant from the election of March 1909,
destined, it was then said, to instil new blood into the socialist parliamentary group as Elena of Montenegro [wife of
King Victor Emmanuel III] has instilled and will instil new
blood into the Savoy line? We look for them, but do not find
them. The grand farce which our group is playing has been
going on for a decade: since the period of obstructionism.
Since that period, the parliamentary platform has ceased to
be—as was desired at the earliest times—a platform of propaganda and protest. For our deputies, Montecitorio is the
supreme point of socialism. Well, we absolutely do not feel
that we are represented by these people who wear themselves
out in the parliamentary merry-go-round and would want to
wear us out in the electoral struggles.*** The socialist deputies are by now too far away from the people who work. In
the political action which they are performing, socialism is
being wrecked. Convince yourselves of this, even you, dear
socialist comrades, who have wreathed pictures of our deputies in your clubs and over your beds as though they were the
newest guardian saints; convince yourselves that socialism
will not be realized in a parliament with a majority of socialist
deputies. You workmen will realize socialism, you and no one
else. You alone will be the artificers of your emancipation.
Karl Marx, who is, after all, not as old and as transcended as

some would have us believe, threw out a cry that will not die:
The emancipation of the workers must be the work of the
workers themselves. Always remember this!"

The editor of the *Class Struggle* deplored the absence of
many socialist deputies from a debate on the military budget.
Representatives of the socialist party had become the petty
lawyers of small clienteles and "in order to speak on behalf of
these clienteles at the ministries, they must keep silent at the
Chamber. This is the bitter, but the real truth." Mussolini
found satisfaction in the vigorous activity of the deputy
Ettore Ciccotti, a noted historian and an independent socialist who was not a member of the socialist parliamentary
group. The fearless independence of Ciccotti, his loyalty to
the socialist ideal despite his dissociation from the socialist
group, and his unusual culture, powerful pen, and caustic
temper endeared him to Mussolini, who was happy to publish
in the *Lotta*, Ciccotti's "powerful and profound" speech on
the military budget.[1]

Like most extreme revolutionists, Mussolini despised lawyers, those bourgeois *par excellence*, who, in his eyes, embraced
socialism in order to advance their careers and who constituted a "plague" on the socialist party. "If the socialist
party", he declared, "has intoxicated itself with electoralism,
it is due to the lawyers.*** All their socialism is in the
ballot." They seek to use the title of "Honourable" in order
to increase their practice. "Their political *conduct* is propor-
tionate to their professional immorality. Lawyers, like priests,
must lie in order to live." They try to monopolize the posts
in the party, but once they are in court, they will take up
the defence of anyone, to-day a thief and to-morrow one
who has been robbed. Mussolini granted that lawyers too
must live, but "not by prostituting socialism. Let them
choose: they are either socialists or lawyers."

Early in the year 1910, Professor Gaetano Salvemini, the
Italian historian, vehemently denounced the political
methods of Giolitti in a book entitled *Il ministro della mala vita*

[1] Ettore Ciccotti must not be confused with Francesco Ciccotti, with
whom Mussolini had close relations for a few years.

(*The Minister of the Underworld*). Mussolini seized upon this description of Giolitti in order to condemn what he regarded as the parliament of the underworld—the parliament of Italy. Salvemini had distinguished himself as an historical scholar by works on the medieval commune, the French Revolution, and Mazzini. His views on Mazzini were well known to Mussolini, who cited them in the course of his polemics with the Forlì republicans. Seeing in the socialist party what many other Italians saw, namely, the only political instrument for genuine democratic progress, Salvemini urged the party to agitate in favour of free trade, educational reform, and universal suffrage. For Salvemini the socialist party was not reformist enough, while for Mussolini the party was too reformist. In 1911, Salvemini founded *L'Unità*, a review devoted mainly to political questions and remarkable for the clarity of its writings, the vigour of its thought, and the distinction of its contributors. It seems certain that Mussolini followed with interest the political as well as the historical writings of Salvemini, for whose intellectual integrity he doubtless had great respect. After the Great War, Salvemini was such a pronounced critic of the anti-liberal and anti-democratic fascist movement (he and Mussolini almost fought a duel in 1920), that he was forced to flee from Italy. His trenchant opposition to fascism, expressed in books, pamphlets and lectures, has commanded wide attention in France, England and the United States, and he is one of the most outstanding anti-fascist exiles. In some ways—the courage of his convictions, the fervour of his political passions and the intensity of his faith in democracy—he reminds us of Mazzini.

In his *Minister of the Underworld*, Salvemini centred his attack on the election to the Italian Parliament of Vito de Bellis, a political henchman of Giolitti. While Salvemini's anti-Giolittian propaganda was motivated by a desire to improve political conditions and reflected optimistic faith in the democratic system, Mussolini's anti-parliamentary propaganda was motivated by a desire to destroy all vestiges of liberal and democratic institutions. In March 1910, Mussolini wrote as follows in an article entitled "The Parliament of the Underworld":

"It is of course the Italian Parliament. The other day, the election of Gioia del Colle was rendered valid, and Vito de Bellis has triumphantly entered Montecitorio. The favourable *rapporteur* was Guarracino, a professor of law at the University of Naples. The immorality of the professorial chair gives its hand to the turpitude of politics." In any other country in the world, Mussolini went on to say, De Bellis would have found the doors of a public body closed to him. "He would be kicked away like a scabby dog with which one fears the least contact.*** Any other Chamber that was not the Italian Chamber would have said 'no' to the deputy of the underworld of the South [of Italy]. But the Italian Chamber is profoundly, irremediably corrupt.*** And the Extreme Left? It indulged a little in the usual verbal battle, with an appendix of insults for the ears of the gallery, but nothing more. None of the 508 deputies has felt the need of resigning his mandate in order not to find himself in contact with the immense political refuse that ferments in the North and the South and of which De Bellis is a typical exemplar. Of the 105 deputies of the Extreme Left, only 66 participated in the voting, and of the 39 in the socialist group, only 21 participated. From good to better! And Morgari [leader of the socialist parliamentary group] talks to us about the 'virginity' of the socialist parliamentary group. And the Executive Committee of the party wishes that in the May 1 platform, there should be included 'the payment of deputies'. Ah, no! I shall never go before a crowd of day-labourers to plead for the payment of deputies. The Italian Chamber is a market-place. And when Gaetano Salvemini documents for us the case of Gioia del Colle, he renders a bad service to corrupt and corrupting parliamentarism."

Sonnino resigned in March 1910 and was succeeded by Luzzatti, who gave evidence of his liberal intentions by taking into his cabinet two members of the radical group in the Extreme Left. Luzzatti's programme for suffrage and social reforms explains the prevailing feeling in the socialist parliamentary group to support his Ministry, a feeling which Mussolini, of course, did not share. In April 1910, he wrote: "We have no illusions. The new coalition ministry leaves us sceptical and indifferent. It is not with these men that Italy can march swiftly on the road of civil progress. They are too old. The Luzzattian ideology is a century behind time. His conception of the social question is lacking in breadth.*** Luzzatti has remained the man who believes 'in the good heart of the ruling classes' and in the miraculous efficacy of reforms. The Luzzatti Ministry is one of transition that prepares the imminent carnival of the coalition-minded democracy, respectful of the king and still more of the pope."

At the national socialist congress of Milan in October 1910, Mussolini indicted the socialist deputies on various counts, and especially for their "moral insensibility" in failing to fight against the increase of sixty-one million lire in the military budget. Later in the year, the socialist deputies withdrew their support from the Luzzatti Ministry. Shortly after Luzzatti resigned in March 1911, Bissolati crossed the Rubicon, so to speak, by seeing the King personally about the formation of a new Ministry, which was eventually organized by Giolitti. He refused to join a cabinet, it is true, but his act was very significant in that it symbolized the readiness of some socialists to hold a ministerial post in a bourgeois government.

Mussolini clearly perceived how the eventual holding of office by socialists was implicit in the logic of reformist socialism. "Ministerialism", he said, "is the inevitable corollary of reformism, and participation in the exercise of political power is the inevitable consequence of ministerialism. This is the real, inescapable result of the reformist logic. But all this is very distant from socialism."

I recall Mussolini's telling me in the course of a conversation I had with him in 1926, that one of the striking events in the history of modern Italy was Turati's refusal of Giolitti's offer to the socialists to have their party represented in his cabinet. It is tempting to consider what would have happened if the reformist socialists had accepted this offer in 1903. Per-

haps it was too early for them to do so. Further oppor-
tunities were offered later. For a decade, between 1901 and
1911, the reformists chose to support various bourgeois
cabinets on occasion, but they refused to favour the participation of socialists in any cabinet. In 1911, it was clear that
men like Bissolati and Bonomi were not averse to holding
office in a "bourgeois" ministry. The following year, they
were expelled from the party which had come under the
dominance of the revolutionary elements represented by
Mussolini and others, while the reformists like Turati and
Treves remained in the minority wing of the party. In 1914,
Mussolini carried with him a small group of revolutionary
socialists and syndicalists who favoured war on the side of
the Allies. Thus by the end of 1914, two extreme socialist
factions, the collaborationists of the right like Bissolati and
the revolutionists of the left like Mussolini, were no longer
parts of the official socialist party. In the difficult post-war
period, the Turati reformist group engaged in a party
struggle with the revolutionary group, which included
Serrati, Lazzari, Bombacci, and others. Again the reformist
socialists hesitated about joining a "bourgeois" ministry. It
was not until July 1922, when it was feared that the Italian
constitutional state would be overthrown by the fascists, that
Turati finally condescended to call on the King with an
offer to join a liberal cabinet. This act of desperation came
too late. The fascist "March on Rome" in October 1922
marked the beginning of the end of the Italian democratic
state, to which the reformist socialists of the Turati school
had, perhaps unwittingly, contributed by their refusal to take
part earlier in a liberal cabinet.

In April 1911, Mussolini was so infuriated by the failure of
the Executive Committee of the socialist party to disavow
Bissolati for visiting the King in regard to the formation of a
cabinet that he induced the Forlì socialist federation to
secede from the party. About two months later, he employed
language against the Italian parliament which can appropriately be applied to contemporary fascist parliaments:
"The Giolittian parliament is in a state of complete decay.

Montecitorio is deserted like the Sahara. In Tuesday after-noon's session, *fourteen* of the five hundred and eight deputies were present. Not so bad! The *Avanti!* goes out of its way to deplore this absenteeism.*** The *Avanti!* is wrong, and the absentees are right. To what avail is it to go to the Chamber since there are no longer any parties, since there are no longer any ideas, since problems are no longer faced and since all political activity is reduced to the rubber-stamping of matters of ordinary administration? What must the deputies do at Montecitorio? Are they not perhaps all in agreement? Well then, it is enough that there is Giolitti. The old and new mercenaries, of the Right and the Left, could very well go into hiding . . . and remain in hiding . . . There would be no harm if the socialist deputies deserted Montecitorio in order to get into touch with the masses. Instead, absenteeism all along the line. We do not know, in truth, why the Italian parliament is kept open. It could be closed. Public hygiene and morality would gain thereby."

Particularly odious to Mussolini was the dependence of the socialist deputies on Giolitti. When a state insurance project came up in 1911, he wrote in an editorial entitled "Carnival Nation": "It is not difficult to predict that the [socialist parliamentary] group—the majority of it—will follow Giolitti with the docility of a dog that follows its master everywhere. Politics in Italy is magnificently carnivalesque. How true is the phrase that we have placed at the head of these lines and with which the English brand us and photograph us! Especially if applied to Giolittian parlia-mentary politics and to the reformism of the socialist deputies ***."

If Mussolini could have his way, he would demand that the socialists rely more on extra-parliamentary activity, direct action, and economic agitation than on parliamentary methods. For him, who was proud to say that he had a "barbaric" idea of socialism, revolutionary aims were better expressed in popular movements and in public squares than in parliamentary votes. Describing the Italian Chamber as a "Chamber of malefactors" because certain deputies had been charged with fraudulent acts, he declared: "And must we continue to hope for something good from such a gang?*** Parliamentarism in its men and institutions is passing through a terrible period of political and moral crisis. The proletariat is sceptical and its scepticism—let us recognize it—is fully justified. After the sad experience, it will perhaps be necessary to revise this very weak point of the socialist tactic. Meanwhile, let us return to the piazza which, despite all the deviations and disillusions, has remained the inexhaustible nursery of all the revolutionary energies!"

Once the socialists were in parliament, however, Mussolini would insist that they constitute a single group, independent of the radicals and the republicans and the Extreme Left coalition of parties, that they give up any idea of holding a ministerial office, and that they refuse to support by their vote any ministry whatsoever. He did not go as far as the anarchists and some syndicalists who believed that revolutionary groups should abstain completely from taking part in elections and, consequently, from sending representatives to parliament. He was not what used to be called an "abstentionist" or an "anti-electionist". Rather, he favoured the participation of the socialist party in elections and in parliament, provided that it did not give an exaggerated importance to parliamentary activity. In a preface to his translation of a book on revolutionary socialism by the French syndicalist Charles Albert, Mussolini remarked: "We do not want parliamentary action to have the first place, the absorbing part in the socialist tactic, but we do not want to give it up completely.*** Parliamentarism must be only one, and not the principal one, among the many forms of socialist activity, not the end and object of this activity."

Mussolini's main ambition was to arouse the revolutionary spirit in the socialist movement, to "oxygenate" it and give it a new tempo. He deplored the absence of real political *passion* in Italian politics. What did parliament do but "domesticate" the Italian socialists? What justification was there for reproaching the socialists of the Romagna like himself because they were supposed to be "impulsive" and hot-headed? In 1910, the twenty-seven year old editor of the *Class Struggle* quoted with approval *La Fronda*, a Milan republican weekly which had discussed the lack of political passion in Italy. Condensed in the lines of the *Fronda*, said Mussolini, "is the whole psychology of this miserable Italy of cowardly subversives. There is indeed lacking *political passion*. The *quieto vivere*: this is the formula of the carnivalesque Italian democracy. How many reproaches, veiled or unveiled, for us socialists of the Romagna, who bring a little *political passion* in our struggles! For the other socialists—the smug—there are no reproaches. For them, politics is an exercise in . . . masturbation. But the absence of political passion which you, O friends of the *Fronda*, deplore and which we too deplore is the consequence of our history that has not had revolutions. Without a revolutionary tradition, there is no political passion."

Unlike the vast majority of socialists, he was convinced that the time for insurrectional movements in the streets had not passed. He still believed in the "barricade, this trench which popular fury, in the hour of great courage, erects in the streets, setting up the heroic impetuosity of the oppressed against the violent repression by the masters". On one occasion in 1912, as he deplored the victory of the clericals in the Belgian elections and the faith of most Belgian socialists in electoral methods, he exclaimed that "twenty-four hours of revolution" would have sufficed to sweep away the clerical "scum". Naturally, he cared little for the scorn of the reformists and the "Marxists". Eventually, his 1848 and Blanquist phraseology as well as his Jacobin ferocity in attacking his enemies earned for him such descriptions as the "man of the barricades", the "Marat" of Italian socialism, and the "Red Barbarossa".

By revolutionary political passion, Mussolini meant violent, direct, and extra-parliamentary action. He could not and cannot conceive of political activity except in these terms, for throughout his entire life, he has never sympathized with democratic and liberal ideals and methods. During his socialist days, he wished to see the Italian proletariat purge itself of democratic and parliamentary illusions and set out to forge the weapons for an aggressive war against the bourgeoisie. He wanted that type of socialist action which would not attenuate, but rather aggravate the antagonism and hatred between classes so that the proletariat would be prepared at some time to effect a *tournant dans l'histoire*. The duty of revolutionary leaders was to stimulate, rather than restrain the bellicose instincts of the proletariat. Mussolini hoped that the day would soon come when he and other revolutionists, instead of writing articles, would participate in the playing of the grand symphony—the social revolution—with instruments of steel. In short, the Italian proletariat needed a "bath of blood" to inure it to the final decisive battle with the bourgeoisie.

He was disappointed in not having led a socialist revolution in Italy, but his love for passionate, direct, and violent political action has been amply requited by his leadership of the fascists. His anti-democratic fascism is the child of his anti-democratic socialism. Both as a socialist and as a fascist, he has been enamoured of the word revolution and he has caressed it so fondly that whatever the movement in which he participates, it must be revolutionary or, at any rate, it must be called revolutionary. When he resigned from the *Avanti!* in 1914 and began to preach Italy's intervention in the Great War, he said he did so in the name of social revolution. When he fathered the fascist movement, he called it a revolutionary movement; and since the fascist seizure of power, he has constantly talked about the "fascist revolution". He has cared more for passionate political combat in itself than for the ultimate social object of such combat—so long as the combat is revolutionary in method. Socialism and Italy, revolution and nationalism have served as ideological masks for his craving to lead or to appear as the leader of an aggressive body of men seeking the conquest of political power. He is a twentieth-century *condottiere* consumed by the lust for dominion over men and ready to embrace any cause so long as this lust can be satisfied.

In his socialist campaign against parliament, Mussolini

always disparaged the Italian Senate, the members of which he described as "old fogies", and naturally, he saw little use in trying to reform it. "For us, the Senate is a relic that could not and should not survive an hour of a political insurrectional storm", he wrote in 1911. The original fascist programme of 1919 included a demand for the abolition of the Senate; but despite the long duration of the fascist "insurrectional storm", the Senate still survives, for the fascist Duce finds that it can be used profitably for his "revolutionary" purposes. Of the two bodies, the Senate and the Chamber, he feigns most respect for the Senate and he prefers it when he wants to make a "serious" political speech. He enjoys the fawning reverence of the majority of the "old fogies". But not all Italian Senators are old fogies. For in their midst, there have risen to speak out their thoughts against fascism, men of principle and of courage who, in defiance of threats of violence, have defended the liberal and democratic traditions of Italy—among them Senators Luigi Albertini, the publisher and editor (until he was forced out by the fascists) of what was once the greatest Italian daily and one of the greatest papers in Europe, *Il Corriere della Sera;* Ettore Ciccotti, the noted historian and political writer; Benedetto Croce, the greatest Italian philosopher since Vico and probably the greatest living philosopher; Luigi Einaudi, one of Italy's leading economists; Gaetano Mosca, the author of remarkable works on political theory; Francesco Ruffini, the distinguished historical scholar, biographer, and canonist; and Count Carlo Sforza, one of post-war Europe's ablest Foreign Ministers. The much-maligned Chamber of Deputies brought out, among others, two martyrs to the right of free discussion: the deputies Giacomo Matteotti, who was brutally murdered by fascists in 1924, and Giovanni Amendola, who died in 1926 as a consequence of injuries inflicted upon him by a fascist mob.

It is obvious that in regard to parliamentary and democratic rule, there is a fundamental coherence in Mussolini's entire political career as a socialist and as a fascist. His apprenticeship in the left wing of the socialist party proved to be an excellent school for his activity as the fascist Duce and for the prostitution by him of representative institutions as free organs of expression. He has done everything in his power to destroy these institutions, at first in the name of social revolution, and later in the name of fascism. All his abusive attacks on parliament are much more applicable to parliament under his own fascist system than to Italian pre-fascist parliaments of this century. Whatever may be said of the defects and imperfections of the latter, it must not be forgotten that they dealt with problems in an atmosphere of liberty and free discussion. And if they were unequal to many burdensome tasks, special thanks are due to men like Mussolini who took advantage of every opportunity to weaken rather than to strengthen them. Giolitti was indeed powerful, but in no sense was he a dictator ruling by martial law. Compared with the total destruction of all forms of liberty under fascism (with the exception, of course, of the liberty of those in the fascist high command), the personal, moral, political, religious, and intellectual liberty enjoyed under the liberal ministers of Italy, let us say of Giolitti, was wide indeed. And yet, in 1911, Mussolini called Giolitti the destroyer of liberty, the "liberticide". To use a phrase that Mussolini once applied to Giolitti, what have the fascist Chamber and Senate done since 1925 but await "the hour for hosannas to their master"—Mussolini? And to use another phrase of Mussolini, what have the fascist deputies and senators done but follow him "with the docility of a dog that follows its master everywhere"?

Nothing could be farther from the truth than the libels and falsehoods that Mussolini and his fascist followers have heaped upon democratic Italy. They have been given so much currency that many so-called objective students of history have been misled into constructing a false picture of pre-fascist Italy. It is rapidly becoming fashionable to regard the history of modern Italy from Cavour to the fascist rule of Mussolini as a sorrowful spectacle. And yet, it is not at all hazardous to assert, after making allowances for her bad heritage, that Italy made as much progress between 1870 and the fascist

"March on Rome" in 1922 as any other country in Europe during the same period of time.

Although Benito Mussolini owes his rapid rise in political power to the democratic system, although he was a beneficiary of this system, he has always despised it and has helped to destroy it, not in order to give men a surer sense of freedom, but in order to enslave them to his personal will. Starting off as "a plebeian of the twentieth century", he ended up in devoting his political gifts to the destruction of liberty. When he was out of office, he decried the censorship and maintained that the freedom of assembly was a sacred and inviolable right; but once he attained power as the fascist Duce, he denied every elementary political and civil right to all but himself and his devoted followers, and he talked of the goddess of liberty as a corpse.

11. THE SECESSIONIST

As editor-in-chief of *The Class Struggle* and as leader of the Forlì socialist federation, Mussolini turned the full force of his polemical ardour against the official Italian socialist party and its three central organizations—the *Avanti!*, the Executive Committee, and the Socialist Parliamentary Group. No newspaper, he boasted in the spring of 1911, had criticized the socialist party, its policies, and its representative men as bitterly as his. By threatening the secession of the Forlì federation from the party, he sought to maintain the revolutionary spirit of his local comrades in high tension and to bring pressure upon the national organization to accentuate its revolutionary stand on all questions.

One of his pet phobias was the *Avanti!*, whose editor-in-chief was Bissolati. It was "as illegible in the moral as in the material sense" and so "bourgeois" that he called it "a liberal national organ". This paper "wearies our soul with long articles in which it very artfully seeks to justify the conduct of the Socialist Parliamentary Group".

The publication of the *Avanti!* at Rome made it so responsive to the parliamentary group that it aroused Mussolini's bitter criticism. Especially during the year 1910, one of the chief topics of discussion among Italian socialists concerned the advisability of publishing the *Avanti!* at Milan or Bologna. Filippo Turati, the leading reformist socialist, still favoured Rome. Mussolini was unalterably opposed to the view of Turati, whom he described as the "Grand Lama of Italian reformism", and he published an envenomed tirade against the city of Rome, which is perhaps unparalleled in the history of modern Italian journalism and political literature. His remarks about the "Eternal City" contrast sharply with his lyrical and almost hysterical exaltation of Rome since the fascists assumed power:

"Rome—parasitical city of furnished-room keepers, boot-blacks, prostitutes, priests and bureaucrats—Rome—city without a proletariat worthy of the name—is not the centre of national political life, but rather the centre and the focus of infection of the national political life. Even Roman journalism is that of a large provincial city, certainly not that of a capital. The great Italian newspapers are not published in the political capital, Rome, but in the moral capital, Milan.*** Why the obstinacy to fight in a city that is also unhappy from a journalistic point of view? Enough then with the stupid unitary prejudice because of which everything, everything must be concentrated in Rome, this huge vampire-city that sucks the best blood of the nation. Dario Papa [a distinguished republican publicist] was fully aware of the nefarious influence that Rome exercises on the life of the nation when he wanted the capital of Italy to be established at Perugia. If it be true that we are federalists and partisans of political and administrative decentralization, let us begin once and for all to put our theories into practice by 'decentralizing' subversive journalism from Rome, taking it away from direct contact with the equivocal parliamentary world and transporting it to a place where the rhythm of our vitality is more passionate."

In October 1910, Mussolini brought to the national socialist congress at Milan all his grievances against the party. This was the first national socialist congress that he attended, and it was here that he made his oratorical debut before the national organization. On the whole, his debut was a fiasco. The congress was dominated by reformists of various gradations, and among those who took a leading part in it were Turati, Bissolati, Cabrini, Morgari, Salvemini, and Modigliani. The small, and at that time rather insignificant, extreme revolutionary group was represented principally by its leader, Lazzari, Giovanni Lerda, Francesco Ciccotti, Serrati, Angelica Balabanoff, and the socialist deputy Elia Musatti. Mussolini was an obscure member of this group which, through a series of circumstances we shall presently describe, obtained control of the party in 1912 with him as its leader.

At the Milan congress, the revolutionary group made a poor showing in the voting, receiving only about 6,000 votes out of about 24,000 ballots that were cast. As the delegate of the Forlì socialists, Mussolini began his speech in his usual straightforward, "telegraphic" manner as follows:

"I shall make a few telegraphic declarations: first, not to prolong this discussion, which savours a good deal of an academy or of an ecumenical council, and then, to heed the recommendations made by the chairman. I have signed the Lazzari [revolutionary] resolution although I have ideas on everything which perhaps would be very much out of tune with the ideas that appear to predominate in this congress, where everyone seems to be playing with mutes-on.[1] Instead, I shall strain the note, and by straining it, it may seem to be out of tune. Meanwhile, I call to the attention of those who have extolled universal suffrage that advanced nations, like Austria and Germany, have universal suffrage; and it is not yet certain that socialism can be attained through it. I call to the attention of those who have extolled social legislation that in the countries where it is most widespread, we are still very far away from socialism. England is a case in point. Finally, I declare that if the Italian proletariat were no longer represented by deputies in parliament, the harm would be slight. And last of all, I declare that the matter of the fatherland, this old *cliché* of the fatherland in danger, is the ideological *cliché* of all the bourgeois democracies, with which *cliché* the blood has been pumped from the poverty-stricken proletariat for the past 30 years. (*Some applause.*)"

Mussolini then denounced the attitude of the national organization toward the economic conflicts between the republicans and the socialists in the Romagna. "You must know that in the Romagna, at Campiano and the surrounding districts, there were hundreds of men who were armed, and not with idle chatter, and you know that when people in the Romagna have weapons in their hands, it is, unfortunately, no joke! (*Rumblings.*)" As for the agreement which the national organization, in its desire for peace, supported, it

[1] In the stenographic report of the congress which I have used, the word "although" in this sentence reads "because" ("*perchè*"). I am fairly sure the word "*perchè*" is a typographical error for the word "*benchè*", meaning "although".

"solves nothing. It is a temporary truce, and I can tell you that the struggle will continue even more tragically than it has hitherto (*Voices*: bad, bad!). Conditions so will it! (*Interruptions*.) Because the Italian socialists have understood nothing about the conflict in the Romagna . . . (*Uuuh, uuuh!*) You have always given us a wailing kind of solidarity and you have always talked about brotherhood, but this is buncombe! There [in the Romagna], people live in full revolution, and this is what you have not understood! (*Rumblings. Some applause.*)"

Despite the interruptions, Mussolini continued to say that the Romagnuole socialists would not change their tactics. "And I shall tell you another thing: that if the socialist party (and may the comparison not seem to you to be irreverent) were a company, let us say a pharmaceutical one, it would very soon go into bankruptcy because an accounting would be asked of its representatives, and when an agent does not do well, does not represent well, what does the company do? It dismisses him. All right, [our socialist] deputies have not at all represented us well!"

Mussolini closed his speech rather abruptly with a bitter attack on the flaccid reformist socialists and their deputies in parliament. "Continue then, if you like, in the policy of a dish of lentils, and you will see where we will end up! I shall cite for you a very recent document which to me is of exceptional gravity. The other day *Le Temps*, the most authoritative representative of the French republican bourgeoisie, eulogized our reformists and said: If we over here had had an *équipe* of Italian socialists instead of this Jaurès who has aligned himself with the most turbulent elements in Paris, this strike [of the French railway men] would have been cut short by their counsels. (*Applause.*)

"Podrecca [interrupting]: And this would have been a good thing! (*Rumblings.*)

"Mussolini: To this certificate of good conduct that the republican bourgeoisie of France has given to our reformists, there will soon be added another: that of the Italian bourgeoisie. And I shall say nothing more. (*Some applause.*)"

While the congress was still in session, Mussolini displayed his utter exasperation with the party when he proposed to a caucus of the revolutionary group that it secede from the party. Perhaps the poor reception of his speech had something to do with this. In any case, it is remarkable that he seems to have been the only member of the revolutionary group to insist upon its immediate secession from the party. Lazzari, Musatti, Lerda, Serrati, Angelica Balabanoff and Ciccotti were opposed to such a drastic step.

Some of the newspaper reports of Mussolini's speech at the congress are interesting. A correspondent of the very conservative Turin daily *Il Momento* persisted in giving his name as Mussolino, not Mussolini, thus calling attention to its similarity with the name of the notorious Italian brigand Musolino: "The quasi-namesake of the ill-famed brigand calmly ascends the platform. There is nothing terrible about him: only a deep bass voice." Farther on, the correspondent, after again noting Mussolini's "magnificent bass voice", stated that he spoke "simply but with great sharpness", and that "his words made a profound impression, especially those referring to the Romagna agreement". The republican weekly of Rome, *La Rivista Popolare*, edited by the republican deputy Napoleone Colajanni, also used the name "Mussolino", but as distinguished from the *Momento's* report, it said that Mussolini "criticizes everything and everybody, but without any originality", adding that the congress had displayed lack of interest in his speech. The conservative Rome daily *La Tribuna* made Mussolini look ridiculous in its summary of his speech which it published under the heading "Intermezzo allegro". Mussolini, it tells us, seemed to have the function of amusing the audience, and when he referred to *Le Temps*, etc., "the delegates still laugh and so loudly that Mussolini is forced to cut short his speech". *La Ragione*, a republican daily of Rome, described Mussolini as an "individualist, syndicalist revolutionist". Goffredo Bellonci, the correspondent of the *Giornale D'Italia* of Rome, observed that Mussolini was "a genuine peasant, whose oratory is characterized by short, staccato sentences".

"I wish I were!" was Mussolini's reaction to Bellonci's description. The future Duce thought his speech was fairly well received "when it is borne in mind that I am not and I shall never be known as one of the jugglers of Montecitorio. On the other hand, my speech was so little keyed to the general symphony and it sounded so heretical that I am surprised I was not stoned. The daily newspapers altered what I had said . . . All the newspapers agreed in saying that my speech had been very brief. After twenty hours of idle chatter, a little conciseness wasn't bad."

As usual, Mussolini likes to emphasize his unconventional, iconoclastic attitudes; he glories in pointing out his pre-eminently individual position on any problem. Not only would he *épater le bourgeois*, but also would he *épater* his own comrades, whether socialists or fascists.

After the Milan congress, Mussolini returned to Forlì filled with contempt for the national party organization. For him, the congress was "a big, useless academy". Instead of facing issues squarely, the reformists, supported by a "devout herd", tried to build up an alibi for their activity and dealt in generalities. "The congress embarked on a large sea of principles, theories and words, and for three very long days, orators of every tendency vomited a diluvium of phrases to the audience.*** Few of the speakers limited themselves to saying what was necessary, to communicating their ideas simply, without oratorical fringes. Instead, almost all of them *orated* in the classic sense of the word."

"There is here," added Mussolini, "on the stage of the political comedy of the third Italy, a big corpse: the official socialist party. Should it be buried?"

The *Lotta di Classe* became more outspoken in its censure of the national socialist leaders and policies. In 1911, Mussolini urged the Executive Committee of the party to do everything in its power to ruin the celebration of the fiftieth anniversary of the founding of United Italy. "Let us spoil the celebration of the monarchy's semi-centennial. Let us find the way to spoil it. This is the task which the Italian socialists must set before themselves in 1911. Dare . . . try . . . Only with new sacrifices will our party get out of the marasmus that is slowly killing it." It was necessary to have a general strike that would lead to a *"tournant* in Italian political history", not the usual futile mass meetings, not "sterile agitations like the masturbating exercises of seminarists", not festive general strikes which do not terrify but amuse the bourgeoisie.

Mussolini's clamours were completely disregarded by the Executive Committee and the *Avanti!* Fully realizing that the party was an unhappy union of diverse and ill-cemented elements and that it could not be a revolutionary instrument as long as it contained so many different currents, from those of right-wingers like Bissolati and Bonomi to those of left-wingers like himself, he took the unusual step of withdrawing from the party and bringing along with him the Forlì socialist federation in April 1911. A few days after Bissolati's visit to the King in connection with the forming of a new ministry to succeed the one headed by Luzzatti, Mussolini, in the name of the Forlì federation, sent the following telegram to the Executive Committee: "Liquidate Giolittian, monarchical, realist Bissolati or fifty sections of the Forlì federation will leave the party." The Executive Committee paid no attention to this telegram and to similar threats from many Italian socialists. Mussolini felt that it was high time to destroy the fetish of the Goddess of Party Unity. "Down with party unity!" was his cry as he convinced the socialist section of Forlì, the Executive Committee of the Forlì federation and the entire federation to secede from the party. Proclaiming the need for audacity, for daring, he wrote on April 15:

"The ice is broken.*** All hesitation has disappeared, must disappear. It is a question not of raising a new political flag, but of saving the old socialist flag from the profanation of those who have gathered under its folds. It is not a new gospel that we want to preach, but it is always the old gospel of socialism, formulated in international congresses, which guides and will guide our propaganda, our action and our battles."

It was while advocating secession that Mussolini made the

following declaration regarding resolutions of protest: "What shall we do? Vote resolutions? Everyone knows what efficacy they have. The risk is run of being taken for fools. We would cut the figure of the good man who finds his wife fornicating with his enemy and instead of throwing him out of his home or going away, rushes to the window and cries out his misfortune to the whole neighbourhood."

The Forlì federation, which is tantamount to saying Mussolini, was, I think, the only local socialist organization that seceded from the party in the period 1910–1912. Mussolini's purpose was to make the Forlì group the nucleus of a nation-wide revolutionary socialist party. Had he succeeded, an organization might have been founded in Italy similar to the Bolshevik organization in the Russian revolutionary ranks. His type of revolutionist would have borne the same relation to the Italian reformists that the Russian Bolsheviks of the Lenin school bore to the Russian Mensheviks. Though he was wholly unsuccessful, he seemed to be happy in his isolation, accentuating his criticism of the official party and refusing to heed those revolutionary socialists who urged him to return to it. For about five months, from the middle of October 1911 to the middle of March 1912, his propagandist work was interrupted because he was in prison for opposing the Turco-Italian War.

Meanwhile, the revolutionary forces in the party were rapidly gaining strength. Despite the absence of the Forlì federation, they made a better showing at the Modena national socialist congress in October 1911 than at the Milan congress a year before. The more marked reformism of the Bissolati group, its ill-disguised support of Italy's war against Turkey, and, above all, its benevolent attitude towards the monarchy after D'Alba's attempt to assassinate King Victor Emmanuel, convinced many socialists that a revolutionary tactic was imperative. Even the reformists of the centre, led by Turati and Treves, notwithstanding their long and warm association with the Bissolati group, admitted that it had veered too far to the right. The numbers of the revolutionary faction were swelled by new recruits in the socialist party, who were resolutely opposed to the Turco-Italian War. So clearly did Bissolati and his friends realize their growing unpopularity in the party that they were prepared to be excommunicated.

Immediately after his release from prison in March 1912, Mussolini went back to his post as editor of the *Lotta* and as leader of the Forlì federation, and he entered upon a feverish anti-reformist campaign. Since it was generally expected that the "crisis" in the party would be squarely faced at the national socialist congress to be held at Reggio Emilia in July 1912, he realized that he could do very little while his federation remained alone and isolated. It was clear to him that he could best serve his own interests and the interests of the revolutionary cause if the Forlì federation re-entered the party. In April 1912, one year after the federation had decided to leave the party at the instance of Mussolini, the federation, again at the instance of Mussolini, decided to rejoin the party with the aim of contributing to its "prompt cleansing".

Under no circumstances would the Duce of the Forlì socialists tolerate peace or compromise with the Bissolatians. He demanded their expulsion. "General absolution. Oh! what a fine holiday! Oh! what a fine holiday . . . is being prepared at Reggio Emilia. But we will spoil it. This is necessary if for no other reason than to render homage to the goddess sincerity.*** Expulsion! This is the word before which so many socialists, of the Right and of the Left, recoil. But is it not an act that is so frequent and so natural in the life of parties? Call this intolerance, if you wish. We shall demonstrate to you that it is not so and that in any case, it is such intolerance that saves parties. It can be a painful operation for those who cause it and for those who undergo it, but it is pain that purifies and liberates. When the wise surgeon realizes the futility of any other cure and wishes to avoid gangrene, he resorts to amputation."

Although his advanced stand at the Milan congress of 1910, his imprisonment for opposing the Turco-Italian War, his striking act in having the Forlì federation secede from the party and his collaboration with the organ of the revolutionists "*La Soffitta*" ("*The Attic*") had made him a familiar figure to members of the extremist group in the national organization, he was almost completely unknown to the reformists of the Right and of the Centre who still controlled the party. In the spring and early summer of 1912, no sign appeared that presaged his rapid rise to leadership in the national organization. And yet, in less than a·year, he was to become the leader of the Italian socialist party. No man in the history of the party had in so short a time risen from a position of almost complete obscurity to a position of commanding importance in the party organization. When, at the congress of Reggio Emilia, Mussolini assumed the rôle of the major speaker on behalf of the revolutionary faction, most of the delegates had to ask who he was. He turned out to be the "dark horse" of the congress. At Milan in October 1910, his speech was a fiasco. At Reggio Emilia in July 1912, his speech was an oratorical triumph. The "mystery" of his meteoric rise to prominence is to be sought, I think, in the paucity of leaders in the revolutionary group of the party and in his close acquaintance with four of its principal representatives, namely, Costantino Lazzari, Angelica Balabanoff, Francesco Ciccotti, and G. M. Serrati. As yet he was not on close personal terms with the other leaders, namely, Giovanni Lerda, his wife Oda Olberg Lerda, Elia Musatti, Giovanni Bacci, Alceste Della Seta, and Arturo Vella.

Lazzari was the real head of the revolutionary faction. He was pre-eminently an able organizer, with no marked ability as an orator or as a writer. Aside from doctrinal differences, he had for many years nourished a personal grudge against the reformists, especially Turati. While a youthful immigrant in Switzerland in 1902, Mussolini cited and agreed with Lazzari's censure of the reformists. They met personally at the Milan congress in 1910 and became better acquainted when Mussolini invited Lazzari to address his Forlì comrades and to write for the *Lotta di Classe*. Lazzari apparently was deeply impressed with Mussolini, and he, more than any other single person, determined Mussolini's rapid rise to leadership. For two years, between 1912 and 1914, while

Mussolini was editor of the *Avanti!*, he and Lazzari worked hand in hand, but when Mussolini began to preach intervention in the Great War, Lazzari denounced him bitterly for his "betrayal" of the socialist movement and regretted whatever help he had given him. As he said in November 1914, it was he who had proposed, supported, and defended the nomination of Mussolini to the editorship of the *Avanti!* in 1912.

Besides Lazzari, Mussolini knew Serrati and Angelica Balabanoff, both of whom he had met during his sojourn in Switzerland between 1902 and 1904. They looked upon Mussolini with great favour and used their influence to his advantage in 1912. Later, in 1914, they became Mussolini's bitter personal and political enemies when he rather abruptly abandoned his anti-war position, left the *Avanti!*, founded *Il Popolo d'Italia*, and joined the proponents of war. Serrati succeeded to the editorship of the *Avanti!*, and for several years, he and Mussolini carried on the most venomous personal feud that the last thirty years of Italian political history record. In her remarkable "Memoirs", published in German at Berlin in 1927 and in Italian at Paris in 1931, Madame Balabanoff presents one of the most disparaging estimates ever made of Mussolini's character. She pours forth her bile against the "traitor" of Italian socialism, accuses him of physical, moral, and intellectual cowardice and attributes the basest qualities to this "ill-famed", "vulgar" man, the "Judas of Italian socialism", who "sold" himself to the enemies of the proletariat. If the name of Mussolini will be remembered in history, writes Madame Balabanoff, it will be because he personifies Judas and Cain, the symbol of what is most infamous and opprobrious, "the venal betrayal, the stabbing in the back of a brother. The modern Judas [Mussolini] surpassed his predecessors: he betrayed a *class*." A full and searching analysis of the "Memoirs" of Madame Balabanoff would take too much space in this volume. Much of what she says about Mussolini is sketchy, questionable, and debatable. She writes from memory, sometimes rather loosely and without proper documentation, of a man with whom she once collaborated and whom she now detests. Her review of Mussolini's activities should have been more thorough.

Other active supporters of Mussolini's advance to leadership were the able journalist Francesco Ciccotti and the prominent socialist deputy from Venice, Elia Musatti, both of whom were more important spokesmen of the revolutionary faction than Mussolini. Musatti had met Mussolini in the Trentino in the early part of 1909, and it was he who had interpellated the Italian Cabinet on Mussolini's expulsion from Austria-Hungary. Ciccotti had come to know and admire Mussolini at Forlì in 1911 and 1912, and during the latter's stay in prison for opposing the Turco-Italian War, he had served as the editor of the *Lotta di Classe*. In January 1912, Ciccotti had written in this paper the first full-length panegyric of Mussolini, a man who "has the brains of a direct descendant of Socrates".

On the eve of the Reggio Emilia congress, Claudio Treves, the distinguished reformist socialist leader and Bissolati's successor as editor of the *Avanti!*, pointed out in a brilliant editorial that the revolutionary group was by no means homogeneous in its views. He singled out Mussolini as an exponent of "revolutionary idealism", of "classic revolutionism", with its "catastrophic" conception of the revolutionary process, its depreciation of reforms like universal suffrage, its disparagement of trade-union work, its exaltation of violence, and its insistence on the immediate conquest of political power. Treves referred to Mussolini's speech at a congress of the Romagna socialist organizations in June 1912, describing it as a "speech of great sweep, worthy of much consideration", and noted how the Romagnuole agitator had "lucidly" expressed the absolute incompatibility between revolutionary idealism and a policy of reforms.

It was a mark of the acute mind of Treves that he recognized in Mussolini a revolutionary leader who had a clear notion of what he wanted. His article is important not only because it clearly set forth the ideological opposition between the reformists and the revolutionists, but also because it prominently brought out Mussolini's name in the daily organ

of the socialist party while he was still obscure. When Mussolini became the Duce of the socialist party, Treves was one of
his *bêtes noires* in the internal party struggles. As editor of the
Avanti!, he saw to it that the contributions of Treves to the
paper were reduced to a minimum. Their personal relations
were never cordial, and after Mussolini left the *Avanti!*, he
and Treves engaged in bitter polemics, even fighting a duel.
The fascists forced Treves and his intimate friend Turati to
flee from Italy. Both died in exile. With their passing, Italy
lost the two principal leaders of its reformist socialist movement and two conspicuous defenders of its democratic
tradition.

The congress of Reggio Emilia held its sessions on July
7, 8, 9, and 10, 1912. Reggio Emilia is situated a few miles
from Gualtieri Emilia, the small town where Mussolini had
his first experience as an elementary school teacher in 1902.
Mussolini's speech, delivered on July 8, was the most
striking address made at the congress, notable less for its
doctrinal content than for its truculent and uncompromising
tone. This time Mussolini was attentively heard and not
ignored or taken lightly as he had been at the Milan congress
two years before. He must have been filled with vindictive
glee at this change of circumstances. His speech was an oratorical success, not a fiasco. He had complete command of
himself and spoke with his usual air of assurance. He was not
disturbed by interruptions; rather, he welcomed them and
enjoyed the pandemonium and confusion that accompanied
his demand that the reformists of the Right be expelled from
the party. Mussolini's speech as the chief prosecutor for the
revolutionary group contains nothing of importance that has
not already been discussed. Most of it was devoted to a violent
arraignment of the socialist parliamentary group, with special
emphasis on the "betrayal" of Bissolati, Bonomi, Cabrini,
and Guido Podrecca. His resolution proposing the expulsion
of these four leaders from the party was approved by a large
vote.

It was when he turned his verbal assault on Bissolati that
Mussolini exclaimed: "Ex ore tuo, te iudico"—the words we

have chosen for the epigraph of this book. Assailing Bissolati's change of position towards the monarchy, Mussolini charged that while Bissolati, in 1900, had justified the censure of the socialist De Marinis for participating in the funeral of King Humbert, who had been assassinated, he had, in 1912, stooped to visit the Quirinal after D'Alba's attempt to kill King Victor Emmanuel.

A few "bourgeois" and non-socialist newspaper reports throw some light on the appearance of "Professor" Mussolini and on the character of his speech. The *Corriere della Sera* of Milan wrote that Mussolini, "lean, bitter, who speaks explosively, with sincerity, is liked by the congress, which feels that it has in him an interpreter of its feelings.*** Mussolini, who spoke with ardour and sincere agitation, leaves the platform, pale and tired." Another Milan daily, *Il Secolo*, spoke of the marked revolutionism, the varied culture, and the deep-rooted rebellious instinct of this "novel Romagnuole agitator". Mario Sobrero, the correspondent of the *Gazzetta del Popolo* of Turin, referred to the phrenetic applause extended to Mussolini, who "hurls himself with vehemence against the parliamentary group". The violence of Mussolini's attack on the reformists of the Right "inflames the congress where there break out disturbances attended by the exchange of insults and put down with great difficulty by the energy of the chairman". With regard to the visit of socialist deputies to the Quirinal after the attempt on the King's life, Mussolini "comes out with judgments of an anarchist complexion, which are very loudly applauded by the audience". Farther on, Sobrero remarked: "The attack of Benito Mussolini, truly sectarian and fierce, received with applause by the assembly, is an evident sign of the psychology of the assembly.*** A dramatic element was not lacking in the situation of the four accused [Bissolati, Bonomi, Cabrini, Podrecca], almost alone, before the openly hostile assembly." The correspondent of the *Resto del Carlino* of Bologna, Angelo Ragghianti, noted Mussolini's "abundance of gestures and expressions that make him resemble a Chinaman".

Among the socialists who praised Mussolini were Paolo

Valera, the publisher and editor of a lively illustrated Milan weekly, *La Folla* (*The Crowd*), and Amilcare Cipriani, the famous Romagnuole, "red" agitator, after whom Mussolini received one of his baptismal names. For many years, Cipriani had been living in exile in Paris, where he often contributed to *L'Humanité*, the French socialist daily edited by Jean Jaurès. In a comment on the Reggio Emilia congress, Cipriani had this to say in *L'Humanité:* "To-day, there is, among those who have triumphed at the Congress of Reggio Emilia, a man, Mussolini, whose resolution was victorious. I like him very much. His revolutionism is mine, I should say, ours—that is, a revolutionism that is called classic." This estimate, coming from one of the chief idols of the Romagnuole revolutionary socialists and anarchists, who was almost in his seventies, was flattering to twenty-nine-year-old Mussolini. In September 1912, Mussolini used capital letters in referring to Cipriani as "HIM".

Valera and Mussolini warmly admired each other ever since their first meeting at Trent in 1909. After the Reggio congress, Valera acclaimed Mussolini in the following language: "Benito Mussolini is an intellectual of revolutionary socialism. He is a personality. He has a style of his own. He writes as he pleases. He gives you an agitated, indignant, furious, tempestuous prose, fighting against everybody. He does not know deviations. He is all of bronze. He is a man with ideas.*** He is a professor of foreign languages.*** He is an orator. He held the floor at the socialist congress of Reggio Emilia. It was he who, with his vehemence, sincere to the point of brutality, demanded the expulsion of the Rightists and won the *Avanti!* for the revolutionists. His speech is memorable. It has made history."

In August 1912, Mussolini began his collaboration with *La Folla* under the pseudonym *L'homme qui cherche*. He enlivened the muckraking, and what he once called the "Zolian", pages of this weekly with trenchant articles, calumniating Italy's war against Turkey and the Italian journalists who indulged in orgiastic glorification of wars of conquest. It was in the *Folla* that Mussolini delivered a furious tirade against those hypocrites, mountebanks, tricksters, and "cartilaginous spines" in the revolutionary ranks, who had betrayed their socialist past in order to support Italy's war, holding up to the scorn of all men such ex-revolutionists as Paolo Orano and Tomaso Monicelli (who are now fascists), for revealing precisely that kind of apostasy and desertion of a cause that he himself was to exemplify with superb completeness when he eventually became the standard-bearer of fascism.

The congress of Reggio Emilia sealed the first complete and sweeping victory of the revolutionary group in the party. The reformists of the Right who had been expelled proceeded to form the "Italian Reformist Socialist Party". The less moderate reformists, the reformists of the Centre, including such men as Turati, Treves, Prampolini, and Modigliani, remained in the official socialist party although they had been routed at the congress. Giovanni Bacci, of the revolutionary faction, replaced Treves as editor of the *Avanti!*, and Francesco Ciccotti became its Rome correspondent. The Executive Committee of the party was completely reorganized and manned by members of the victorious revolutionary group. As it was a tradition of the party to have on its Executive Committee representatives of its minority sections, the reformists of the Centre were invited to choose two of their men to serve on the Committee, but they refused on the ground that they preferred to have the revolutionists assume full responsibility for their experiment. On the basis of conversations I have had with several socialists who attended the congress, it seems to me that this refusal was predicated on the general feeling among the reformists that the revolutionists would fail to administer and carry on successfully the work of the party. They were confident that the untried and inexperienced revolutionists, upon showing their incapacity, would be either turned out of the party or relegated again to their minority position. In this view, they were sadly disappointed, for the revolutionary group proved to be more than equal to its task, in the success of which Mussolini played a dominant rôle.

The revolutionists had now gained control of two of the most powerful organs of the party, the *Avanti!* and the Executive Committee. The third organ was the Socialist Parliamentary Group which was still dominated by reformists like Turati and Treves. In order to bring it into line with the revolutionary policies sanctioned at the Reggio Emilia congress, the revolutionists deprived the Group of its autonomy in settling matters of socialist policy in parliament and insisted that in such matters, the Group should be under the control of and responsible to the Executive Committee.

The new Executive Committee included, among others, Costantino Lazzari as secretary-general of the party, Arturo Vella as vice secretary-general, Adolfo Zerbini as secretary-general for administrative matters, Bacci, the lawyer Alceste Della Seta, Angelica Balabanoff, Mussolini, and the deputies Gregorio Agnini and Elia Musatti. The election of Mussolini to the powerful post of member of the Executive Committee was an immediate recognition of his abilities and of his striking performance at the congress of Reggio Emilia. An important, though not decisive, element in his election was the fact that the Romagna region would thereby have a delegate on the Committee. It was customary to have as many Italian regions as possible represented on the Committee.

After the congress of Reggio Emilia ended its sessions on July 10, Mussolini resumed his work as editor of the *Lotta di Classe* and as secretary of the Forlì socialist federation. In October, he became secretary of the socialist federations of the electoral colleges of Forlì, Cesena, San Arcangelo, and Rimini, which had formed a single organization. His attendance at meetings of the Executive Committee in various Italian centres made him better known to the leading figures of the party, and his signed contributions to the *Avanti!*, including an enthusiastic review of an Italian translation of Daniel Halévy's *Life of Nietzsche*, brought his name before a large socialist public.

Even then, in the autumn of 1912, no one suspected that Mussolini would soon be entrusted with an unusual rôle in the party. His great opportunity to assume a post of commanding importance may be said to have arisen quite accidentally, as a result of circumstances centring about the editorship of the *Avanti!* Giovanni Bacci, who had been selected by the revolutionary group, was a good-natured man with some capacity for administrative work, but he was utterly unfit to edit the *Avanti!*; from a journalistic point of view, he was decidedly inferior to his predecessors—Bissolati, Enrico Ferri (in many other respects a charlatan), Morgari, and Treves. It must be said that Bacci, realizing his shortcomings as a journalist, had accepted his appointment conditionally, until a more suitable man could be found. While he was editor, the *Avanti!* fared badly.

Francesco Ciccotti, who had had considerable experience as a journalist, was considered, but he preferred to serve as its Rome correspondent, a key position because of the political doings at the capital. The Hon. Elia Musatti was also approached. Personal reasons played a large part in his refusal. His home and law office were in Venice; his duties as a deputy required his frequent presence in Rome; and he could not arrange to establish his residence at Milan where the *Avanti!* was published. Other active revolutionary social- ists who were available for the *Avanti!* post were G. M. Serrati and Giovanni Lerda. As editor of *"La Soffitta"* (*"The Attic"*), the organ of the revolutionary socialists in 1911 and 1912, Lerda had achieved an important position among the revo- lutionists, but he was disqualified for the editorship of the *Avanti!* because of his membership in the Masonic Order which was steadily encountering the disfavour of many socialists who insisted that a person should not be at once a Freemason and a member of the socialist party.

Although Serrati was well known as a socialist agitator and journalist and although he was older than most of the leaders of the revolutionary faction (he was, incidentally, about ten years older than Mussolini), he was generally unpopular in socialist circles. I think that the chief reason why Serrati was not selected for the editorship of the *Avanti!* in 1912 was that in the year 1903, while he was editing *Il Proletario*, the paper of the Italian socialists in the United States, he became involved in a violent polemic with Italian anarchists at Barre, Vermont. The polemic and a scuffle between Italian anarchists and socialists resulting in the killing of an anarchist caused the anarchists to denounce Serrati as a "spy" and as an instigator of "assassination". The "American incident" lent such an unsavoury element to Serrati's career that the future leader of the Italian communists had to wait until Mussolini's resignation from the *Avanti!* in 1914 before he could become its editor-in-chief.

Interesting but fruitless negotiations were also carried on with the socialist deputy Ettore Ciccotti, who must not in any way be confused with Francesco Ciccotti. We have referred to him in our chapter on Mussolini as a hater of parliament. He was one of a dozen or so Italian socialists who had really studied Marx. In the year 1904, owing to a series of circumstances which we need not discuss here, he dissociated himself from the official socialist party; but although he ceased to be a member of the party, he remained a socialist. After his election to parliament in 1909 as an independent socialist and not as a candidate of the socialist party, he declined the invitation of the socialist deputies Bertesi and Morgari to join the Socialist Parliamentary Group. Lazzari, hoping for Ciccotti's help in combating the reformists, also requested Ciccotti to rejoin the party. In June 1912, about three weeks before the congress of Reggio Emilia, when it appeared certain that the revolutionary group would gain control of the party, Arturo Vella wrote to Ciccotti asking him to allow his name to be put forth as the revolutionists' candidate for the editorship of the *Avanti!* In addition, Vella orally made similar requests of Ciccotti before and after the congress. Ciccotti turned a deaf ear to these requests. It is noteworthy that Mussolini, who had a great admiration for Ciccotti's independence, wrote in the *Lotta di Classe* as early as June 1910, that he hoped to see Ciccotti made editor of the *Avanti!* after the Milan congress of October 1910.

The negotiations that were carried on with Francesco Ciccotti, Musatti, and Ettore Ciccotti were unknown to the

general public. In November 1912, when the Executive Committee met to settle, among other things, the problem of the
Avanti!, it accepted Bacci's resignation from the editorship
of the paper and named Mussolini in his place. Although
contemporary reports state that the Executive Committee
appointed Mussolini to his new post by a unanimous vote, it
seems quite clear from several sources, both written and oral,
that one member of the Committee, Arturo Vella, did not
approve of Mussolini's appointment. He felt that Mussolini
was not a genuine exponent of the dominant point of view in
the revolutionary, intransigent faction that had just gained
control of the party. On the whole, there was no real opposition to Mussolini's appointment.

The Forlì socialists were elated by Mussolini's appointment.
Their leader, the editor of what had been a small and rather
obscure weekly, had now been elevated to one of the highest
positions in the national socialist organization. As the new
editorial board of the *Lotta di Classe* put it, they all felt proud
that they had contributed to the success of a "man, who is
a method and a symbol ***, who for three years, fearless
and penetrating, bold and imperturbable, had given his all,
leaving a profound impression on our passionate Romagna".

At a banquet in Mussolini's honour, held at Forlimpopoli
in December 1912, the socialist lawyer Gino Giommi voiced
the sentiments of the Forlì socialists when he spoke of twenty-
nine-year-old Mussolini as the man "who for three years was
our upright duce". Several months earlier in the same year,
Mussolini had been described as the "duce" of the Forlì
socialists by a writer for "*The Attic*." In 1904, when he was
twenty, he had been called the "great duce" of the Italian
socialist club of Geneva, Switzerland, by a correspondent of
the Rome daily *La Tribuna*. He heard Giommi's tribute with
his own ears; he doubtless read the tribute paid to him in
"*The Attic*"; and it is in this book that he will read for the
first time the reference in *La Tribuna*.

Mussolini left Forlì and settled at Milan late in November
1912, assuming his duties as editor-in-chief of the *Avanti!* on
December 1 of that year. Thereafter, in one capacity or

another, he was a national figure. From December 1912 until the middle of October 1914, he was editor of the *Avanti!* Under his brilliant editorship, the paper increased its daily circulation from about twenty-eight thousand to ninety-four thousand copies, a number never before reached in the history of the paper. He asserted himself not only as a journalist but also as a political leader of the first order. For about two years, he was in effect the Duce, the dominant personality in the national socialist movement, in much the same way that he had been the Duce and dominant personality in the provincial Forlì socialist movement and in much the same way that he was to become the Duce and dominant personality in the fascist movement.

CHAPTER VII

IL DUCE

MUSSOLINI's eventual shift from internationalism to nationalism, from socialism to fascism, is merely an external event in
the career of a man who has always had a pre-eminently
individualistic conception of life. He has individualized
everything in his lifetime, including, of course, both socialism
and fascism. Born in a family of miserably poor people, in a
region where revolutionists, sincere and insincere, abound, this
révolté by instinct, temperament, and upbringing aligned himself with the socialist movement because this movement was
easily adapted to give full scope to his rebellious impulses. He
followed in the wake of his father, Alessandro, a courageous
and articulate socialist whose memory is being continually
insulted by fascist authors who have written travesties on his
life. Those who ramble about Mussolini's intellectual father,
be he Nietzsche or Sorel, would do well to pause and consider the influence of his real father.

Mussolini's training as an elementary school teacher raised
him above the condition of the average socialist party member. With his extraordinary and facile power of assimilation,
he read extensively, especially in the field of periodical
literature. A young man of uncommon intelligence and dis-
cernment, he had a predilection for the literature of revolt,
which buttressed and lent an intellectual air to his refractory
nature. He was receptive to that literature which harmonized
with his temperament. He appropriated what he wanted.
Never has he been interested in learning, research or ideas
except in so far as he could use them for his self-advancement
as a man of action. His sole preoccupation is himself. It
would be unjust to the anarchist tradition established by such
men as Bakunin, Kropotkin, Reclus, and Malatesta who
emphasized the spirit of solidarity among men, to call Mussolini an anarchist. Mussolini has always been an authoritarian.

If the term anarchist is to be applied to him at all, because of his emphasis on individualism, it must be interpreted as meaning an individualist who cares nothing for the masses, nothing for human solidarity. What Mussolini said in April 1920 thus becomes clear:

"I start with the individual and strike at the state. The number of individuals who are in potential revolt against the state, not this or that state, but against the state in itself, is a minority that is not unaware of its fate, but it exists.*** Down with the state in all its forms and incarnations: the state of yesterday, of to-day and of to-morrow; the bourgeois state and the socialist state. To us, who are the dying symbols of individualism, there remains, during the present gloom and the dark to-morrow, only the religion, at present absurd, but always consoling, of Anarchy!"

Mussolini gave his real personal estimate of the masses when he said in 1911 that they were cowardly. He did indeed speak in the name of the masses, of the need for their elevation, but this was a part of the conventional socialist technique. Mussolini was among them, not of them. He was an individualist in their midst, with that disdain or disregard for the masses, for the people, for humanity that has found its most complete literary expression in Max Stirner, the German author of *The Ego and His Own*, a book which appealed so strongly to him that in 1911, when he was twenty-seven years old, he enthusiastically described it as "the Gospel of individualism and the greatest poem that has ever been sung to the glory of man become god". Both as a socialist and as a fascist, Mussolini has been a rather lone, solitary figure. Sceptical of the efficacy of mass action, he placed his faith in the action of small, resolute, audacious *élites* to which he, of course, appointed himself, whether their object was socialism or fascism.

And yet, with all his overwhelming concentration upon himself, he has been an effective, even an inspiring, orator and propagandist. Haranguers like him can readily be found at Hyde Park or Union Square. He is an adept in every trick of the demagogue; he is a genuine *blagueur*, uttering short, staccato sentences, declaiming instead of arguing, dictating instead of persuading, and usually with a threatening tone. Whether assailing the enemies of the masses—the bourgeoisie, the church, and the state—or the foreign and domestic enemies of the fascist, totalitarian state—his personal state— his oratorical mannerisms have remained unchanged.

Mussolini has a low warm voice that sometimes becomes monotonous. He can make it raucous when he likes, and this is true especially when he speaks at a mass meeting in a public square and when he speaks "down to" the four hundred or so sheep-like men who make up his fascist Chamber of Deputies. He generally seems excited, but, at bottom, he is quite calm. He is not carried away by emotional frenzy when he speaks. Indeed, he is always appealing to and exciting the emotions and passions of his audience, be it fascist or socialist, but he himself is not imbued with the emotions and passions which he voices. He derives keen pleasure from playing with the emotions of a crowd, which he has compared to a woman, but he does not respect it. In evaluating his power over fascist audiences, it must be remembered that they are notoriously "packed" audiences and that applause is mandatory. And yet, he has revealed the salient quality of making his audience believe and feel that he is sincere. He is capable of communicating enthusiasm without being himself carried away by enthusiasm, of producing fanatics without being himself a fanatic. Like many false ministers and priests of God, like many confidence men and rabble-rousers, he invests his speeches, his writings, and his activities with a ring of sincerity. That is doubtless why the anarchist Armando Borghi wrote as early as 1910 that Mussolini had the appearance of an apostle. Little did Borghi then dream that fascist persecution would force him into exile and that he would publish, in three languages, an unusually scathing attack on the "apostle" who had turned his back on the revolutionary cause. Mussolini's uncanny faculty for making it appear that he has been completely absorbed by zealous devotion to a cause, whether it be socialism or fascism, internationalism or nationalism, is one of the great sources of his strength as a political agitator and leader. It accounts for the many people in Italy who are Musso-liniani—Mussolinians, followers of Mussolini—without believing in fascist ideology and explains his tremendous personal following when he was preaching the socialist gospel. Though he never has had faith in anything but himself, Mussolini has always been fully aware of other men's need for faith. The value of this criterion, manipulated by a man with his political ingenuity, cannot be over-estimated. When he was the Duce of Italian socialism, this superb actor stressed the need for faith in much the same way that he stressed the need for faith when he became the Duce of Italian fascism. The following illuminating statement by him in 1912 will be more instructive if the reader will substitute the word fascist for the word proletarian and the word fascism for the word socialism: "What does it matter to the proletarian to understand socialism as one understands a theorem? And is socialism perhaps reducible to a theorem? We want to believe in it; we must believe in it. Humanity needs a *credo*. It is faith that moves mountains because it gives the illusion that mountains move. Illusion is perhaps the only reality of life."

In the past several years, Mussolini has used to advantage his experiences as an emigrant, a poverty-stricken person, a political prisoner, a labour organizer, a journalist, and a leader of the socialist movement and of the early fascist movement, all of which had brought him into contact with different types of people and circumstances. With consummate agility, he adapts himself to a large variety of situations and personalities. He could make most foreign visitors believe anything. He plays on their vanity, on their desire for publicity. To industrialists, he will speak of bringing order out of chaos. To professors, he will speak of the "higher things". And so on. Of course, he finds it much easier to bamboozle the Italians because behind his words are the material power of a militia, an army, and all the organs of a state. He is a master of the art of political deception. On the morrow of the Matteotti murder in June 1924, when he was at the most critical point of his career as head of the fascist government, he solemnly promised to "normalize" the situation in Italy. So sincere and convincing did he appear that many Italian liberals, including several liberal members of the Senate and the Chamber of Deputies, helped to give him a new lease of power. Once he had emasculated and disarmed the opposition, he set out creating the fascist totalitarian state.

Mussolini has always had a poor opinion of the human race. As a socialist and as a fascist, he has repelled humanitarian impulses. He is completely lacking in generosity. Friendship is foreign to him. Either he has disdained it or he has never had the capacity for it. Possibly with the exception of members of his immediate family, Mussolini has never loved or trusted anyone, and he has rarely, if ever, shown any liking for people. Neither in the socialist nor in the fascist movement has he had a single trusted and intimate friend. His brother Arnaldo, who died in 1931, is perhaps the only person who enjoyed his continued confidence.

His lack of generosity towards his former acquaintances, his personal and political enemies, and even those who disagree with him probably constitutes his worst quality. I think he himself regards it as one of his best traits, for it enables him to act unhampered by any sentimental considerations. He would rather be feared than loved. It may be that his lack of generosity and his incapacity for or aversion to making friends are among the principal reasons for his political success. With his thorough, almost fiendish, knowledge of all that is weak and bad in human nature, Mussolini derives sadistic satisfaction in degrading men and in bringing out their worst qualities. He seeks to humble, not to elevate a man. And this he does with no compunctions whatever. He is a great corrupter. I do not know of a single fascist whom he respects. That scowl of contempt which his face often expresses became one of his physical characteristics as he saw passing before him that array of sycophants, hypocrites, office-seekers, intellectual traitors, and journalists who fawningly begged a favour, some form of recognition from him. He cynically allows men whom he once regarded as pimps and personifications of Rabagas in Italian political life, to call themselves fascists, even to write laudatory books about him. Note the nationalists of the Corradini, Federzoni, Rocco school. Note the ex-revolutionist Paolo Orano, now a prominent spokesman of fascist policy, and author, besides, of one of the most idiotic books ever written on the Duce.

Mussolini has seen mankind at its worst, and this he gloats over. He has always had little respect for human life, defending assassination in the name of socialism, allowing it under his fascist regime. He disapproves of assassination not because he believes in the inviolability of human life, but because it so frequently is inexpedient for certain political ends. He was not in the least moved as a man when members of his party butchered Matteotti. He was furious over this murder not because it was a crime, but because he deemed it to be a political blunder which might cost him his power. As editor of the *Avanti!*, he yearned for a "bath of blood", the "historic day" of judgment in the battle between the proletariat and the bourgeoisie. As leader of the fascists, he has viewed more than one "bath of blood", more than one "historic day" of judgment in his effort to seize and maintain unlimited power for himself. Whatever his alleged social objective, socialism or fascism, he has always been certain that "it is blood which gives movement to the resounding wheel of history". Once entrenched in power, he translated into imperialist terms his former bellicose socialist exhortations and he told the world that "war alone brings up to its highest tension all human energy and puts the stamp of nobility upon the peoples who have the courage to meet it". The ex-Hervéiste was one of the most vociferous exponents of Italy's entrance into the Great War. After the war, he excited those passions in Italy that would lead to civil war. The contemporary event he has perhaps admired most, outside of the fascist movement which he regards as his personal creation, is the Bolshevik Revolution—particularly its achievement in violently overthrowing an old regime. He has not hatred, but contempt for the Italian communist leaders because they failed miserably to effect a revolution in Italy, because they talked too much about revolution without resorting to the weapon of violence with sufficient success. Mussolini has utilized to the full his masterful knowledge of revolutionary technique. Ideas do not count for him; power does—power achieved through violence, maintained by violence. Two legends adorned his newspaper *Il Popolo d'Italia*, the organ he founded in November 1914 in order to advocate Italy's intervention in the war: one, "Whoever has arms has bread—Blanqui"; the other, "Revolution is an idea that has found bayonets—Napoleon". Almost all the writers on Mussolini's life cite these mottoes as though Mussolini had been the first to make use of them, but I am quite sure that he had found them at random on the title page of *La Conquête de l'Armée*, a book written by Gustave Hervé and published in 1913.

Mussolini assimilated these mottoes for his own purpose, emphasizing arms and bayonets, not revolution, although with his abiding fascination for "revolution", he persists in calling the fascist seizure and exercise of power a revolution. He is a master in the manipulation and exploitation of sentiments. In this respect, he has displayed veritable political genius at certain times in his career, notably in the immediate post-war period when he was at the nadir of his political fortunes. He exalts nationalism in much the same way that he used to exalt internationalism. It makes little difference to him what the flag is, whether that of fascism or of socialism, so long as he is its standard-bearer. The innumerable changes in his fascist programme before and after the "March on Rome" did not disturb him, for his eye was set on one thing only: the seizure of power and its maintenance. For example, in 1919 and 1920, when "bolshevism" was supposed to have threatened Italy, Mussolini fomented the passions of discord and conflict in the peninsula. He championed an advanced radical programme. He favoured the occupation of the factories by Italian workers in September and October 1920, and he supported their economic grievances. Later, he was able to exploit the "horror" and "fear" engendered in vast strata of the Italian public by the occupation of the factories, which was represented as the high-water mark of Italian "bolshevism".

In July 1920, Mussolini wrote one of his many articles denouncing the Bolshevik regime and Lenin. We are not at present interested in the truth or falsity, the soundness or unsoundness of his observations. Rather, we are interested in noting that he later built up his fascist state in Italy along the lines he had condemned in the Bolshevik state. His attack on Lenin and Soviet Russia gives us an excellent description of the later fascist, totalitarian, Mussolinian state. Substitute the word Mussolini for Lenin, the word Italy for Russia, the words fascist party for communist or socialist party, and an accurate idea will be formed of the Italian fascist state. Mussolini really was fond of what he appeared to hate. According to him, the Bolshevik state was a "state in the most concrete meaning of this word: a state, that is, a government, composed of men who exercise power, imposing an iron discipline upon individuals and groups and practising 'reaction' whenever necessary ***. In the Russia of Lenin, there is only one authority: his authority. There is only one liberty: his liberty. There is only one opinion: his opinion. There is only one law: his law. One must either submit or perish.*** No crisis, therefore, of state authority in Russia, but a state, that is, a super-state ***, a state that swallows up and crushes the individual and governs his entire life. It is understood that the zealots of the 'strong', Prussian or iron-fisted state find that their ideal has been realized there. In order to maintain the authority of the state in full force, no speeches, manifestos or lachrymose invocations are wanted; armed force is wanted. The most powerfully armed state, for domestic and foreign purposes, that exists in the world to-day is precisely Russia. The army of the Soviets is formidable, and as for the 'police', it has nothing to envy in the Okrana of the time of the Romanoffs. Whoever says state necessarily says the army, the police, the judiciary and the bureaucracy. The Russian state is the state *par excellence*, and it is clear that having *statetized* economic life in its innumerable manifestations, a huge army of bureaucrats has been formed. At the

base of this pyramid, on the summit of which stands a handful of men, there is the multitude; there is the proletariat
which, as in the old bourgeois regimes, obeys, works, and
eats little or allows itself to be massacred. Dictatorship of the
proletariat? The members of the wine clubs in their 'drinking'
meetings still believe in it. In Russia, there exists, indeed,
a dictatorship of the proletariat, exercised not by the
proletarians, but rather *** by the communist party which,
if it has, as is said,*** scarcely 700,000 members, represents
a very small minority of the total population. In reality, it is
a few men of this party who govern Russia. Their republic,
'with absolute and unlimited power', is a genuine and
veritable autocracy ***. The reality is this ***: In Russia,
there does not exist anything that even distantly resembles
socialism; in Russia, owing to a series of well-known historical circumstances, a small fraction of the socialist party
has seized power.*** That of Lenin is a gigantic, terrible
experience in *corpore vili*. Lenin is an artist who has worked
men, as other artists have worked marble or metals. But men
are stronger than stone and less malleable than iron. There is
no masterpiece. The artist has failed. The task was superior
to his capacities."

Whatever doubts Mussolini may have had about Lenin, he
has certainly entertained none about his own capacity to
work men, to subdue them to his own will and to cast them
in any mould he wished. He is the prey of a boundless ambition which was whetted early in his life by the extraordinary
power he wielded in the socialist movement and which is still
far from being satisfied despite his enormous personal success
in many fields. We find it easy to believe that apparently
when he was only twenty-six years old, he told one of his close
Romagnuole acquaintances, Torquato Nanni, that he had
found few men in Italy who were his equals. Always in search
of an ideological lever with which to move the masses and to
assert the supremacy of his ego, he found it first in socialism
and later in an extreme form of nationalism. During the
Great War, as he quoted the saying "Give me a fulcrum for a
lever and I will move the world", he thought of Buddha,

Christ, and Mahomet as men who had found a point of support and had moved three worlds in different ideological directions. With his flair for whatever will impress the masses, Mussolini has been superlatively successful in identifying his person with such popular causes as socialism and nationalism, exploiting every opportunity and occasion that would advance his quest for personal power. He has had the singular good fortune to be the Duce both of extreme revolutionary socialism and extreme reactionary fascism. Is it any wonder that he has wished to make his own life his masterpiece? A little more than a year before the fascist "March on Rome", when certain fascists were recalcitrant to his will, he brusquely declared that if fascism, his child, would not follow him, no one could oblige him to follow fascism. "The man who has guided and led a movement and has given it the best of his energy, has the right to go beyond the analysis of a thousand local elements in order to view in its synthesis the political and moral panorama *** which is not that of Bologna, of Venice or of Cuneo, but which is Italian, European, world-wide.*** I am a leader who leads, not a leader who follows. Besides and above all, I go against the current; I will never yield and I will always be on the watch, especially when the changing wind swells the sails of my destiny." After achieving power, he spoke to his coquettish and official biographer Signora Sarfatti about his desire to be *someone:* "Yes, I am possessed by this mania. It inflames, gnaws and consumes me, like a physical malady. I want to make a mark on history with my will, like a lion with his claws."

All Mussolini's doctrinal and moral somersaults and divagations, all his outward allegiance to varied and contradictory political theories become intelligible only if it is borne in mind that he cannot pay even lip-service to ideas unless he can utilize them as instruments of his ambition for power, unless he can convince himself of the identity between an idea and his will for power. With him, as with so many men of action, the utterance of an idea and the conviction that he alone can be its standard-bearer are inseparable.

Since his dominant passion is the pursuit of personal power, his apostasy does not disconcert him in the least. A few years before the Great War, he castigated the corrupters of political principles by hurling at them the definition of conscience as a pair of breeches that can be lowered whenever necessary. In later years, he offered history his own person as one of the most shameless symbols of political hypocrisy, glorifying everything he once condemned, allying himself with his former political and personal enemies, and tearing to pieces whatever sense of solidarity he had at any time professed with the humble and the underprivileged. The same man who warned his socialist comrades against adopting the Nietzschean maxim "Nothing is true, everything is permitted" has made this maxim the cornerstone of his fascist philosophy of life. As a hater of the bourgeoisie, he saw no reason for becoming sentimental if a "bourgeois son of a bitch" were killed by a bomb. Why should he later become sentimental over the murder of an anti-fascist "son of a bitch"? Why get sentimental if someone should try to kill the King, asked Mussolini before the Great War? Since an attempt on the King's life is an accident to be expected in a King's profession, "why be moved and why weep for the King, 'only' for the King? Why this hysterical, excessive sensibility when it is a question of crowned heads?" After the war, Mussolini's fascist programme demanded a republic in Italy. But after the "March on Rome", a law was passed establishing the death penalty in cases involving the assassination of or the attempt to assassinate the King, the Queen, the Crown Prince, or the Head of the Government—Mussolini.

It remained for him—who once consigned a little volume on John Huss to the press in order to arouse in its readers "hatred of every form of spiritual and secular tyranny, whether it be theocratic or Jacobin"—to establish in Italy a reign of secular tyranny. Where in anti-clerical and atheistic literature can there be found anything approaching Mussolini's statements about the love affairs of Christ with Mary Magdalene and the wife of Pontius Pilate? and yet, he negotiated the Lateran Accord with the Church, restoring the Papacy to a measure of power in the Italian peninsula that it has not enjoyed in several decades.

A fundamental consistency in Mussolini's career has been his predilection for extreme points of view, be they revolutionary or reactionary, red or black. Both his defamation and exaltation of religion, patriotism, militarism, monarchy, and the state have been characterized by the same truculence. He has turned his vehement clamour for war between proletarian and capitalist classes into vehement clamour for war between proletarian or poor and capitalist or rich nations. Before the Great War, at a time when Italy was steadily progressing under a system of democracy and liberty, he railed at the Italian judiciary for following Torquemada instead of Beccaria. It took him to degrade the Italian judiciary, to legislate Beccaria out of existence in his own native land and to install Torquemada as the symbol of fascist justice. At one time an articulate dissenter only because he was without power, going so far as to express the hope that the rulers of Italy would choke in their own blood, he saw to it, when he achieved power, that no man could enjoy the right of dissent from, let alone that of opposition to, his personal will. In relationship to himself, he can see men only as slaves or servants, never as equals or collaborators.

The destroyer of every elementary civil and political right would allow no one in fascist Italy to paraphrase what he had to say in 1914 when he vindicated in a court-room his right to censure the "massacre" of workmen: "Imagine an Italy in which thirty-six million citizens should all think in the same way as though their brains were cast in the same mould and you would have . . .

"President of the Court [interrupting]: An insane asylum.

"Mussolini: Or rather, the kingdom of boredom and imbecility. The King himself, faced by thirty-six million monarchists, would feel the need of insisting on the existence of a republican ***. It is necessary that beside those who say *no* there be those who say *yes*, that beside those who exalt the army there be those who decry it, and that beside those who acclaim bourgeois society there be those who wish to destroy this bourgeois society.*** Unanimity, uniformity mean acephaly, death. Gentlemen of the jury, pay homage to the ancient philosopher Heraclitus, the melancholy man of Ephesus, who declared: 'Strife is the origin of all things.' Well then, allow us to struggle, give us the liberty to struggle, and you will render homage to a great philosopher and to a very great principle: the principle of liberty!''

Surely, Mussolini has always sought movement, strife, action, struggle. He cannot be a neutral spectator of events; he must be an active participant in them; he must take sides. He would defy fate and shape his course with his will if he could. In the midst of his orgiastic activism, he has frequently and without conscience trampled upon every principle he may have once held sacred. Hence it is questionable if there is anything heroic in his life, for can a leader be a hero unless he symbolizes an idea, a mode of life that ennobles men instead of degrading them?

On March 23, 1919, the official date of the founding of the fascist movement, the future dictator proclaimed: "We are positively against every form of dictatorship, from that of the sword to that of the three-cornered hat [the church], from that of money to that of the masses." In the same year, the future liberticide cried out: "Down with the dictatorship of a party!", for he, the self-styled individualist, was then certain that the freedom of the individual could not be crushed by the "dictators of the Leninist barracks", just as it was not crushed by the "corporals of the Prussian barracks".

His first published article—in his nineteenth year—was a cry of indignation against the Kurdish oppression of the Armenians. His most clamorous fascist deed has been the suppression of the Ethiopians as an independent people. The execution of Ferrer in 1909 excited his ire. He has recently given material aid and comfort to virtually the same forces in Spain that willed the execution of Ferrer. In his twenty-fourth year, when the police authorities of Oneglia asked the Directorate of the school where he was teaching to dismiss him, he raised the following questions: "Is not the attempt to take away bread from an individual criminal?***

Is not this persecution of ideas sincerely professed revolting?"
And yet, as the head of the fascist state, he proceeded without
the slightest qualm to order the dismissal or the persecution
of the most independent minds in Italian universities. Under
his fascist rule, justice is not "the beautiful Themis of the
pagans", but, as he once wrote, "an old idler who prostitutes
herself to the first one who comes along, provided he belongs
to the police, to this ignoble collection of hirelings". He
would relegate the law to the flames only when it interfered
with his personal liberty. The same man who railed against
Swiss authorities for expelling him from their borders as
though he were a "mangy dog that might infect everybody",
and who began to ask himself whether his face was one for a
guillotine, has learned from his bitter experiences only to hate
any man who questions his power or will as the fascist Duce.
One thing he fears is assassination, he who sang pæans of
praise to the sacred acts of the avengers—the assassins of
tyrants. Does he not fear assassination because his own early
preachings constitute an incitement to his own assassination,
now that he has come to rule tyrannically? He once made
humble workers shiver with horror and weep as he told them
of the brutalities of the Italian police against workers. And
yet, when he became the fascist Duce, he embarked on a
policy of violent reprisal against all his enemies, urging his
followers with unrestrained fury to have no mercy on his
opponents. The same man who once defined martial law as
the unchaining of brutal police instincts has erected martial
law into a system of government, compared to which the
Austrian rule of various parts of Italy in the nineteenth
century seems like the reign of enlightened government. He
has strengthened those institutions he once excoriated—the
monarchy, the church, the army, and the police. He has
established a special tribunal of the fascist state, that pitilessly
metes out heavy sentences to Italians who do not agree with
fascism, and as he observes the verdicts of this tribunal, the
memory of his own prison experiences does not in the
slightest disconcert him or give him pause.

Amid all these contradictions, the one concern from which

he has never swerved has been his search for power. Truly, he has given us the best definition of fascism by calling it a hierarchy culminating in a pin-point—the pin-point, of course, being himself. Both as a socialist and as a fascist, he has conceived of himself as the infallible leader who must be obeyed. By order, by discipline, by law, by duty, he means subservience to his own person. Perhaps the record of no statesman in history offers as many illogical, inconsistent, and contradictory elements and yet such inflexible faith in his own capacity for leadership as that of Mussolini. Whether at Forlì, as the Duce of a small band of socialists, or at Rome, as the Duce of a large army of fascists, the autocratic bent of his mind, the ex-cathedra character of his pronouncements and the brisk gestures of finality with which he clothes his decisions have always been in evidence. His demand for the conquest of Ethiopia offered him occasion to display in all its plenitude his arrogant sense of pride in his own leadership. With rare political subtlety combined with audacious truculence, he achieved the most resounding personal triumph of his entire career by suppressing the independence of Ethiopia. Little did the fate of his own people matter to him as long as his personal prestige was at stake. When the fall of Addis Ababa sealed the victory of his personal policy, he said to a group of Italian peasants: "I am with you because I know you are with me." And yet, great as his victory in Ethiopia has been, it has by no means appeased his thirst for personal glory. As long as Mussolini lives as the head of the Italian State, the world will know no peace, for this man's constant and restless search for power knows no bounds and no restraint. He has taken advantage and he will continue to take advantage of any situation that will help him to project his personality, so as to make it dominant not only in Italy but also in Europe and even the rest of the Western world. Having satisfied his ambition to become the undisputed master of forty million people, he has achieved success in crushing a free African state; he has aided and abetted in the establishment of clerical fascism in Austria, the Nazi victory in Germany, the breakdown of the League of Nations system, and the fascist attempt to control Spain. He will never stop fomenting disorder, arousing hatred, and threatening war as long as he envisages himself as the founder of a new world politic, as long as there lies before him the formidable temptation of seeing the fascist mentality, as incarnated in his own person, dominate the Western world.

Mussolini the socialist was as imperious, fiery, dictatorial, and disdainful as is Mussolini the fascist. He has always been refractory to any law, to any norm tending to restrict his personal will. Hence his aversion to liberalism, to democracy and to parliamentary institutions. The closer one studies his socialist career, the more one realizes how irregular he was as a party member. He thoroughly enjoyed being the Duce of the socialist party, but when it refused to embrace his views contemplating intervention in the Great War though he had for weeks insisted upon a policy of absolute neutrality, he resigned his post as editor of the *Avanti!* and advocated intervention. For several years, from 1914 until 1920, he played a minor rôle in national politics. The years of his greatest isolation were those immediately following the war; the socialists were too strong, but it must be said that he never despaired. Fighting for power with an extraordinary singleness of purpose, an astute political sense, and a complete disregard for scruples, he manœuvred himself into a strong position with the "March on Rome" in October 1922. By 1925, after ruthlessly destroying all traces of serious opposition, he found his way clear to establishing a totalitarian regime. Thereafter, the Duce of a political party and a well-organized militia became the Duce of a state.

Nationalism, patriotism, Italy, the interests of the Italian people are mere words to him, mere symbols of sentiments which he can and does use and exploit to his own advantage with superlative effectiveness. Italy, the nation, the national interest are shibboleths to him, just as socialism, the social revolution, human welfare were shibboleths to him. Few are the men in history who have seen their consuming ambition and love of power as effectually realized as Mussolini. He has had the satisfaction of becoming what he always wanted to be—a duce, a superman beyond good and evil, a "man become god". No one has more effectively described Mussolini than Mussolini himself, when in the year 1910, at the age of twenty-seven, he uttered the words: "Within me, I recognize no one superior to myself."

CHRONOLOGY

SOME IMPORTANT DATES IN MUSSOLINI'S CAREER

July 29, 1883. Born in district of Dovia, Commune of Predappio, Province of Forlì, Italy. Father a blacksmith and socialist; mother an elementary school teacher and devout Catholic.

1901. Receives normal school diploma.

February 1902. Goes to Gualtieri Emilia to teach in elementary school.

July 1902. Emigrates to Switzerland. Arrested for vagrancy at Lausanne.

August 1902. Begins career as socialist agitator.

June 1903. Expelled from Canton of Bern for revolutionary activities.

October or November 1903. Returns to Italy.

January 1904. Leaves again for Switzerland. Prefecture of Forlì begins to keep a secret police record of his activities.

March 1904. Plays a leading rôle at Zurich Congress of Italian socialists in Switzerland.

April 1904. Declared a *réfractaire* or draft-dodger in Italy. Expelled from Canton of Geneva for using falsified passport.

September 1904. Amnesty in Italy for certain *réfractaires*.

November or December 1904. Returns to Italy.

1905–1906. Performs compulsory military service in Italy.

1906–1907. Elementary school teacher at Tolmezzo.

March–June 1908. High school teacher at Oneglia.

July 1908. Sentenced by Forlì Court to three months' imprisonment for having threatened armed violence against a "scab" labour organizer.

November 1908. On appeal, sentence reduced to 12 days' imprisonment.

February 1909. Goes to Trent, in Austria-Hungary, as socialist journalist and labour leader. Provokes hatred of clericals and government officials.

September 1909. Expelled from Austria-Hungary.

October 1909. Returns to Forlì. Speaks against the execution of the Spanish anarchist Francisco Ferrer.

January 1910. Becomes editor of the weekly *La Lotta di Classe* (*The Class Struggle*) at Forlì and leader of the Forlì socialist federation.

October 1910. Delivers speech at Italian socialist congress at Milan.

November 1911. Sentenced to one year of imprisonment for agitating against the Turco-Italian War.

February 1912. On appeal, prison term reduced to five months.

March 1912. Released from prison. Resumes editorial work on *The Class Struggle*.

July 1912. Delivers famous speech at Italian socialist congress at Reggio Emilia as spokesman of revolutionary group in the party. Made member of party's Executive Committee.

December 1, 1912. Becomes editor of the *Avanti!*, daily organ of Italian socialist party, published at Milan.

October 1913. Defeated as socialist candidate for parliament.

April 1, 1914. Acquitted of charge of inciting to crime, vilifying the army, etc.

April 27, 1914. At socialist congress at Ancona, demands expulsion of Freemasons from the socialist party.

June 1914. Enthusiastic supporter of revolutionary "Red Week".

THE DICTATOR ADDRESSES THE PEOPLE.

July–October 1914. One of the originators and vigorous proponents of formula of "absolute neutrality" for Italy in the Great War; then advocates formula of "relative (or conditional) neutrality", i.e. socialist position in the event of Italy's intervention to be determined according to changing circumstances. Passionate controversy in socialist party regarding its neutrality stand.

October 20, 1914. Party's Executive Committee refuses to adopt Mussolini's "relative neutrality" formula. He resigns editorship of the *Avanti!*

November 15, 1914. Founds *Il Popolo d'Italia*, a daily at Milan, advocating Italy's intervention in the Great War on the side of the Allies. Begins feverish interventionist campaign.

November 24, 1914. Expelled from Milan club of Italian socialist party.

November 29, 1914. Party's Executive Committee ratifies act of Milan club.

February 1915. Duel with lawyer Libero Merlino.

March 1915. Duel with socialist deputy Treves.

May 23, 1915. Italy declares war on Austria-Hungary.

August–September 1915. Conscripted and goes to the front.

August 27, 1916. Italy declares war on Germany.

February 23, 1917. Severely wounded by shrapnel when shell exploded during trench-mortar practice. Taken to hospital near front and later to hospital in Milan.

c. August 1917. Leaves hospital on crutches and resumes regular editorial work on *Il Popolo d'Italia*. Does not return to the front.

March 23, 1919. Founder of fascist movement at Milan, with advanced radical programme.

September 1919. Supports D'Annunzio's occupation of Fiume.

November 1919. Defeated as fascist candidate for parliament.

May 1921. Elected deputy to parliament as a fascist.

October 1921. Duel with former socialist comrade Francesco Ciccotti.

November 1921. Organization of fascist movement into a political party called *Partito Nazionale Fascista.*

May 1922. Duel with journalist Mario Missiroli.

October 24, 1922. Threatens fascist march on Rome.

October 27, 1922. Facta Ministry resigns. Beginning of mobilization of armed fascists for march on Rome.

October 29, 1922. King asks him to form ministry.

October 30, 1922. Forms a coalition ministry with himself as Prime Minister. Armed fascist squads begin to enter Rome.

October 31, 1922. He and other members of ministry take formal oath of office. Armed fascist squads parade (or march) through Rome and are reviewed by Mussolini and by the King.

November 25, 1922. Chamber of Deputies grants extensive powers to the Mussolini Ministry.

August 1923. Orders occupation of Corfu as measure of retaliation against Greece, after the assassination of Italians on Albanian–Greek border.

September 1923. Orders evacuation of Corfu after exacting satisfaction from Greece.

January 1924. Annexation of Fiume to Italy by treaty with Yugoslavia.

June 1924. Murder of socialist deputy Matteotti by fascists.

June–December 1924. Widespread unrest and growing opposition to fascist rule.

January 1925. Beginning of fascist totalitarian state and suppression of opposition to fascist rule.

1926. Three attempts to assassinate him.

February 1929. Concludes Lateran Accord with Catholic Church.

1935–1936. Conquest of Ethiopia.

1936–1937. Aids Spanish insurgents.

INDEX